Song of the Righteous

Song of the Righteous

by Darwin Wolford

ISBN: 1-55517-193-1

Published and Distributed by:

Cedar Fort, Incorporated
925 North Main, Springville, Ut 84663 801-489-4084

Cover Design by Lyle Mortimer
Page Layout and Design by Stephen J. Bons
Printed in the United States of America

1 2 3 4 5 6 7 8 9 10

If I would teach with power
The doctrine and the plan,
I'd wish for gentle music
To prepare the soul of man.

And then to press forever
These truths upon his mind,
We'd sing the hymns of Zion,
With their messages sublime.

—Elder Stephen D. Nadauld
Second Quorum of the Seventy

Acknowledgments

A published volume such as this is never the product of one person's labors. My deepest gratitude is expressed to everyone who has contributed in any way to the creation of this book.

Lyle Mortimer, publisher, conceived of a book about *music* and the *prophets,* and had the confidence to ask me to write it.

Michael F. Moody and Herbert Klopfer of the General Music Committe continually expressed their enthusiasm for this project, and offered guidance and a considerable amount of information.

The Thomas E. Ricks Foundation at Ricks College provided financial assistance for my research and the preparation of the manuscript.

Robert R. Worrell, chairman of the Division of Performing Arts at Ricks College, continually reinforced my conviction of the importance of this subject, especially when I might have been a little discouraged.

M. David Chugg, chairman of the Music Department at Ricks College, offered constant encouragement and provided practical assistance.

Marie Withers, a talented artist, provided beautiful and sensitive portaits of the prophets, as well as the illustrations used for the cover.

Lisa Williams provided invaluable input as editor and Stephen J. Bons' attention to detail while typesetting further improved the overall work.

LuWana Roberts provided considerable input, corrected many errors, and offered tremendous help both at the computer and away from it.

Cyndee Meyers and Alicia Johnson Sheehy painstakingly typed the manuscript.

Shirley S. Calder repeatedly directed me to and located sources and materials in the Ricks College Library.

Apologies and deep appreciation are extended to my wife, Julie, for allowing me to monopolize the studio in our home for more than a year, and the use of the rest of the house as an overflow for notes, pages of manuscript, and open books.

FOREWORD

Perhaps the official statement of the First Presidency least familiar to Latter-day Saints is the preface to the 1985 edition of the hymnbook. In that pronouncement, the members of the First Presidency declare that

> Inspirational music is an essential part of our church meetings. The hymns invite the Spirit of the Lord, create a feeling of reverence, unify us as members, and provide a way for us to offer praises to the Lord.
>
> Some of the greatest sermons are preached by the singing of hymns. Hymns move us to repentance and good works, build testimony and faith, comfort the weary, console the mourning, and inspire us to endure to the end.
>
> We hope to see an increase of hymn singing in our congregations. We encourage all members, whether musically inclined or not, to join with us in singing the hymns. We hope leaders, teachers, and members who are called upon to speak will turn often to the hymnbook to find sermons presented powerfully and beautifully in verse....
>
> Music has boundless powers for moving families toward greater spirituality and devotion to the gospel. Latter-day Saints should fill their homes with the sound of worthy music.
>
> Ours is a hymnbook for the home as well as for the meetinghouse. We hope the hymnbook will take a prominent place among the scriptures and other religious books in our homes.

This statement is not just an afterthought or an attempt to justify a new hymnbook, as Darwin Wolford clearly shows in *Song of the Righteous*. Leaders of the Church in the dispensation of the fullness of times as well as prophets from past ages have regarded music as an essential part of worship and as a means to supplicate and thank the Lord. We learn from Dr. Wolford's timely compilation of scriptural references to music that, in addition to the Saints' expressing joy in singing unto the Lord, so also do they who dwell in His presence. The Lord Himself, as the author points out, gave the words to *The Song of the Lamb* by revelation to the Prophet Joseph Smith, as recorded in the Doctrine and Covenants, in anticipation of the Millennial Day when all "shall see eye to eye, and shall lift up their voice, and with the voice together sing this new song."

From the time the Lord commanded Emma Smith, through her husband, the Prophet, to compile a "selection of sacred hymns," until the present day, presidents of the Church have had an intimate acquaintance with music and have made profound comments about it. In this book, one learns about a prophet who, deprived of the privilege of enjoying music in his youth, promoted it on all fronts as president of the Church. Another shares a vision of the kind of music that is sung in the heavens, exhorting the Saints to enjoy music and dance but to leave out the corruption the world ordinarily puts into them.

Church presidents have urged missionaries to learn the hymns and to sing them as part of their labor in preaching the gospel. Some have been accomplished musicians themselves or have written hymn texts to be set to music by composers. The prophet least gifted in singing spent the most time to learn the art and to perform in public. One, as a missionary, saved his life by singing, and another formed a professional band at age seventeen. The author gives the details of these and other fascinating connections of the prophets with music, along with a delightful characterization of each president.

Statements by the prophets give insight into the sacred nature of music and warnings of its possible misuse. For example, President Mckay called music a "divine art," and President Lee said, "the most effective preaching of the gospel is when it is accompanied by beautiful, appropriate music." President Kimball urged artists and musicians of the Church to purify themselves, to become worthy to produce compositions that will appropriately tell "the full story of Mormonism." On the other hand, President Benson warned,

> Evidence of the dastardly work of evil forces is increasingly evident.... The devil-inspired destructive forces are present in our literature, in our art, in the movies, on the radio, in our dress, in our dances, on the TV screen, and even in our modern, so-called popular music.

Dr. Wolford is particularly well-qualified to write this book, being a widely-published composer, arranger, music teacher, and former member of the committee that compiled the current *Hymns of the Church of Jesus Christ of Latter-day Saints*. In his lucid style, he brings to the foreground many prophetic exhortations regarding the use of hymns and other music probably unknown to the general membership of the Church—commandments and concepts that should be taught in every home where Latter-day Saints dwell.

Robert R. Worrell, Chairman
Division of Performing and Fine Arts
Ricks College

To Julie, for her love of music and devotion to the living prophets, and to Paul, Annalee, Andrew, and Sarah, who provided their own unique inspiration.

TABLE OF CONTENTS

MUSIC IN BIBLICAL TIMES

"Praise him with the sound of the trumpet: praise him with the psaltery and harp." (Psalm 150:3)

Ancient Israel sang the songs of Jehovah and, with instruments of various kinds, made music in praise of God. They sang and danced when they were merry, and pled for solace when they were mourning. Their songs expressed joy and thanksgiving and begged for mercy.

For God's chosen people, music and religion were inseparable. Well over one hundred references to music and singing in the Old Testament attest to this. These few quotations are perhaps typical:

"Then sang Moses and the children of Israel this song unto the Lord, and spake, saying, *I will sing unto the Lord*, for he has triumphed gloriously" (Exodus 15:1).

"*Jehovah is my strength and my song*: he also is become my salvation" (Isaiah 12:2).

"*Sing unto the Lord, praise ye the Lord*: for he hath delivered the soul of the poor from the hand of the evildoers" (Jeremiah 20:13).

The people of Zion cried to the Lord for deliverance from the enemies of Israel, and they offered thanksgiving through songs when their enemies were subdued:

And when he [Jehosphaphat] had consulted with the people, *he appointed singers unto the Lord, and that should praise the beauty of holiness*, as they went out before the army, and to say, Praise the Lord; for his mercy endureth for ever.

And when they began to sing and to praise, the Lord set ambushments against the children of Ammon, Moab, and mount Seir, which were come against Judah; and they were smitten (2 Chronicles 20:21-22).

Then sang Deborah and Barak, the son of Abinoam on that day, saying,
Praise ye the Lord for the avenging of Israel, when the people willingly offered themselves.
Hear, O ye kings; give ear, O ye princes; *I, even I, will sing unto the Lord; I will sing praise to the Lord God of Israel* (Judges 5:1-3).

It is God that avengeth me, and bringeth down the people under me,
And that bringeth me forth from mine enemies: thou also hast lifted me up on high above them that rose against me: thou has delivered me from the violent man.
Therefore I will give thanks unto thee, O God, among the heathen, and I will sing praise unto thy name (2 Samuel 22:48-50).

After Moses led the children of Israel out of Egypt, and the Red Sea was parted, and the Egyptian armies were left to drown, Israel sang a lengthy song of gratitude for their deliverance:

Then sang Moses and the children of Israel this song unto the Lord, and spake, saying, I will sing unto the Lord, for he hath triumphed gloriously: the horse and his rider hath he thrown unto the sea (Exodus 15:1-19).

The Lord, through his prophet, Ezekial, enumerated the sins of Judah and the punishments that would befall them if they did not heed the Lord's warnings. Finally, the Lord made this awful promise:

"I will cause the noise of thy songs to cease, and the sound of their harps shall be no more heard" (Ezekial 26:13).

The Jews loved their land. They loved to sing and play the songs of Zion, and they loved Jehovah. Psalm 137 reflects their deep sorrow when taken captive to a strange land:

> By the rivers of Babylon, there we sat down, yea, *we wept, when we remembered Zion.*
> We hanged our harps upon the willows in the midst thereof.
> For there they that carried us away captive required of us a song; and they that wasted us, required of us mirth, saying,
> Sing us one of the songs of Zion.
> *How shall we sing the Lord's song in a strange land?* (Psalm 137:1-4).

Shortly before the betrayal and the crucifixion, Jesus met with the Twelve for the Last Supper. There he initiated the sacrament.

> And as they were eating, Jesus took bread, and blessed it, and brake it, and gave it to the disciples, and said, Take, eat; this is my body.
> And he took the cup, and gave it to them, saying, Drink ye all of it;
> For this is my blood of the new testament, which is shed for many for the remission of sins.
> But I say unto you, I will not drink henceforth of the fruit of the vine, until that day when I drink it new with you in my Father's kingdom. (Matthew 26:26-29)

And then Matthew added this one verse:

> And when they had sung an hymn, they went out into the mount of Olives (Matthew 26:30).

Then followed the terrible ordeal at Gethsemane, and eventually the crucifixion.

References to music are less numerous in the New Testament than in the Old, but the New Testament is shorter than the Old Testament and covers a fraction of the time. From these references to music, we learn that the apostles taught the Saints that music is a necessary part of religion as well as the well-ordered life.

In the fifth chapter of Ephesians, Paul admonished the Saint in Ephesus in day-to-day living: "walk in love toward each other," "avoid filthiness and foolish talk," "walk as children of the light," and walk "circumspectly." Paul cautioned, "Be not drunk with wine...but be filled with the spirit." And then he explained how to invite the Spirit into our lives:

> [Speak] to yourselves in psalms and hymns and spiritual songs, singing and making melody in your hearts to the Lord. Giving thanks always for all things unto God and the Father in the name of our Lord Jesus Christ (Ephesians 5:19, 20).

Paul, in his letter to the Colossians, admonished the saints:

> Let the word of Christ dwell in you richly in all wisdom; teaching and admonishing one another in psalms and hymn and spiritual songs, singing with grace in you hearts to the Lord (Colossians 3:16).

The Saints in the Church of Christ positioned music and worship together similar to the Hebrews of the Old Testament. Predictably, the revelations to the prophets of this dispensation are consistent with the teachings of the apostles and prophets of old, and are reflected in music in the lives of our Latter-day prophets.

JOSEPH SMITH

JOSEPH SMITH
(1805-1844)

"The song of the righteous is a prayer unto me." (D&C 25:12)

At fourteen, Joseph Smith had already developed a strong inclination toward religion and the deeper questions of life. Of the many denominations soliciting membership in western New York where he lived, he felt an intense desire to know which church to join. On a spring morning in 1820, Joseph went into the woods near his home to pray. His prayer was indeed answered, but in a far more dramatic way than Joseph had imagined. In perhaps the greatest vision ever seen by mortal man, *both* God the Father and Jesus Christ appeared to Joseph and spoke with him. Joseph was told to join none of the existing churches, for he would become *the* instrument through whom the original Church of Jesus Christ would be restored to the earth. Joseph, a boy of fourteen, had gone to the grove to inquire of the Lord. He returned a prophet.

Opportunities for education in rural New York were limited to the basic subjects, and Joseph's formal education in those days was meager. Yet in other matters, Joseph came to know what Abraham, Moses, and Isaiah knew. Like the Old Testament prophets, Joseph had been taught by the great Jehovah. Other mentors included some of the Old Testament prophets.

One of Joseph's special tutors was the Angel Moroni, an ancient prophet who had lived on the American continent. His three visitations to Joseph during a September night in 1823 lasted until the roosters announced the rising of the sun. With each appearance, Moroni repeated the same message. After young Joseph had tried unsuccessfully to work in the field with his father, and his father suggested that he return to the house, Moroni returned again with the same message.

A little later, Joseph climbed the Hill Cumorah where he was shown plates, containing an ancient record of the prophets and peoples of the American continent. Joseph wrote, "I left the field, and went to the place where the messenger had told me the plates were deposited; and owing to the distinctness of the vision which I had had concerning it, I knew the place the instant that I arrived there."[1] Joseph was shown the plates, but was not permitted to take them at that time.

According to the instructions from Moroni, Joseph returned to the same spot for four annual visits, with continued instruction from the angel. These four years were an important time of preparation before Joseph was able to translate the divinely inspired record. Finally, in the late summer or early fall of 1827, Joseph was entrusted with the important records.

As the Prophet Joseph translated the Book of Mormon, completing it in July, 1829, he encountered *nineteen* references to music and singing. The verses in the Book of Mormon dealing with music sound remarkably similar to those found in the Old or New Testaments:

> And being thus overcome with the Spirit, [Lehi] was carried away in a vision, even that he saw the heavens open, and he thought he saw God sitting upon his throne, *surrounded with numberless concourses of angels in the attitude of singing and praising their God* (1 Nephi 1:8).

> I say unto you that I have caused that ye should assemble yourselves together that I might rid my garments of your blood, at this period of time when I am about to go down to my grave, that I might go down in peace, and *my immortal spirit may join the choirs above in singing the praises of a just God* (Mosiah 2:28).

> How beautiful upon the mountains are the feet of him that bringeth good tidings; that publisheth peace; that bringeth good tid-

ings of good; that publisheth salvation; that saith unto Zion, Thy
God reigneth;

Thy watchmen shall lift up the voice; *with the voice together
shall they sing;* for they shall see eye to eye when the Lord shall
bring again Zion;

Break forth into joy; sing together ye waste places of Jerusalem;
for the Lord hath comforted his people, he hath redeemed Jerusalem
(Mosiah 12:21-23; also Isaiah 52:7-9).

And now behold, I say unto you, my brethren, if ye have experienced a change of heart, *and if ye have felt to sing the song of
redeeming love,* I would ask, can ye feel so now (Alma 5:16-26)?

Blessed be the name of our God; *let us sing to his praise,* yea, let
us give thanks to his holy name, for he doth work righteousness forever (Alma 26:8).

And he hath brought to pass the redemption of the world,
whereby he that is found guiltless before him at the judgment day
hath it given unto him to dwell in the presence of God in his kingdom, *to sing ceaseless praises with the choirs above, unto the
Father, and unto the Son, and unto the Holy Ghost, which are one
God;* in a state of happiness which hath no end (Mormon 7:7).

*And they did sing praises unto the Lord; yea, the brother of
Jared did sing praises unto the Lord,* and he did thank and praise the
Lord all the day long, and when the night came, they did not cease
to praise the Lord (Ether 9:9).

And their meetings were conducted by the church after the
manner of the workings of the Spirit, and by the power of the Holy
Ghost; *for as the power of the Holy Ghost led them whether to
preach, or to exhort, or to pray, or to supplicate, or to sing, even so
it was done* (Moroni 6:9).

We learn from these and other quotations in the Book of
Mormon, that music, to the righteous, is a companion to worship: *to praise God is to sing to God.* And the children of God
who are found worthy to return to their Father will join with
celestial choirs in singing for joy and thanksgiving. The
Prophet Joseph Smith learned from many verses in the Book of

Mormon the relationship between music and worship. He also learned, elsewhere, that singing and dancing may sometimes accompany rude behavior. As Lehi and his family were on board their ship traveling to the promised land, part of the family apparently ignored the power of the Lord in delivering them out of Jerusalem:

> And after we had been driven forth before the wind for the space of many days, behold, my brethren and the sons of Ishmael and also their wives began to make themselves merry, insomuch that they began to dance, and to sing, and to speak with much rudeness, yea, even that they did forget by what power they had been brought thither; yea, they were lifted up unto exceeding rudeness (1 Nephi 18:9).

President Ezra Taft Benson said that the Book of Mormon brings men to Christ, while the Doctrine and Covenants brings men to Christ's Kingdom on earth, or the Church. As the revelations that comprise the Doctrine and Covenants were received by Joseph Smith, beginning in 1823, Joseph came to understand the Lord's attitudes regarding music in His Church. In a dozen references to music, in particular singing, Joseph learned of music in a variety of contexts.

The dedicatory prayer of the Kirtland Temple was revealed to Joseph in what is Section 109. In verses 38 and 39 of the revealed prayer, the servants who would go forth to proclaim the gospel are blessed, and those who would accept it, we are told, would come forth singing:

> Put upon thy servants the testimony of the covenant, that when they go out and proclaim thy word they may seal up the law, and prepare the hearts of thy saints for all those judgements thou art about to send, in thy wrath, upon the inhabitants of the earth, because of their transgressions, that thy people may not faint in the day of trouble.
>
> And whatsoever city thy servants shall enter, and the people of that city receive their testimony, let thy peace and thy salvation be upon that city; that they may gather out of that city the righteous,

that they may come forth to Zion, or to her stakes, the places of thine appointment, with songs of everlasting joy.

The expression "songs of everlasting joy" is used many times in the Doctrine and Covenants, and is found in Isaiah and also the Book of Moses. The scriptures would indicate that songs are sung by the righteous and the repentant as they discover they are the recipients of the Lord's redeeming love, suggesting that songs are an expression of deepest gratitude and highest praise. Just as *every* knee shall bow and *every* tongue shall confess, every righteous soul, we may infer from the scriptural references, will sing the songs of everlasting joy. We may assume that all whose hearts are full of gratitude and praise, will express that with a voice of singing.

In an epistle to the brethren of the Church in what is now Section 128 of the Doctrine and Covenants, Joseph speaks in detail of baptism for the dead. Verses 22 and 23 describe how *the dead will sing with joy upon their deliverance,* and the *earth will also rejoice with them:*

Brethren, shall we not go in so great a cause? Go forward and not backward. Courage, brethren; and on, on to victory! Let your hearts rejoice, and be exceedingly glad. *Let the earth break forth into singing. Let the dead speak forth anthems of eternal praise to the King Immanuel,* who hath ordained, before the world was, that which would enable us to redeem them out of their prison; for the prisoners shall go free.

Let the mountains shout for joy, and all ye valleys cry aloud; and all ye seas and dry lands tell the wonders of your Eternal King! And ye rivers, and brooks, and rills, flow down with gladness. Let the woods and all the trees of the field praise the Lord; and ye solid rocks weep for joy! *And let the sun, moon, and the morning stars sing together, and let all the sons of God shout for joy!* And let the eternal creations declare his name forever and ever!

In 1833, when the Saints were suffering what must have been indescribable persecution—driven from their homes in Jackson County—Joseph received the revelation now found in

Section 101. Here the Lord comforts His children who thought that in the place of Zion they would find peace:

> Therefore, let your hearts be comforted concerning Zion; for all flesh is in mine hands; be still and know that I am God.
>
> Zion shall not be moved out of her place, notwithstanding her children are scattered.
>
> *They that remain, and are pure in heart, shall return and come to their inheritances, they and their children, with songs of everlasting joy, to build up the waste places of Zion—*
>
> And all these things that the prophets might be fulfilled (D&C 16-19).

Music is associated with missionary labors, as seen in this revelation to William E. McLellin, who, incidentally, did not remain faithful to the Church.

> Keep these sayings, for they are true and faithful; and thou shalt magnify thine office, *and push many people to Zion with songs of everlasting joy upon their heads* (D&C 66:11).

The Lord, in Section 29:4, speaks of missionary work in musical terms:

> Verily, I say unto you that ye are chosen out of the world to declare my gospel *with the sound of rejoicing, as with the voice of a trump.*

The Lord describes Zion at the time of the Second Coming, and talks about the state of the righteous as well as the wicked:

> And the glory of the Lord shall be there, and the terror of the Lord also shall be there, insomuch that the wicked will not come unto it, and it shall be called Zion.
>
> And it shall come to pass among the wicked, that every man that will not take his sword against his neighbor must needs flee unto Zion in safety.
>
> And there shall be gathered unto it out of every nation under heaven; and it shall be the only people that shall not be at war one with another.

And it shall be said among the wicked; Let us not go up to battle against Zion, for the inhabitants of Zion are terrible; wherefore we cannot stand.

And it shall come to pass that the righteous shall be gathered out from among all nations, *and shall come to zion, singing with songs of everlasting joy* (D&C 45:67-71).

The "songs of everlasting joy" are spoken of when the lost tribes return:

And an highway shall be cast up in the midst of the great deep.

Their enemies shall become a prey unto them.

And in the barren deserts there shall come forth pools of living water; and the parched ground shall no longer be a thirsty land.

And they shall bring forth their rich treasures unto the children of Ephraim, ye servants.

And the boundaries of the everlasting hills shall tremble at their presence.

And there shall they fall down and be crowned with glory, even in Zion, by the hands of the servants of the Lord, even the children of Ephraim.

And they shall be filled with songs of everlasting joy (D&C 133:27-33).

Later in Section 133, the Lord speaks of the resurrection.

Yea, and Enoch also, and they who were with him; the prophets who were before him; and Noah also, and they who were before him; and Moses also, and they who were before him;

And from Moses to Elijah, and from Elijah to John, who were with Christ in his resurrection, and the holy apostles, with Abraham, Isaac, and Jacob, shall be in the presence of the Lamb.

And the graves of the saints shall be opened; and they shall come forth and stand on the right hand of the Lamb, when he shall stand upon Mount Zion, and upon the holy city, the New Jerusalem; *and they shall sing the song of the Lamb, day and night forever and ever* (verses 54-56).

Unique to the Doctrine and Covenants, indeed, all scripture, are the words given to the Prophet Joseph from the Lord to a great exultant anthem, called the "Song of the Lamb."

This lofty poem, *composed by Jehovah*, is contained in what is
Section 84, which Joseph Smith called a "revelation on priesthood." This will be sung by the Saints at a time when "all
shall know me, even from the least unto the greatest, and shall
be filled with the knowledge of the Lord, and shall see eye to
eye, and shall lift up their voice, and with the voice together
sing this new song":

> The Lord hath brought again Zion;
> The Lord hath redeemed his people, Israel,
> According to the election of grace,
> Which was brought to pass by the faith
> And covenant of their fathers.
> The Lord hath redeemed his people;
> And Satan is bound and time is no longer.
> The Lord hath gathered all things in one.
> The Lord hath brought down Zion from above.
> The Lord hath brought up Zion from beneath.
> The earth hath travailed and brought forth her
>   strength;
> And truth is established in her bowels;
> And the heavens have smiled upon her;
> And she is clothed with the glory of her God;
> For he stands in the midst of his people.
> Glory, and honor, and power, and might,
> Be ascribed to our God; for he is full of mercy,
> Justice, grace and truth, and peace,
> Forever and ever, Amen (D&C 84:98-102).

This is the same "Song of the Lamb" that is mentioned in
the fifteenth chapter of Revelation. Other interesting details
regarding it are provided.

> And I saw another sign in heaven,...
> And I saw as it were a sea of glass mingled with fire: and them
> that had gotten the victory over the beast, and over his image, and
> over his mark, and over the number of his name, stand on the sea of
> glass, having the harps of God.
> *And they sing the song of Moses the servant of God, and the
> song of the Lamb,* saying, Great and marvelous are thy works, Lord

God Almighty; just and true are thy ways, thou King of saints (Revelation 15:1-3).

The most familiar quotation in the Doctrine and Covenants regarding music—and one of the most frequently quoted statements—is the directive to Emma Smith to compile a "selection of sacred hymns" for the infant Church:

> And it shall be given thee, also, to make a selection of sacred hymns, as it shall be given thee, which is pleasing unto me, to be had in my church.
> For my soul delighteth in the song of the heart; yea, the song of the righteous is a prayer unto me, and it shall be answered with a blessing upon their heads (D&C 25:11-12).

This familiar quotation is part of the short section given Emma through her husband—the only section in the Doctrine and Covenants directed to a woman! Considering all that Joseph and his colleagues had to be taught to complete the establishment of the Church, special significance is seen is the commandment to compile a hymnal in July, 1830, just three months after the formal organization of the Church!

The work on this important book continued until 1835, when it was published in August of that year. This tiny book, consisted of ninety hymn texts only. (In a technical sense a *hymn* is a poem; the music which accompanies it is called the *hymn tune*.)

The inspiration that guided Emma's compilation of hymns is seen in the fact that of the ninety hymns included, twenty-six are included in our current hymnbook, published in 1985, 150 years later!

We see little, if any, from the pen of Joseph Smith regarding the hymnbook or hymn singing in the Church. Six years later, however, in 1841, a second hymnbook was published in Nauvoo. This volume now contained 304 hymns, more than three times the length of the first hymnal published in 1835.

In a letter to Parley P. Pratt, dated December 22, 1838, the Prophet's brother, Hyrum, wrote the following:

> I should...strongly advise, yea, urge you and all the Elders of Israel, when they meet those who have means, and a disposition to forward this work, to send them to this place, where they may receive counsel from time to time.
>
> If when Brothers Joseph and Rigdon return we should deem [it] prudent to avail ourselves of the facilities offered in New York for reprinting the Book of Mormon, it is probably that a delegation will be sent to accomplish that object....
>
> *The above observation will apply to the book of the Doctrine and Covenant, Hymn Book, etc, which publications I long to see flowing through the land like a stream, imparting knowledge, intelligence, and joy to all who shall drink at the stream.*[2,3]

A poignant sentence near the end of Hyrum's letter to Parley says this:

> The families of the Twelve are generally well, but not altogether so comfortably situated as I could wish, *owing to the poverty of the Church.*

Yet, in spite of the poverty that Hyrum refers to, Joseph records in his diary one week later, Sunday, December 29, the following:

> The High Council of Nauvoo voted to print ten thousand copies of the hymn-books, and an edition of the Book of Mormon, under the inspection of the First Presidency at Nauvoo, *so soon as means can be obtained.*[4]

The Saints had been driven from place to place, suffering one atrocity after another. However, they looked hopefully toward "Zion" in Jackson County, Missouri, as a permanent place of peace and safety. Then in November and December of 1838, the Saints were expelled from Jackson County.

In February of 1834, Parley P. Pratt and Lyman Wight returned from Missouri to Kirtland to talk with the Prophet about assisting the Missouri Saints in reclaiming their lands and offering relief. The Lord, in Section 103, then directed Joseph to organize a contingency of able-bodied men to form "Zion's Camp" and travel to Missouri and do whatever possible to assist them.

In May, with Joseph Smith as commander-in-chief, 207 of the best men available left on their 700-mile journey across four states. Zion's Camp included, besides Joseph, Brigham Young, Wilford Woodruff, Parley P. Pratt, and many other future leaders of the Church.

> In many respects the daily routine of Zion's Camp was similar to that of other armies. Most able-bodied men walked beside the heavily loaded wagons along the muddy and dusty trails. Many of them carried knapsacks and held guns. It was not unusual for them to march thirty-five miles a day, despite blistered feet, oppressive heat, heavy rains, high humidity, hunger, and thirst. Armed guards were posted around the camp at night. At 4 a.m. the trumpeter roused the weary men with reveille on an old, battered French horn. Each company gathered for prayer, then went to work at their respective assignments.[5]

Parley P. Pratt painted a "pen-picture" of a typical evening of Zion's Camp:

> As he (Joseph Smith) warms under the glow of the Spirit of God, he tells them of the future glory of Zion—of the temple to be overshadowed by a pillar of cloud by day and of fire by night—of her being a place of refuge—a city of peace in which the saints of God shall safely dwell, and how the wicked shall say, "let us not go up to battle against Zion, for her inhabitants are terrible." But listen! In another part of the camp a number of the brethren are singing; and as the melody floats out on the calm stillness of the night, you recognize one of the familiar songs of Zion:
>
> > Glorious things of thee are spoken
> > Zion, city of our God!
> > He, whose word can not be broken,
> > Chose thee for his own abode.

> On the Rock of ages founded,
> What can shake thy sure repose!
> With salvation's walls surrounded
> Thou may'st smile on all thy foes.[6]

> The song was scarcely concluded when the sharp, thrilling notes of the bugle summon to prayer. All promptly retire to their tents and are engaged in solemn devotion. Few leave the tents after prayers. The guards have been notified to take their places, and their comrades stretch out their tired limbs upon their rude pallets.[7]

The march of Zion's Camp was undoubtedly a preparation for the westward exodus of the pioneers. The division of Saints into companies, with company leaders, a chain of command, plus the bugle calls to announce the time of rising and going to bed, continued to be the way the pioneers made their journey westward to the valley of the Great Salt Lake.

The Saints who joined the new Church brought with them favorite hymns from their former denominations. Gradually, however, a number of Church members began creating a repertoire of hymns reflecting the restored gospel; Parley P. Pratt, W. W. Phelps, Joel H. Johnson, Eliza R. Snow, William Clayton, and John Taylor, to name a few. Some of the first generation of LDS poets wrote inspired texts that have not been surpassed in quality in the years since. The creative talents of such writers were obviously inspired by their new-found faith. But, at the same time, their writing skills and their message were ignited by the charisma of the Prophet Joseph Smith.

Joseph organized the first choirs in the Church, and was very attentive to their progress, attending rehearsals and offering encouragement.

> When this subject (music) is studied and sought after by the singers of the Saints, with their whole hearts, their songs and anthems, and their minstrelsy, will soften into celestial melody, melt the hearts of the Saints and draw them together, as the magnet needle is drawn to the loadstone. When these graces and refinements and all the kindred attractions are obtained that characterized

the ancient Zion on Enoch, then the Zion of the last days will become beautiful, she will be hailed by the Saints from the four winds, who "will gather to Zion with songs of everlasting joy." Then Zion will be free, and to God and the Lamb will be the glory, to Saints, the boundless joy."[8]

Nauvoo, apparently, was a hive of entertainments of various kinds, as well as a variety of cultural activities. The volume, *The Story of the Latter-day Saints*, by James B. Allen and Glen M. Leonard, offers this characterization of activities in Nauvoo relating to music:

> Local initiative created most leisure activities, and except for such voluntary educational organizations as the lyceum and the debate and literary clubs, the choir, and the bands, most fraternizing was carried out by families, at home or between households.
> Entertainments for larger groups were held in the Concert Hall, north of the temple, or in the Masonic Hall. The Mansion House, an official residence built for the church president in 1843, rapidly became a social center. Self-improvement was fostered by the Nauvoo Lyceum, organized in 1842 to conduct weekly debates on current issues, and by the Nauvoo Library and Literary institute, founded two years later to encourage the reading of good books. University music professor Gustavus Hills helped create the Teacher's Lyceum of Music in December 1841 to foster improvements. The church choir offered occasional concerts, as did two brass bands, led by William Pitt and Domenico Balloo. The bands played for private parties, where dancing became a religiously acceptable practice among the Latter-day Saints.[9]

With Joseph Smith as President of the Church, hymn singing became a regular part of worship. A sampling of journal entries from the pen of the Prophet reveals much:

> January 21, 1836
> Our meeting was opened by singing, and prayer was offered up by the head of each quorum; and closed by singing, and invoking the benediction of heaven, with uplifted hands. Retired between one and two o'clock in the morning.[10]

March 3, 1836
After singing and prayer, President Oliver Cowdery, chairman of
the committee...arose and made report in behalf of the committee.[11]

Minutes of General Conference, Saturday, April 6, 1844, include these comments:

The President arrived at the stand at half-past two o'clock, p.m.
The choir sang a hymn; after which prayer by Elder John P. Greene,
when the choir sang another hymn.

Minutes for Sunday, April 7, 1844, include the following:

Very pleasant morning. The President arrived at ten o'clock,
the largest congregation ever seen in Nauvoo having assembled.
The choir sang the hymn, "Ye slumbering nations that have
slept."

President Rigdom offered an affectionate appeal for the prayers
of the Saints on behalf of the sick, and then prayer by Elder George J.
Adams.

Choir sang the hymn, "The Spirit of God like a fire is burning,"
etc.[12]

Other sessions of conference included similar comments. Minutes for Monday, April 8, 1844, include the following:

At three-quarters past 9 a.m., President Joseph Smith took his
seat on the stand and requested the choir to sing a hymn. He called
upon Elder Brigham Young to read 1st Corinthians, 15th chapter, as
his own lungs were injured.

Elder Brigham Young said—to continue the subject of President
Smith's discourse yesterday, I shall commence by reading the 15th
chapter of 1st Corinthians, from an old Bible; and requested W. W.
Phelps to read it.

Prayer by Elder Brigham Young, after which the choir sang a
hymn.[13]

"The Prophet," wrote B.H. Roberts, "lived his life in crescendo."[14] As the revelations and spiritual powers increased during this life, so did the abuse and persecution. The culmination of both were reached with the great King Follet discourse delivered April 7, 1844, and the assassination of Hyrum and Joseph less than three months later.[15]

The record indicates that at 3:15 on that fateful afternoon of June 27, "the guards began to be more severe in their operations, threatening among themselves, and telling what they would do when the excitement was over."[16]

About three hours later, Jospeh and Hyrum were dead.

This scene in the Carthage jail was not unlike that in the Upper Room. Alexander Schreiner drew this comparison:

> John Taylor and Willard Richards, intimate friends of the Prophet and the Patriarch, were in Carthage Jail with Joseph and Hyrum. John Taylor sang to cheer the group. This was an occasion similar to that one long ago when Jesus sang with His disciples that night he was betrayed. The hymn which Jesus and His disciples sang has been lost. But the hymn by John Taylor was "A Poor Wayfaring Man of Grief."[17]

1 Joseph Smith—History 1:50.

2*Referring to the Doctrine and Covenants and the hymnbook together, while pointing out that the two books will "impart knowledge, intelligence, and joy," reminds one of the statement by Boyd K. Packer in General Conference, October, 1991, that"...the hymns of the restoration are, in fact, a course in doctrine!"

3 *History of the Church*, Vol IV, pp. 47-48.

4 Op cit, p. 49.

5 *Church History in the Fulness of Times*, Church of Jesus of Christ of Latter-day Saints, 1989, p. 143.

6 Hymn #46 in the current (1985) hymnal.

7 *Readings in L.D.S. church History*, by Berrett and Burton, Deseret Book, Co, 1956, Volume I, pp. 192-193.

8 *History of the Seventies* by Joseph Young Sr., Deseret News Printing, 1878, p. 15.

9 Op Cit, p. 174, Deseret Book co. Second Edition, 1992.

10 Joseph Smith: *History of the Church*, Volume II, p. 382.

11 Ibid., p. 402.

12 *History of the Church*, Volume VI, p. 297.

13 Ibid., p. 318.

14 B.H. Roberts, TPJS, p. 356, footnote.

15 Op Cit, p. 356, also reported in *Joseph Smith the Prophet* by Truman Madsen, Bookcraft, 1989, p. 116.

16 *The History of the Church*, Volume VI, p. 614.

17 *Music and the Gospel*, CFI p. 107.

BRIGHAM YOUNG

Withers '94

BRIGHAM YOUNG
(1801 - 1877)

===

*"We cannot preach the gospel without
good music."[1]*

John Young, Brigham's father, fought in the Revolutionary
War under General George Washington. One of eleven children, Brigham Young was born in New England in extreme
poverty. When he was two, his family moved to New York
where economic conditions were somewhat better.

With only eleven days of schooling, Brigham said years
later:

> We never had the opportunity of letters in our youth, but we
> had the privilege of picking up brush, chopping down trees, rolling
> logs, working amongst the roots and getting our shins, feet and toes
> bruised...I learned how to make bread, wash the dishes, milk the
> cows, and can make butter and beat most of the women in this com-
> munity at housekeeping. Those are about all the advantages I gained
> in my youth.[2]

Brigham's father was a strict disciplinarian. Brigham
observed that discipline from his father, "used to be a word and
a blow...but the blow came first."[3] When Brigham was fourteen, his mother died, and Brigham left home to find his own
way in life.

Commenting on his strict Puritan upbringing, Brigham
recalled:

> When I was young, I was kept within very strict bounds, and
> was not allowed to walk more than half an hour on Sundays for
> exercise. The proper and necessary gambols of youth having been
> denied me, makes me want active exercise and amusement now. I

had not a chance to dance...and never heard the enchanting tones of the violin until I was eleven years of age; and then I thought I was on the highway to hell, if I suffered myself to linger and listen to it. I shall not subject my little children to such a course of unnatural training, but they shall go to the dance, study music, read novels, and do anything else that will tend to expand their frames, add fire to their spirits, improve their minds, and make them feel free and untrammeled in body and mind....

Tight-laced religious people of the present generation have a horror at the sound of a fiddle. They do not realize that all good music belongs to heaven; there is no music in hell. We should delight in hearing harmonious tones made by the human voice, by musical instruments, and by both combined. Every sweet musical sound that can be made belongs to the Saints and is for the Saints. Every flower, and every sensation that gives to man joy and felicity are for the Saints, who receive them from the Most High.[4]

In 1830, Brigham first saw a copy of the Book of Mormon, which had been given to his brother by Samuel Smith. The book circulated among the members of the Young family, all of whom accepted it as the Word of God. Brigham, however, studied the book methodically for two years before joining the Church. Then in 1832, Brigham was baptized. All of the other members of his family had accepted the Gospel and joined about the same time. That same year brought tragedy to Brigham's life—his wife, Miriam, passed away leaving two small children.

Brigham Young was 31-years old when he joined the Church in 1832 and met Joseph Smith for the first time later that year. Joseph was four years younger than Brigham.

Here my joy was full at the privilege of shaking the hand of the Prophet of God, and I received the sure testimony, by the spirit of prophecy, that he was all that any man could believe him to be, as a true Prophet.[5]

Joseph, also was impressed with the new convert, and remarked that one day Brigham would "preside over this Church."[6] Brigham was made a member of the first Quorum of the Twelve Apostles in 1835 when it was organized.

Brigham and several members of the Twelve were called on a mission to England. On April 6, 1840, Brigham and the other apostles arrived "sick and almost penniless" to do the Lord's work in the British Isles. Ten days later, Brigham wrote a letter to Joseph Smith summarizing their activities and progress:

> To President Joseph Smith and Counselors:
>
> Dear Brethren:
>
> You no doubt will have the perusal of this letter and minutes of our conferences; this will give you an idea of what we are doing in this country....
> Concerning the Hymnbook—when we arrived here, we found the brethren had laid by their old hymn books, and they wanted new ones; for the Bible, religion and all is new to them. When I came to learn more about carrying books into the states, or bringing them here, I found the duties were so high that we never should want to bring books from the states.[7]

In England, Brigham Young supervised the publication of 5,000 copies of the *Book of Mormon*, and with the assistance of Parley P. Pratt and John Taylor, 3,000 copies of the hymnbook. Like Emma Smith's hymnbook, this was a volume of poetry without music, and was titled *A Collection of Sacred Hymns for the Church of Latter-day Saints in Europe*. It was later known as the *Manchester Hymnal* and continued to be published in England until 1890. With Parley P. Pratt as editor, the monthly periodical entitled *The Latter-day Saint's Millennial Star* was born.[8] It continued to be published for 130 years!

Brigham Young details their publishing enterprises in Great Britain:

> We went to Preston and held our first conference, and decided we would publish a paper. Brother Parley P. Pratt craved the privilege of editing it, and we granted him the privilege. We also decided to print 3,000 hymnbooks, though we had not the first cent to begin with and

were strangers in a strange land. We appointed Brother Woodruff to
Herefordshire and I accompanied him on his journey to that place. I
wrote to Brother Pratt for information about his plans, and he sent me
his prospectus, which stated that when he had a sufficient number of
subscribers and money enough on hand to justify his publishing he
would proceed with it. How long we might have waited for that, I
know not, but I wrote him to publish 2,000 papers and I would foot
the bill. I borrowed two hundred and fifty pounds of Sister Jane
Benbow, one hundred of Brother Thomas Kington and returned to
Manchester, where we printed 3,000 hymn books and 5,000 Books of
Mormon, and issued 2,000 Millenial Stars monthly, and in the course
of the summer gave away 60,000 tracts. I also paid from five to ten
dollars a week for my board and hired a house for Brother Willard
Richards and his wife, who came to Manchester, and sustained them;
and gave sixty pounds to Brother P. P. Pratt to bring his wife from
New York. I also commenced the emigration in that year.

I was there one year and sixteen days, with my brethren, the
Twelve, and during that time I bought all my clothes except one pair
of pantaloons, which the sisters gave me in Liverpool soon after I
arrived and which I really needed....

I paid three hundred and eighty dollars to get the work started
in London and when I arrived home in Nauvoo, I owed no person
one farthing. Brother Kington received his pay from the books that
were printed, and Sister Benbow, who started to America the same
year, left names of her friends to receive two hundred and fifty
pounds, which amount was paid them, notwithstanding, I held her
agreement that she had given it to the Church.

We left two thousand five hundred dollars' worth of books in
the office, paid our passages home, and paid about six hundred dollars to emigrate the poor who were starving to death, besides giving
sixty thousand tracts; and that, too, though I had not a sixpence
when we landed in Preston, and I do not know that one of the
Twelve had.[9]

Brigham had been in England one year and sixteen days,
landing "as strangers in a strange land and penniless." Yet,
besides the publication of 5,000 *Books of Mormon*, 3,000
hymnbooks, 2,500 volumes of the *Millenial Star* and 60,000
tracts, along with Parley P. Pratt, John Taylor and Wilford
Woodruff, they baptized between seven and eight thousand and
assisted one thousand converts in emigrating to Zion.

On June 27, 1844, the Saints were stunned to learn that assassin's bullets had claimed the lives of Joseph and Hyrum. After Sydney Rigdon's unsuccessful campaign to become the "Guardian of the Church," Brigham Young, the senior apostle, rightfully assumed the leadership of the Church.

On January 14, 1847, while at Winter Quarters, the revelation known as "The Word and Will of the Lord concerning the Camp of Israel in their journeyings to the West," Section 136 of the Doctrine and Covenants, was given to Brigham Young. Practical advice about the organization of the Saints into companies, with captains and presidents acting under the direction of the Twelve Apostles was given, including specific duties, supplies that were needed, and advice on getting along efficiently and peacefully together. Included are these lines that appear in verses 28 and 29:

> If thou art merry, praise the Lord with singing, with music, with dancing, and with a prayer of praise and thanksgiving
> If thou art sorrowful, call on the Lord thy God with supplication, that your souls may be joyful.

One week later, January 23rd, with temperatures about twenty degrees below zero, a celebration and dance were held in the Council House. William Clayton, the camp historian, provided this description of the happening:

> President Young told the brethren and sisters he would show them how to go forth in the dance in an acceptable manner before the Lord. President Young then knelt down and prayed to God in behalf of the meeting, imploring his blessings upon those present and dedicating the meeting and house to the Lord. At the sound of music the President then led forth in the dance.[10]

Other "entertainments" similar to this were held in the Council House during the lonely winter months.

On Monday morning, April 5, 1847, the Saints departed on the exodus to the West. Historian Preston Nibley described their departure:

> Almost in military formation and under the guiding genius of
> Brigham Young, the Pioneers moved out across the plains towards
> the setting sun....
>
> Brigham rode horseback most of the way, at the head of his car-
> avan, to select the safest and most feasible route. He led the way;
> always in the foreground; a natural leader. Day after day (the) camp
> journalist records: "Progress was slow but steady, from five to twen-
> ty miles being made, Sundays excepted. Early in the morning a bugle
> would sound. The brethren would arise, prepare their breakfast, har-
> ness their teams or yoke up their oxen, and then push forward."[11]

About fifteen members of the Pitt Brass Band were among
the first company of Saints that left Nauvoo during the cold
days between February 10th and 14th, 1845. William Clayton,
who played the violin, was one of the group who did not actually play a brass instrument. The band had responsibilities
other than boosting the morale of the weary saints:

> Brigham Young gave them specific permission to remain togeth-
> er as a group. Thus, they were not only available to sustain the
> Saints' morale with dances and musicals, but provided a much-need-
> ed boost to the Saints' faltering financial affairs by giving paid con-
> certs at Iowa settlements of Farmington and Keosagua.[12]

Upon arriving in the Salt Lake Valley, the pioneers began
preparing the ground for planting and building log cabins.
Within one month, the first choir was formed, suggesting, no
doubt, the priorities of their prophet. Soon a brass band was
playing, and as the settlements extended beyond the Salt Lake
Valley, other bands and choirs began making their contribu-
tions to their communities and the Church.

In 1852, an adobe building known as the "Old Tabernacle"
was built where the present Tabernacle stands. This structure
was used for religious gatherings as well as a variety of musical
events. In the meantime, an English carpenter with a passion
for organs left England with his wife for Australia. There

Joseph and Adelaide Ridges converted to Mormonism. "I found out what a Mormon was," wrote Joseph Ridges, "and I became one joyfully."[13]

After building a home in Sydney, Ridges returned to his hobby to build a small pipe organ, which was perhaps the very first pipe organ made in Australia. This pleased the local Church authorities, and they suggested that the organ ought to be shipped to Utah, and presented as a gift to the Church there. Brother Ridges agreed, and then sent word to Brigham Young that the pipe organ was to be sent, as a gift from the Saints in far away Australia. Ridges, with help from some of the local elders, dismantled it, crated it up and sent it to California. On June 12, 1857, Joseph Ridges and his family arrived in Utah, along with the organ, coming from San Pedro, California in twelve wagons pulled by fourteen mule teams.

J. Spencer Cornwall related this interesting incident that took place as the organ was being "set up" in the "Old Tabernacle":

> As it was being completed, someone asked Brigham Young who would play it. The President replied with that same assurance which was the motivating principle of his life, "The Lord will provide men to do all things that are necessary." Joseph J. Daynes, a young convert from England and a highly musical lad, was the answer. It was here on October 11, 1857, that this talented youngster began a thirty-three year career as the chief organist of the community."[14]

Others who played the organ in the "Old Tabernacle" were Fannie Young, daughter of the President, and Karl G. Maeser, a convert from Germany, who later founded Brigham Young University.

When the new Tabernacle was begun in 1863, Brigham made known his strong desire for a new and bigger organ. "The Tabernacle must have a big organ which would be commensurate with beauty and vastness of the building."[15] Ridges made a sketch of an organ he thought feasible for the new building and presented it to the President. When Brigham saw the sketch, he exclaimed, "Joseph, if you will make that organ, there is nothing you want which you cannot have!"[16]

The construction of a new pipe organ for the Tabernacle went ahead with Brigham's encouragement, though building such an instrument in the middle of the desert in the 1860's presented great challenges. Joseph Ridges described some of the challenges that faced him in this massive undertaking:

> We had no material except wood in that early day in Utah, so I went to Boston and New York and purchased what material we had to have, expanding about $900.00—all that could be spared from the Church fund.
>
> That was the start of it. I returned to Salt Lake over the old stage line with the material and erected a shop right inside the Tabernacle walls. President Young asked me how much the organ would weigh. I told him between eighty and ninety tons, so he had a platform built capable of supporting that weight. In the shop, I put up a small model of the organ, and every pipe that went into the instrument was tested and voiced and tuned from this little instrument.
>
> For a while we were in doubt as to whether the wood in the canyons of Utah would be suitable for the work. I went out in the territory north and south with a teamster, and together we selected and hauled much of the wood that was put into the organ. It was nearly all yellow pine....
>
> But finally we had enough timber inside the walls of the Tabernacle and the year following, while they were putting on the roof, the first piece of wood in the frame of the organ was put into place.
>
> Now there was not a man in Utah who knew the first thing about an organ. I had to take each one of the ten assistants they gave me and instruct him in every move. The trees had been sawed at President Young's mill in the canyon, and from large timbers about the size of half logs we had to saw out by hand every piece and place them one at a time.
>
> No wonder it took years of toil. We were twelve years building the organ. It had over 2,000 pipes when I got through with it, and these pipes were nearly all of wood, ranging in size from two feet to thirty-two feet length.[17 & 18]

Brigham Young's interest in the building of the Tabernacle organ was like that of a proud father, or *grandfather*, since

Joseph Ridges was really the father of this organ! President Young visited the organ shop inside the Tabernacle to check on the organ's progress regularly. The work was tedious. Occasionally, Ridges, who had "prospector's blood" in his veins, left for a few days at a time to search for ore in the mountains east of Salt Lake. Impatiently, Brigham would go in the canyons, find Ridges, and bring him back to work.

On one of his visits inside the Tabernacle, Brigham Young enthusiastically exclaimed, "We cannot preach the gospel unless we have good music. I am waiting patiently for the organ to be finished, then we can sing the Gospel into the hearts of the people."[19] J. Spencer Cornwall suggests that in this statement, Brigham Young prophetically points to the interrelationship between the Tabernacle organ and Choir that would exist in future years.

The Tabernacle was first used for General Conference Sunday morning, October 6th 1867. Though the Tabernacle Organ was far from completion, it was played and heard publicly on that auspicious occasion. Preston Nibley describes the first conference:

> On the stand, in addition to the Presiding Authorities...were the Salt Lake Choir, under the leadership of Elder Robert Sands, numbering about 150, with Organist Joseph John Daynes. To the left of the speakers' benches was a large choir, uniting the choirs of Springville, Payson and Spanish Fork, under their respective leaders, Elders Frederick Waight, William Clayton, and William R. Jones.[20]

President Young, according to reporters covering the conference

> thought it proper to say something of the unfinished condition of the organ. Not over one-third of the pipes were up, and till the casing was built, they had thrown around it a loose garment. It was now only about fifteen feet high, but when completed it would be forty feet high. Brother Ridges, and those who had labored with him, had done the best they could and notwithstanding their diligence by early day, noon and night, they had been unable to have it properly

tuned. It was, however, in a condition to accompany the choir, and he was pleased with it.

The conference continued for four days.

While the Tabernacle Organ has been expanded, refurbished, and replaced several times since 1867, the organ would not have come into being without the vision of Brigham Young and the devoted labor of Joseph Ridges. It is symbolic, no doubt, that some of the pipes from Ridges' original organ are still part of the present organ.

The Tabernacle Organ, today, is the most famous organ in the world, and the Tabernacle Choir is the most famous choir in the world. An essential aspect of that "special sound," recognized by radio and TV audiences throughout the nation, results from the unique acoustics of the building itself, which Brigham Young reportedly conceived of while contemplating a hard-boiled egg one morning at breakfast.

In addition to Brigham Young's position as President of the Church, he served for many years as Governor of the State of Deseret. As the music in the Church reflects the attitudes of President Brigham Young regarding music, so does the music performed at public and civic gatherings.

Brigham Young's daughter, Clarissa Young Spencer, makes this comment about the bands that were expected to march in every parade:

> There were sure to be a number of bands in any parade, bands having always played an important part in life among our trek across the country. Although they didn't have sufficient food for their needs, they had *two* bands to help uphold their morale, one evidently not being deemed sufficient for the purpose.[21]

Formal celebrations in early Utah would often border on the spectacular. Naturally, music was ostensibly a part of these festivities. Clarissa describes the second anniversary of the coming of the pioneers to the Salt Lake Valley, July 24, 1849:

A large cannon had been brought from Nauvoo the first year, part of the way on its own wheels, and the rest of the journey in a wagon, and on the day before the celebration several of the brethren spent the day making cartridges for firing salutes. Forty-niners, on their way to California had obligingly furnished seventy-five pounds of power toward the venture. At 7:30, on the morning of the twenty-fourth, when the great sixty-five foot national flag was unfurled, it was saluted by the firing of this cannon, the firing of guns, the ringing of the Nauvoo bell, and spirit-stirring airs from the band.

The main events of the day were held in the Bowery, an open-air building on the Temple grounds, and hither at 3:15, father and his counselor were escorted by the following retinue: (1) Horace S. Eldredge, marshall, on horseback, in military uniform; (2) brass band; (3) twelve Bishops bearing the banners of their wards; (4) seventy-four young men dressed in white; with white scarves on their right shoulders and coronets on their heads, each carrying in his right hand a copy of the Declaration of Independence and the Constitution of the United States, and each carrying a sheathed sword in his left hand. One of them carried a beautiful banner which bore the inscription, "The Zion of the Lord"; (5) Twenty-four young ladies dressed in white with white scarves on their shoulders and wreaths of white roses on their heads, each carrying a copy of the Bible and Book of Mormon and one carrying a very beat banner inscribed, "Hail to our Captain."

As they left our house and marched through the streets the young men and women sang a hymn, the Nauvoo bell pealed, and the band played. When all had arrived at the Bowery, the audience, which had been waiting for an hour, shouted, "Hosanna to God and the Lamb" and "Hail to the Governor of Deseret!" A meeting followed in which songs were sung and the Constitution of the United States was read and received with cheers."[22]

Brigham Young is more readily remembered as a 19th century Moses, leading an entire people across America in the most dire of circumstances, or the *great colonizer*, having directed the settlement of about 350 cities and towns across the West, in Canada and Mexico. But Brigham Young was also a prophet who understood the place of music in the Church and in the lives of its members. In the life of Brigham Young, this is exemplified most remarkably.

Brigham Young may or may not have read music or played an instrument, but he loved music of all kinds. He loved the sound of a fine choir, and he loved the hymns of Zion. Performances by the choir were expected for most, if not all, religious services. Moreover, he delighted in the sound of a brass band, and there was usually a band for every parade or civic occasion. In addition, Brigham was very fond of dancing, and was considered "one of the best" dancers around.

One of our recent prophets taught that the work that goes on within the walls of our home is at least as important as the work that we do away from home. Brigham's enthusiasm for music in Church or in the community is reflected in his enthusiasm for beautiful music at home.

In the book *Brigham Young at Home*, his daughter, Clarissa Young Spencer, describes the nightly ritual of family prayer:

> Father would step to the glass cupboard, take down the prayer bell, go to the door, and give three distance rings. After a moment he would put the bell back and take his place by his brothers in the center of the room. In a very short time the patter of feet would be heard in the long hallway upstairs and down, and the children would come tripping in to be followed by their mothers with a more sedate tread. Father and his brothers sat on the west center part of the room. On their right, in an honored place, sat Aunt Eliza R. Snow, and on around the room with the rest of the family, each wife having her own place with her children about her.
>
> Father usually discussed the topics of the day, and then we would all join in singing some familiar songs, either old time ballads or songs of religious nature. Finally, we would all kneel down while father offered the evening prayers.[23]

Singing and playing of musical instruments were characteristic of life in the Young home. Yet, writes Clarissa, "If we indulged in singing or reading [on a Sunday], the music or books must be of a nature appropriate to the day."[24]

One bitter-sweet story is told of Fanny:

> She was very gifted musically and could come home from the theatre and play through the score of an entire opera after having heard it once. Father had given her a beautiful golden harp which,

naturally, she loved dearly. One day he came home and said to her, "Fanny, would you be willing to give your harp to a blind musician?"

Fanny looked up at him very much concerned that her treasure should be threatened, but after a moments' hesitation she said, "Why, yes, Father, if you wish it."

"There is a man by the name of Giles," said Father, "who has just come over from England. Over there he made a living by playing the harp but he was unable to bring one with him. If you are willing, I should like to give him yours." Without more ado, the precious harp which had been hauled a thousand miles over plains and mountains by ox team was given to an almost complete stranger.[25]

Brigham Young believed music to be a gift from God, given to man for entertainment as well as edification, comfort and cheer.

Some wise being organized my system, and gave me my capacity (and) put into my heart and brain something that delights, charms, fills me with rapture at the sound of sweet music.... Who gave...a love for those sweet sounds, which with magic power fill the air with harmony, and cheer and comfort the hearts of men, so wonderfully affect the brute creation? It was the Lord, our Heavenly Father, who gave the capacity to enjoy these sounds.[26]

1 J. Spencer Cornwall, *A Century of Singing—The Salt Lake Mormon Tabernacle Choir* (Salt Lake City: Deseret Book, 1958), p25.

2 Leonard J. Arrington: *The Presidents of the Church* (Salt Lake City, Deseret Book, 1986) p. 44.

3 Ibid., p. 44.

4 Ibid., pp. 44–45.

5 Ibid., p. 49.

6 Ibid., p.49.

7 Joseph Smith: *History of the Church*, Volume IV, pp. 121–122.

8 Parley P. Pratt composed "The Morning Breaks" to appear on the front of the first issue of the *Millennial Star*. It was also published on the first page of the *Manchester Hymnal*.

9 Preston Nibley, *Brigham Young—the Man and His Work* (Independence, Missouri: Zion's Printing and Publishing Co.), p. 34.

10 Ibid., p. 87.

11 Ibid., pp. 91–92.

12 *Ensign*, July 1980, p. 22.

13 Barbara Owen, *The Mormon Tabernacle Organ An American Classic* Salt Lake City: The American Classic Organ Symposium, 1990, p. 2.

14 J. Spencer Cornwall, *A Century of Singing—The Salt Lake Mormon Tabernacle Choir* (Salt Lake City: Deseret Book, 1958) pp. 21–22.

15 Barbara Owen, *The Mormon Tabernacle Organ An American Classic* Salt Lake City: The American Classic Organ Symposium, 1990, p. 5.

16 J. Spencer Cornwall, *A Century of Singing—The Salt Lake Mormon Tabernacle Choir* (Salt Lake City: Deseret Book, 1958), p22.

17 Ibid., pp. 22–23.

18 In organ terminology the length of the pipes in feet refers to the longest pipes of the set.

19 Ibid., p. 25.

20 Preston Nibley, *Brigham Young—the Man and His Work* (Independence, Missouri: Zion's Printing and Publishing Co.), p. 427.

21 Clarissa Young Spencer, *Brigham Young at Home* (Salt Lake City: Deseret Book, 1961) pp. 201–202.

22 Ibid., pp. 198–200.

23 Ibid., pp. 32–33.

24. Ibid p. 183.

25 Ibid. pp. 280–281.

26 *Church News*, August 28, 1983.

JOHN TAYLOR

MWithers '94

JOHN TAYLOR
(1808-1887)

"We have no idea of the excellence, beauty, harmony and symphony of the music in the heavens."[1]

John Taylor stands as a striking contrast to both Joseph Smith and Brigham Young. Joseph and Brigham were American, born and raised on the frontier. Various writers have referred to them as "homespun," with little formal education. European born, John Taylor came to the United States by way of Canada. Before coming into the Church, he had received an excellent education in Great Britain. With opportunities never afforded Joseph or Brigham, John Taylor blossomed into a highly cultured, polished and articulate gentleman. He studied Greek, Latin, and higher mathematics. With a beautiful voice, even from an early age, he developed a love for music.

John Taylor was born in the scenic mountain and lake regions of northern England, the second of ten children. His family moved to the port city of Liverpool when John was seven. Baptized as a member of the Church of England as an infant, John grew up in an Episcopalian home, and as a boy developed a sensitivity towards spiritual things. Even from his early years, John had dreams and visions. He wrote, "I often heard sweet, soft melodious music, as performed by angelic or supernatural beings."[2] B. H. Roberts describes John Taylor, as a boy, seeing, "in vision, an angel in the heavens, holding a trumpet to his mouth, sounding a message to the nations."[3] He would recall the image of the angel, with a trumpet to his lips, many times during his early years, though he would not fully understand the meaning of this spiritual manifestation until years later.

Little by little, John realized that the Church of England was not able to answer some fundamental questions about religion. At sixteen, he joined the Methodist Church. One year later, he was made a lay minister and assigned to serve in a small town near Penrith. While walking with a companion, also from this church, he stopped. Standing in the road, he exclaimed, "I have a strong impression on my mind, that I have to go to America to preach the gospel!"[4] The vividness of this manifestation remained with him for years.

In 1830, the Taylor family emigrated to Canada, hoping to find a brighter future with improved economic conditions. Since John's oldest brother, Edward, had passed away, it was necessary for John to remain in England to sell the family property and finalize family business. He arrived in Toronto in 1832.

In Canada, John continued to preach for the Methodists. It was in that work that he met Leonora Cannon and married her. Together, they gradually became aware of limitations in the teachings of the Methodist Church. Finally, in 1836, the Taylors formed a study group that consisted of former Methodist preachers who sought the truth. These people, mostly men, were "gentlemen of refinement and education and generally talented."[5]

Elder Parley P. Pratt, while on a mission to Canada, discovered John Taylor's study group some months after and began teaching the gospel to them. Many of the group joined. John was ordained an elder shortly thereafter, and soon began teaching his new-found religion, baptizing many into the Church. Later, after he was ordained a high priest, he had a strong impression that he would one day become an apostle. John and Leonora left Canada for Kirtland, Ohio, and there John Taylor met Joseph Smith for the first time. John and the Prophet Joseph became life-long friends. John was a strong defender of Joseph to his enemies—in and out of the Church.

1838 marked one of the blackest chapters in church history, with widespread apostasy within the Church and violent persecution from without. Joseph and several hundred saints were forced to flee Kirtland to Missouri for their safety. Then in Missouri, Governor Boggs issued his infamous Order of Extermination. Historian B. H. Roberts assesses events of that year:

> Some four hundred of the Saints were either murdered outright or died from exposure and hardship inflicted upon them in this unhallowed persecution; from twelve to fifteen thousand citizens of the United States were expelled from Missouri—from the lands they had purchased of the general government; while their homes were destroyed, and their stock and much other property were confiscated. Many of the leaders in the Church, among them the Prophet Joseph and his brother Hyrum, were cast into prison.[6]

On a quiet Tuesday afternoon, October 30, 1838, Colonel Williams O. Jennings and 240 of the Illinois militia descended on the village of Haun's Mill, slaughtering twenty of the saints—men, women, and children, wounding many others, and hauling off anything of value. On December of that year, John Taylor, age thirty, was ordained an apostle by Brigham Young.

On April 26, 1834, after the official expulsion of the Saints from Missouri, five apostles and several other members of the Church returned to the temple site at Far West, meeting in the moonlight hours before dawn for their own safety. B. H. Roberts recounts this poignant occasion:

> At this meeting they excommunicated a number of persons from the church, ordained Wilford Woodruff and George A. Smith apostles, and others were ordained to the office of seventy. Prayer was offered up by the apostles in the order of their standing in their quorum. It was a brilliant, moonlight night, according to Elder Taylor, and out of the still air, strong and clear rose that glorious song of Zion—
>
> ADAM-ONDI-AHMAN
>
> The earth was once a garden place,
> With all her glories common;
> And men did live a holy race,

And worship Jesus face to face—
In Adam-ondi-Ahman.

We read that Enoch walked with God,
Above the power of mammon;
While Zion spread herself abroad,
And saints and angels sang aloud—
In Adam-ondi-Ahman.

Her land was good and greatly blest,
Beyond old Israel's Cannon;
Her face was known from east to west,
her peace was great, and pure the rest
Of Adam-Ondi-Ahman.

Hosanna to such days to come—
The Savior's second coming,
When all the earth in glorious bloom
Affords the saints a holy home,
Like Adam-ondi-Ahman.[7]

No doubt the strong, clear voice of John Taylor could be heard leading out in the singing of that hymn. Before departing, the south-east corner stone was laid in position to await the time when the Lord should open the way for its completion. Then, with hardly a cent among the five apostles, they left the sacred spot for New York, and then on to their missions in Great Britain.

The sadness of this occasion is reminiscent of the occasion when the Jews were taken captive to Babylon:

By the rivers of Babylon, there we sat down, yea we wept, when we remembered Zion (Psalm 137:1).

By the 6th of April, eight of the Twelve were in England, teaching the Gospel and making converts by the thousands.

Heavy duties made shipping Books of Mormon or hymn books from America prohibitive. Brigham Young, the senior apostle, directed that an edition of 5,000 copies of the Book of

Mormon and 3,000 copies of a new hymnbook were to be published. Brigham Young, John Taylor and Parley P. Pratt began the work of selecting hymns for the hymnbook. Including 271 hymns, with 78 from Emma Smith's 1835 hymnal, the volume was published in 1840 with the title: *A Collection of Sacred Hymns for the Church of Latter-day Saints in Europe.* This historic volume was published in Manchester, and came to be known as the *Manchester Hymnal.*

In his book, *John Taylor Mormon Philosopher, Prophet of God*, Francis Gibbons describes the working relationship of the three apostles:

> President Young was concerned primarily with financing and expediting the printing of the book so that it would be in the hands of the British Saints as soon as possible. John and Parley, on the other hand, were equally concerned about the quality of the hymns, about the make-up of the volume, and about the proofreading of the galleys to guard against typographical errors. President Young was prepared to sacrifice literary perfection on the altar of speed, and being the chairman of the committee, his views prevailed, sometimes to the annoyance of his precise brethren. This was nothing more than the kind of collision that occasionally occurs between powerful men of different talents and temperaments but does not indicate a dislike for each other.[8]

Forty-four of the hymns were from the pen of Parley P. Pratt, who, also, was given the responsibility of editing the monthly periodical, *The Millennial Star.*

John Taylor introduced the gospel into Ireland, the Isle of Man, and Scotland. Before his return to Nauvoo, July 1, 1841, John Taylor and the other apostles baptized between seven and eight thousand souls.

Monday morning, June 24, 1844, Joseph and Hyrum, accompanied by John Taylor and Willard Richards, left Nauvoo on horseback for Carthage, the county seat. A group of about sixty of the state militia stopped them. Holding an order from the governor for the Nauvoo Legion to surrender their arms, they took Joseph and his companions back to Nauvoo to see that this was done. Following this, Joseph, Hyrum, John Taylor, and Willard Richards were taken to Carthage and jailed.

During the next three days, the group comforted themselves inside the jail by reading the Book of Mormon and praying. Outside, the crowd of mobsters increased in numbers and became progressively rowdier.

Hyrum, who was five years older than Joseph, was faithful and loyal to his younger brother and to his sacred office. "Hyrum," wrote Joseph Fielding Smith, "guarded his younger and more favored brother as tenderly as if the Prophet had been his son instead of his younger brother." Willard Richards—cousin to Brigham Young, physician, member of the Quorum of the Twelve and private secretary to Joseph—was asked if he would like to accompany the Prophet to the inner cell of the jail. Without hesitation, he responded:

> Brother Joseph, you did not ask me to cross the river with you—you did not ask me to come to Carthage—you did not ask me to come to jail—and do you think I would forsake you now? but I will tell you what I will do; if you are condemned to be hung for treason, I will be hung in your stead, and you shall go free.[9]

John Taylor—apostle and devoted, faithful friend to the Prophet—was one of Joseph's favorite singers. A little after three in the warm, sultry afternoon, Joseph asked John if he would sing "A Poor Wayfaring Man of Grief," a song that had recently been introduced in Nauvoo. John, like the others, was "dull and languid." Perhaps sensing the inevitable, his heart was heavy. Reluctantly, however, with his beautiful rich baritone voice, John Taylor sang the melancholy ballad to comfort his beloved Joseph:

> A poor wayfaring Man of Grief
> Hath often crossed me on my way,
> Who sued so humbly for relief

That I could never answer nay.
I had not pow'r to ask his name,
Whereto he went or whence he came;
Yet there was something in his eye
That won my love; I knew not why.

Once, when my scanty meal was spread,
He entered; not a word he spake,
Just perishing for want of bread.
I gave him all; he blessed it, brake,
And ate, but gave me part again.
Mine was an angel's portion then,
For while I fed with eager haste,

The crust was manna to my taste.
I spied him where a fountain burst
Clear from the rock; his strength was gone.
The heedless water mocked his thirst;
He heard it, saw it hurrying on.
I ran and raised the suff'rer up;
Thrice from the stream he drained my cup,
Dipped and returned it running o'er,
I drank and never thirsted more.

'Twas night: the floods were out, it blew
A winter hurricane aloof.
I heard his voice abroad and flew
To bid him welcome to my roof.
I warmed and clothed and cheered my guest
And laid him on my couch to rest;
Then made the earth my bed, and seemed
In Eden's garden while I dreamed.

Stript, wounded, beaten nigh to death,
I found him by the highway side.
I roused his pulse, brought back his breath,
Revived his spirit, and supplied
Wine, oil, refreshment—he was healed.
I had myself a wound concealed,
But from that hour forgot the smart,
And peace bound up my broken heart.

In pris'n I saw him next, condemned
To meet a traitor's doom at morn.
The tide of lying tongues I stemmed,
and honored him 'mid shame and scorn.
My friendship's utmost zeal to try,
He asked if I for him would die.
The flesh was weak; my blood ran chill,
But my free spirit cried, "I will!"

Then in a moment to my view
The stranger started from disguise.
The tokens in his hands I knew;
The Savior stood before mine eyes.
He spake, and my poor name he named,
"Of me thou hast not been ashamed.
These deeds shall thy memorial be;
Fear not, thou didst them unto me." [10]

After singing all seven verses of James Montgomery's plaintive ballad from memory, John was asked if he would sing it again. He responded, "Brother Hyrum, I do not feel like singing." Hyrum replied, "Oh, never mind; commence singing, and you will get the spirit of it." John sang it again. Like the Savior before his death, Joseph was comforted by the apostolic singing of a hymn.

Less than two hours later, a barrage of gun shots claimed the lives of Joseph and Hyrum, and left John Taylor seriously wounded. A pocket watch, however, prevented another bullet from penetrating the heart of the man who, thirty-six years later would assume the mantle of the prophet. One bullet lodged beneath John Taylor's left knee, which he carried for the rest of his life. Of the four men, Willard Richards was the only one that was not hurt.

John's intense devotion for the Prophet led him to later write the hymn, "Oh give me Back My Prophet Dear," which appeared in the LDS hymnbook until the 1948 edition. The hymn was published with the musical setting by George Careless:

Oh give me back my Prophet dear
And Patriarch, Oh give them back
The Saints of latter days to cheer,
And lead them in the gospel track!
But oh they're gone from my embrace,
From earthly scenes their spirits fled.
Two of the best of Adam's race
Now lie entombed among the dead.

Inspired by the song, "The sea! The sea! the open sea!", John Taylor wrote "The Seer, Joseph, the Seer," which, too was included in LDS hymn books until 1948, with music by Neukomm, arranged by Ebenezer Beasley:

The Seer!, Joseph, the Seer!
I'll sing of the Prophet ever dear,
the Prophet ever dear:
His equal now cannot be found By searching the
     wide world around.
With Gods he soared in the realms of day.
And men he taught the heavenly way,
And men he taught the heavenly way.
The earthly Seer! the heavenly seer!
I love to dwell on his memory dear;
The chosen of God and the friend of man,
He brought the priesthood back again;
He gazed on the past and the future too,
And opened the heavenly world to view.
And opened the heavenly world to view.

John later completed a second mission to Great Britain, as well as a mission to France. He learned the French language well enough to write missionary tracts in French and assisted with the translation of the Book of Mormon into both French and German.

John Taylor's zeal for missionary work is reflected in the hymn text, "Go, Ye Messengers of Glory" which he wrote. This stirring and lofty hymn is published today in the Church's 1985 hymnbook, with a musical setting by Leroy J. Robertson for congregation, plus a setting for male voices by F. Christensen:

> Go, ye messengers of glory;
> Run, ye legates of the skies.
> Go and tell the pleasing story
> That a glorious angel flied,
> Great and mighty, Great and mighty,
> With a message from the skies.
>
> Go to ev'ry tribe and nation;
> Visit ev'ry land and clime.
> Sound to all the proclamation;
> Tell to all the truth sublime:
> That the gospel, That the Gospel
> Does in ancient glory shine.
>
> Go, to all the gospel carry;
> Let the joyful news abound.
> Go till ev'ry nation hear you,
> Jew and Gentile greet the sound.
> Let the gospel, Let the gospel
> Echo all the earth around.[11]

Upon the death of Joseph Smith, Brigham Young became the second president of the Church. John Taylor then assumed the responsibilities of President of the Quorum of the Twelve, though he was not formally sustained to that position until the general conference held in Salt Lake City on October 6, 1877.

> This action formalized Elder Taylor's status as the presiding officer of the Church of Jesus Christ of Latter-day Saints and set him on the road toward which his whole life had been treading since those early days in England when the impressionable boy had often heard soft, melodious music, ostensibly performed by angelic and supernatural beings, and had received spiritual impressions that he was to go to America "to preach the gospel."[12]

John Taylor was a forceful speaker and writer of prose as well as poetry. With his beautiful voice, he sang often. Recorded incidents suggest that he committed the poetry to memory and sang often without music.

Francis M. Gibbons recalls this interesting story:

> Two Latter-day Saint veterans of Nauvoo and the exodus...were at odds and had refused to submit to the counsel of their local leaders. Being personally acquainted with them, John had agreed to hear and to try to resolve their grievances. After the pair had entered his office and were comfortably seated, John said that with their approval he would like to sing one of the songs of Zion to them. They agreed, of course, whereupon the host proceeded to sing a familiar Mormon hymn in his melodious baritone voice. We might logically infer that these listeners were not a little awed by this rendition, coming from the head of the Church, who, they would not have failed to recall, had similarly serenaded the Prophet Joseph Smith during his last hours in the Carthage jail. Any awe they experienced no doubt would have turned to amazement at what followed. The arbiter, turned singer, told them he never heard one hymn but that he wanted to hear another, whereupon, with their approval, he sang song number two. Then, telling his audience he understood there was luck in odd numbers, he sang a third hymn before they could protest or approve. And finally, Elder Taylor ended his impromptu recital by singing a fourth hymn, assuring his dumbfounded visitors that if they would indulge him just once more, he would then consider their case. At the end, the erstwhile enemies, touched by the Spirit, were melted to tears, and, standing to thank their host, shook hands and left without having said anything about the dispute that had brought them to his office.[13]

When Brigham Young passed away in 1880, John Taylor became the third President of the Church.

In 1886, President John Taylor announced his desire to publish a new hymnbook for the Church, this time with words *and* music (all previous hymnbooks had included only the words). He called a committee of five prominent Latter-day Saint musicians to produce the book: George Careless, Ebenezer Beasley, Joseph J. Daynes, Evan Stephens, and Thomas C. Griggs. President Taylor wanted, so far as possible, original music "by our mountain home composers." Finally, the volume was published in May, 1889, with the title, *Latter-*

day Saints' Psalmody. In the preface, the committee made these interesting statements:

> [A] feature which we feel confident will prove acceptable to many, is the presentation of a number of old and familiar tunes, which, together with the words, are associated by many with the incidents of the most pleasing experiences in their first acquaintance with the gospel; while to others, scenes of trial and suffering will be vividly brought to their remembrance.
>
> That this work may be a means of still further extending a knowledge of the Gospel of Salvation; and aid to the congregations of the Saints in singing the praises of the Lord, and of assistance in their gatherings the world over, is the prayer of your brethren in the Gospel of peace.

The *Psalmody* had the distinction of being "the largest and most important musical work yet published in Utah."[14] It was the first hymnbook published by the Church with music as well as words. Sadly, President John Taylor did not live to see this important work in print. Nevertheless, through this hymnbook which he had directed to be published, the influence of John Taylor is reflected in the music of the Church today.

John Taylor firmly believed that music was part and parcel of religion and may elevate us to celestial heights, as illustrated by this quotation:

> Consider for a moment how much sacred music enters into the very life, exercise and progress of religion!... The very spirit of religion is breathed into music.... Never, indeed do we feel so near heaven as when listening to the performance of some grand anthem, in which the angels themselves might fitly take their parts.[15]

The latter part of this quotation also points out John Taylor's strong desire for high quality in the music we compose and perform in church today. Music, in his opinion ought to lift the listener, and give him a glimpse of heaven:

> We have no idea of the excellence of the music we shall have in heaven. It may be said of that, as the apostle Paul has said in rela-

tion to something else—"Eye hath not seen, nor ear heard, neither have entered into the hearts of man, the things which God hath prepared for them that love him" (I Corinthians 2:9). We have no idea of the excellence, beauty, harmony and symphony of the music in the heavens.[16]

Mormonism, John Taylor passionately believed, ought to embrace and include *all* that is good and true, including good music:

> Is there a true principle of science in the world? It is ours. Are there true principles of music, or mechanism, or of philosophy? If there are, they are all ours. Is there a true principle of government that exists in the world anywhere? It is ours, it is God's; for every good and perfect gift that exists in the world among men proceeds from the "Father of lights with whom there is no variableness, neither shadow of turning." It is God that has given every good gift that the world ever did possess.[17]

Perhaps President John Taylor is best remembered today for the prophecy that Zion, with all of her intellectual and cultural attainments, *will*, and *must*, become the "praise and glory of the whole earth:"

> *You will see the day that Zion will be as far ahead of the outside world in everything pertaining to learning of every kind as we are today in regard to religious matters.* You mark my words, and write them down, and weep if they do not come to pass....
> *God expects Zion to become the praise and glory of the whole earth so that kings, hearing of her fame, will come and gaze upon her glory....*
> We ought to foster education and intelligence of every kind; cultivate literary tastes, and men of literary and scientific talent should improve that talent; and all should magnify the gifts which God has given them. Educate your children, and seek for those to teach them who have faith in God and in his promises, as well as intelligence.... If there is anything good and praiseworthy in morals, religion, science, or anything calculated to exalt and ennoble man, we are after it. But with all our getting, we want to get understanding, and that understanding which flows from God.[18]

This is not to say, however, that John Taylor did not see a place in our recreation or entertainment for music. Men are meant to enjoy life to the fullest, in all wholesome ways. The following statements echo the thinking of Brigham Young:

> There are some people who think that the fiddle, for instance, is an instrument of the devil and it is quite wrong to use it. I do not think so, I think it is a splendid thing to dance to. But some folks think that we should not dance. Yes, we should enjoy life in every way we can....

> Our object is to get and to cleave to everything that is good, and to reject everything that is bad. One reason why religious people in the world are opposed to music and theatres is because of the corruption that is mixed up with them. Wicked and corrupt men associate themselves with theses things, and degrade them; but is this any reason that the saints should not enjoy the gifts of God? Is that a correct principle? Certainly.... It is for them to grasp at everything that is good, and calculated to promote the happiness of the human family.[19]

This point is reiterated in an *Epistle of the First Presidency,* dated April 8, 1887. This epistle further states that instead of forbidding the entertainments of the world, members of the Church ought to create our own secular music, drama, and literature, but purify these of unclean or unwholesome elements. This point has a very contemporary ring to it, having been reiterated by church leaders today.

> We have given the religious world a lesson upon this point. We have shown that the social enjoyment and amusements are not incompatible with correct conduct and true religion. Instead of forbidding the theatre and placing it under ban, it has been the aim of Latter-day Saints to control it and keep it free from impure influences, and to preserve it as a place where all could meet for the purpose of healthful enjoyment.[20]

With the Edmunds Act of 1882, the U.S. Government began to track down, arrest and jail polygamous men of the

Church. In particular, the government seemed to target the more visible leaders in the Church. This situation forced President John Taylor to spend the last two years of his living "under-ground," moving from place to place, trying to stay ahead of the prosecutors. He died in Kaysville, Utah, July 25, 1887, nearly seventy-nine years of age.

B.H. Roberts described the funeral held in the Salt Lake Tabernacle July 29, 1887:

> Though (the services) lasted for two hours and a half, and many had been sitting in the building from early morning, there was no sign of weariness. The most profound silence was maintained. Nothing was heard in the vast building but the sweet strains of music, the voice of the speakers as they recounted the noble deeds and virtues of the illustrious dead. A spirit of profound sorrow brooded over that great congregation. Israel sincerely mourned the departure of their great leader.[21]

Among the cortege that accompanied the body of John Taylor to the place of burial were the following musical organizations: Held's Cornet Band, Ogden Brass Band, Garfield Beach Band, Olsen's Brass Band, Provo Silver Band, the Salt Lake City Band and a choir that sang at the grave site:

> O My Father, thou that dwellest
> In that high and glorious place!
> When shall I regain thy presence
> And again behold thy face?
> In thy holy habitation
> Did my spirit once reside?
> In my first primeval childhood,
> Was I nurtured near thy side?[22]

1 John Taylor: *The Gospel Kingdom* (Salt Lake City, Utah; Bookcraft, 1990, p.62.

2 B. H. Roberts: *The Life of John Taylor* (Salt Lake City: Bookcraft, 1963), pp. 27-28.

3 Ibid, p. 28.

4 Ibid., p. 29.

5 Ibid, p. 31.

6 Ibid, pp. 63.

7 Ibid, p. 65-66.

8 Op. Cit, p. 40.

9 *History of the Church*, Volume VI, p. 616.

10 Hymn No. 29 in the current (1985) hymnal.

11 Hymns 262 and 327 in the current 1985 hymnal.

12 Francis Gibbons: *John Taylor Mormon Philosopher, Prophet of God* (Salt Lake City, Deseret Book, 1985) p. 195.

13 Op Cit, pp. 203-204.

14 *The Latter-day Saints Psalmody*, 1889, Preface.

15 "The First Presidency on Music," *Utah Musical Times*, Volume II, No. 7, (1877), p. 105.

16 *Gospel Kingdom*, p. 62.

17 Ibid. p. 5.

18 Ibid. pp. 275-277.

19 Ibid, p. 62.

20 Ibid, p. 339.

21 B. H. Roberts: *Life of John Taylor*, p. 461.

22 Hymn No. 292 in our current (1985) hymnal.

WILFORD WOODRUFF

M Withers '94

WILFORD WOODRUFF
(1807-1889)

*"When I shall leave this life...I would like
to visit my loved ones and enjoy their
sweet singing."*[1]

Wilford Woodruff was President of the Council of the Twelve in 1887, when John Taylor passed away, and succeeded John Taylor to become the fourth Prophet of this dispensation.

Born in rural Connecticut in 1807, Wilford became an accomplished hunter and fisherman. Though he attended schools in the area, he was more interested in religious truth than the subjects taught at school.

A spirit of revival spread through New England during his boyhood years. While attending meetings with other members of his family, he earnestly "tried to get religion," but the preaching brought more "darkness than light."

Wilford recorded in his journal:

> At an early age my mind began to be exercised upon religious subjects, but I never made a profession of religion until 1830 when I was twenty-three years of age. I did not join any church for the reason that I could not find a body of people, denomination, or church that had for its doctrine faith, and practices those principles, ordinances, and gifts which constituted the gospel of Jesus Christ as taught by Him and His apostles.[2]

In 1833, when Wilford was twenty-six, Mormon elders scheduled a meeting in the village schoolhouse and circulated notices throughout the area. Wilford learned of the meeting from his sister-in-law as he returned home for the evening:

> I immediately turned out my horses and started for the school-

house without waiting for supper. On my way I prayed most sincere-
ly that the Lord would give me His spirit, and that if these were the
servants of God I might know it, and that my heart might be prepared to receive the divine message they had to deliver.[3]

After a prayer and the singing of a hymn, even before the
elders began to preach, Wilford knew that these were men of
God, and the church they represented was the church he had
been searching for:

> Elder Pulsipher opened with prayer. He knelt down and asked
> the Lord in the name of Jesus Christ for what he wanted. His man-
> ner of prayer and the influence which went with it impressed me
> greatly. The spirit of the Lord rested upon me and bore witness that
> he was a servant of God. *After singing,* he preached for an hour and a
> half. The spirit of God rested mightily upon him and he bore a
> strong testimony of the divine authenticity of the Book of Mormon
> and of the mission of the Prophet Joseph Smith.[4]

After two days' instruction by the elders, Wilford and his
brother, Azmon, were baptized by Zera Pulsipher on December
31, 1833, in water "mixed with ice and snow." Upon his joining the Church, Wilford began writing a daily journal which he
continued faithfully for sixty-four years until his death.
Considering it a sacred obligation, he wrote in great detail of
the events of his daily life, the lives of those around him, and
of the Church. He developed the mental discipline necessary
to write "nearly word-for-word" two or three sermons in a row,
after they were given. The many volumes of his journals provide the single most important record of Church history during
these years.

Four months after his baptism, Wilford met the Prophet
Joseph for the first time. After hearing the Prophet preach,
Wilford wrote:

> There was more light, knowledge, truth and good sense made
> manifest in this meeting respecting the gospel and the kingdom of
> God than I had ever received from the sectarian world during my

life. I rejoiced much in being made acquainted with a Prophet of God and the Saints of God. I felt that it was a fulfillment of the promises of God to me in former days. It was what my soul had desired for many years. And I had now found the people, Church, and the Kingdom of God, and I was satisfied.[5]

From his baptism until the end of his life, Wilford's total focus was on the building up of the Kingdom of God. Wilford Woodruff was to become one of the greatest missionaries in the history of the Church. His expansive travels, the inordinate trials and extreme hardships, and his brilliant successes are reminiscent of the Apostle Paul.

Though still a priest in the Aaronic Priesthood, Wilford Woodruff and his companion, Henry Brown, departed on January 13, 1835 for a mission to Tennessee and Arkansas. With a valise packed with copies of the Book of Mormon, the hymn book,[6] and little more, they arrived in Memphis on March 27, tired and hungry. After locating one of the nicer taverns in town, where they hoped to find lodging for the night, they introduced themselves as ministers of the Gospel. Surprised at the appearance of the travelers, the proprietor said to Wilford that "he did not look much like a preacher." Wilford recorded:

> I did not blame him, as most of the preachers he ever had been acquainted with rode on fine horses or in fine carriages, dressed in broadcloth, had large salaries, and would likely see this whole world sink to perdition before they would wade through one hundred and seventy miles of mud to save the people.[7]

In wanting to have some fun at the missionaries' expense, the landlord offered to keep them overnight if Wilford would preach. Sensing the proprietor's motives, Wilford did not want to do so, but finally he reluctantly agreed.

> He took my valise, and the landlady got me a good supper. I sat down in a large hall to eat. Before I got through, the room began to be filled by some of the rich and fashionable people of Memphis,

dressed in their broadcloth and silk, while my appearance was such as you can imagine, after traveling through mud as I had done. When I had finished eating, the table was carried out of the room over the heads of the people. I was placed in the corner of the room, with a stand having a *Bible, hymnbook, and candle on it,* hemmed in by a dozen men, with the landlord in the center.

There were present some five hundred persons, who had come together, not to hear a gospel sermon, but to have some fun. I read a hymn, and asked them to sing. Not a soul would sing a word. I told them I had not the gift of singing, but with the help of the Lord, I would pray and preach. I knelt down to pray, and the men around me dropped on their knees. I prayed to the Lord to give me His spirit and to show me the hearts of the people. I promised the Lord, in my prayer, that I would deliver to the congregation whatever He would give me. I arose and spoke one hour and a half, and it was one of the best sermons of my life. The lives of the congregation were opened to the vision of my mind, and I told them of their wicked deeds and the reward they would obtain. The men who surrounded me dropped their heads. Three minutes after I closed I was the only person in the room.[8]

This less-than-successful meeting did not begin with the singing of a hymn as Wilford had hoped. Perhaps if the men had been willing to sing, the Spirit of the Lord might have attended the gathering of listeners. Even though the men were indifferent to the message, the landlord did offer them a good breakfast before they left the next morning, and he invited them to return whenever they were in the area.

Seven months after his return from the southern states, on April 13, 1837, Wilford married Phoebe Carter at Kirtland. Even though he loved her deeply, "one month and a day" later, Wilford left her in the care of a friend and departed for a second mission, this time to the Fox Islands, off the coast of Maine.

Wilford completed a year-long mission with remarkable success. It was during his second mission to the islands that he received a letter from Thomas B. Marsh, President of the Quorum of Twelve Apostles, informing him that he had been called to fill a vacancy in the Quorum by one of the "Twelve who had fallen." He was instructed to travel to Far West, Missouri, and, "on the 26th of April next, take your leave of the Saints here and depart for other climes across the mighty deep."[9]

Because the Mormons had been driven from Missouri by order of the Governor, Far West was now practically a ghost town. Nevertheless, Wilford joined Brigham Young, John Taylor, Heber C. Kimball, and John A. Smith at the temple site in Far West on April 26, 1839 for this sacred meeting. Because the brethren were now back in enemy territory, they chose to meet in the early pre-dawn hours. Sadly, it was necessary to excommunicate about thirty people who had apostatized. Then they sang a hymn, "The Mission of the Twelve." Following this, the brethren set in place the southeast corner-stone of the temple, symbolically at least, to await the time when the Lord would permit the building of the temple. Wilford and George A. Smith, in turn, sat on the cornerstone while they were ordained to the apostleship. Each of the five then offered a prayer in order of their standing of the Quorum. Having left their wives in the care of the Lord, the brethren sang the tender hymn "Adam-ondi-Ahman," and left for New York and then to the British Isles.

After twenty-three days at sea, the *Oxford* arrived at Liverpool on January 11, 1840, carrying Wilford and his companions. In England, an item of high priority was to publish the Book of Mormon, as well as a new hymnbook.

> Not surprising, the apostles decided to publish [a hymnbook] without delay, a decision that was ratified at the April 1840 conference in Preston. Brigham Young, Parley P. Pratt and John Taylor were assigned to choose the hymns. They moved quickly. By May the apostles had granted a printing contract for three thousand copies to W. R. Thomas. Writing to Brigham Young on May 4, Parley said that he wrote new hymns every day and hoped to contribute one hundred to the new book. "There is indeed a great call for hymn books suited to our worship," he added.[10]

Wilford Woodruff and Brigham Young went south to Herefordshire where the two of them set out to raise funds for the publication of the hymnbook. In six months, seventy-eight hymns from Emma Smith's hymnbook had been selected as the core of the new collection. To these were added 193 other hymn texts that were newly composed or selected from other sources. With the addition of an index, *A Collection of Sacred Hymns for the Church of Jesus Christ by Latter-day Saints in Europe* was soon published. The historic *Manchester Hymnal*, as it was to be called, went through thirteen editions. Moreover, its influence was felt in all subsequent Latter-day Saint hymnbooks published in the 19th century. Of course, the selection and editing of the hymns that were included were absolutely necessary for the creation of this volume, but so was the procuring of funds which fell to Brigham and Wilford.

The successes of the eight Apostles who served missions in Great Britain between 1837 and 1841 are not unlike those of the Apostles of the New Testament, or of the great missionaries recorded in the Book of Mormon. The story of Wilford Woodruff's life shows a man who was ever-sensitive to the whisperings of the Spirit. So often when there was a spiritual prompting, there had been singing. Wilford writes of one such incident:

> March 1st, 1840, was my birthday; I was thirty-three years of age. It being Sunday, I preached twice during the day to a large assembly in the city hall...and administered the Sacrament to the Saints. In the evening I again met with a large assembly of the Saints and strangers, *and while singing the first hymn, the spirit of the Lord rested upon me* and the voice of God said to me, "This is the last meeting you will hold with this people for many days." I was astonished at this...and when I arose to speak to the people, I told them that it was the last meeting I should hold with them for many days.... At the close of the meeting four people came forward for baptism; we went down into the water and I baptized them.[11]

Wilford then went to the Lord for an explanation. "The answer I received was that I should go to the south; for the

Lord had a great work for me to perform, as many souls were waiting for His word."

> Over six hundred...had broken off from the Wesleyan Methodists, and taken the name of United Brethren. They had forty-five preachers among them, and for religious services had chapels and many houses that were licensed according to the law of the land. This body of United Brethren were searching for light and truth, but had gone as far as they could, and were calling upon the Lord continually to open the way before them and send them light and knowledge, that they might know the true way to be saved.[12]

Over 600 baptisms resulted from this journey "to the south," including that of the constable who was sent with a warrant for Wilford's arrest. When the constable was impressed with the message and refused to serve the warrant, the rector sent two clerks of the Church of England as spies. They, too, were baptized. The prompting that there were many souls waiting for the gospel message came during the singing of a hymn.

Early in the spring of 1840, Wilford went to the Weston home near Gloucester to introduce the Gospel to the Weston family. Mary Ann, the only one at home, invited Elder Woodruff in to warm his hands by the fire. She described his sitting by the fireplace, singing a hymn:

> There was no one at home but me. He sat by the fire and soon commenced singing [a song of Zion].... While he was singing I looked at him. He looked so peaceful and happy, I thought he must be a good Man and the Gospel he preached must be true.[13]

Mary Ann Weston was the only member of her family to "obey the gospel." She immigrated to America, and married Peter Maughn in Kirtland. Eventually they settled in Cache Valley in northern Utah.

Wilford returned to Great Britain in 1844 to serve a second mission. His travels took him to Europe twice more, to Canada and twenty-three of the United States. He participated in the march of Zion's Camp in 1834, and arrived with the pioneers in the Salt Lake Valley in 1847. He calculated that he traveled more than 175,000 miles altogether. His life extended through most of the nineteenth century. He was protected from serious injury and death on many occasions and he witnessed the power of the adversary and enjoyed the comfort of ministering angels. His journal recounts frequent miracles and visions.

At 82, Wilford Woodruff was sustained as President of the Church on October 10, 1880. The early years of his administration witnessed continued persecution by the enemies of the Church. Law enforcement and government officials began enforcing the Edmunds Act which prohibited polygamy with "stern rigidity." Like John Taylor who spent the last two years of his life underground to prevent arrest and imprisonment, Wilford Woodruff spent a considerable amount of time in southern Utah and Arizona, away from his family, evading the federal officials. Having seen in a vision what would become of the Church should it continue its practice of plural marriage, on September 25, 1890, Wilford issued the now-famous Manifesto which forbade plural marriage in the Church.

Apostle Wilford Woodruff had been present in July, 1847 when Brigham Young plunged his cane into the ground and said, "Here we will build the temple to our god!" Forty years later—an entire generation of sacrifice, adversity and the most arduous labor—President Wilford Woodruff saw the completion of the Salt Lake Temple, and dedicated this great monument to the Lord on April 6, 1893.

Music was an important part of the dedicatory services, as it had been for each of the previous temple dedications. William W. Phelps wrote the stirring text to "The Spirit of God Like a Fire is Burning" to an anonymous tune for the dedication of the Kirtland Temple in 1836. Evan Stephens composed the "Hosanna Anthem," a powerful musical elaboration of "The Spirit of God" for the dedication of the Salt Lake Temple. Evan Stephens' "Hosanna Anthem" was written either by the request of President Woodruff, or with his approval, and has been sung at every temple dedication since.[14]

Five months later, on August 28, President Woodruff and his two counselors, George Q. Cannon and Joseph F. Smith left Salt Lake City with the Tabernacle Choir to perform at the World's Fair in Chicago. Enroute, the Choir visited Denver, Kansas City and Independence, Missouri. In Independence, the Tabernacle Choir and the First Presidency were received by the mayor and city council, as well as other dignitaries. On this auspicious occasion, President Woodruff gave a brief address, and the Tabernacle Choir performed. Writing in his journal, the Prophet made these comments about this occasion:

> The mayor of Independence had lost one arm in the war, but the one he had left was kindly given to me while I was with him. One striking incident worthy of record is this; I went through Jackson County with Harry Brown in 1834 on a mission to the Southern States. At the time we travelled secretly lest our lives should be taken by mobocrats; now in 1893, the mayor of the Independence and hosts of others bid us welcome to the city. How great the contrast, and we ascribe the honor and praise to God, our Heavenly Father.[15]

In his history of the Tabernacle Choir, *A Century of Singing*, J. Spencer Cornwall adds further details of this historic occasion:

> The whole town was in holiday attire. Fifty carriages met the choir party at the depot and were at once filled to overflowing. The remainder of the party walked up the slight eminence from the depot, through a beautiful shaded street to the well-remembered Temple square, where several thousand people had congregated. Presidents Wilford Woodruff, George Q. Cannon, and Joseph F. Smith were escorted to the platform, and there a rousing song was sung and greatly applauded. At the invitation of Mayor Mercer, the whole gathering then adjourned to the handsome gray stone church of the Josephites, who numbered about eight hundred.
>
> The building was crammed to overflowing. The choir was singing, the audience applauding, and brief remarks were made by

Major Mercer and Presidents Woodruff and Cannon. The choir was immensely applauded, especially Easton's rendition of "O My Father."[16]

Cornwall then included this description of the Tabernacle Choir's performance from the *Globe-Democrat* of St. Louis:

> A thrill of surprise was felt at the announcement that a large band of accomplished singers from the Mormon Tabernacle would appear in St. Louis en route to Chicago, there to contend for a prize of substantial proportions. The idea of musical culture in the heart of the Rocky Mountains is new to most people not familiar with that region, and yet the fact was emphasized with not little force by the appearance of 250 singers, Mormons all, the trained choir of the principal Church in the Mormon Country, who gave an entertainment that may justly be pronounced one of the events of the season.
>
> From a purely technical and professional point of view, there was little to be desired in the chorus work. There was what is often lacking in concerts of professional people, a spirit of enthusiasm among the singers that more properly rendered the chosen selections that could have been done by professional skill alone. But when to the skill of the professional is added the enthusiasm of the amateur, the result is perfection.
>
> There was a lack of conventionality in the concert that both surprised and pleased the hearers. The leader read the program in an old-fashioned style that both interested and amused the people; he pulled the conductor's stand from the platform with an energy that showed he was accustomed to wait on himself: he forgot to bow on entering and leaving, and generally exhibited unfamiliarity with the tricks of a professional conductor. But so far from being offended, the change was evidently agreeable to the audience, and they applauded his old-time ways as heartily as they would have done the most Chesterfieldian bow that was ever made from a platform.[17]

Under the direction of Evan Stephens, the Tabernacle Choir went on to the World's Fair at Chicago where they performed for the Eisteddfod competition. Required selections performed by each of the competing choirs consisted of the following: "Worthy is the Lamb" from Handel's *Messiah*, "Blessed are the Men that Fear Him" from Mendelssohn's *Elijah*, and "Now the Impetuous Torrents Rise" from Jenkin's *David and Saul*.

The first price of $5,000 was awarded to the Choral Union of Scranton, Pennsylvania; the second prize of $1,000 was given to the Tabernacle choir, with a gold medal going to Evan Stephens. How Wilford Woodruff must have felt on this occasion, realizing that the Saints were driven from Illinois less than fifty years before!

The *Deseret News* published this quotation by W. Apmadoc, secretary of the International Eisteddfod:

> Had it not been for a little unfortunate 'flatting' in the last chorus there is no doubt that they (the Tabernacle Choir) would have been accorded the first prize.... Had the Mormon choir sung as well at the great contest as they did on the Saturday after at the Grand Central Music hall, they would have easily defeated all competitors.[18]

While in Chicago, the Tabernacle Choir received invitations to sing in Carnegie Music Hall in New York, and also in Boston and Philadelphia. Because of other engagements in Chicago and a concert scheduled in Omaha, Nebraska on the return trip home, the invitations had to be declined.

When traveling throughout the church, President Woodruff was frequently greeted upon arrival in a city with the music of a brass band or a choir, which pleased him very much. He also enjoyed the music provided by his family in the privacy of their home:

> I am fond of music and singing gatherings, and when I shall leave this life I hope my family would gather often to sing. If I was permitted, I would like to visit my loved ones and enjoy their sweet singing.[19]

Wilford believed music to be an important part of a young person's education, as indicated by this statement:

> Singing exercises can be made a great attraction and also a valuable addition to the education of the young. The interest that is now taken among us in vocal and instrumental music is a marked feature of the times.[20]

We may assume from this short comment made in
Wilfords' journal on June 11, 1897, that he was able to play the
piano to some extent, and apparently enjoyed sitting down to
play: "Played on the piano."[21]

On Sunday after, February 28, 1897, and continuing again
on Monday morning, a special commemoration of Wilford
Woodruff's 90th birthday was held in the Tabernacle. The
Sunday afternoon session, presented by the Sunday Schools of
the Church, opened with the hymn, "We Thank Thee O God,
for a Prophet," sung by the congregation and directed by Evan
Stephens. Matthais F. Cowley observed that the "rendition vis-
ibly affected President Woodruff, and made it necessary for the
honored veteran to wipe the tear-drops from his eyelids."[22]
Other hymns included "God Speed the Right" and "In Our
Lovely Deseret." Tabernacle organist Joseph J. Daynes played
an organ solo, "My Father's Growing Old."

Elder George A. Smith talked of the life and labors of
Wilford Wooddruff:

> In his lifetime, he had traveled 175,000 miles to preach the
> gospel. He had baptized 2,000 souls into the Church, and had writ-
> ten a journal of 7,000 pages, covering his work for a period of sixty-
> two years.[23]

President Woodruff was then presented with a basket of 90
fresh roses.

A special trio was written for the occasion by H. A. Tucket
and arranged by Evan Stephens. "We Ever Pray for Thee" was
sung by three young ladies:

> We every pray for thee, our prophet dear,
> That God will give to thee comfort and cheer;
> As the advancing year furrow thy brow,
> Still may the light within shine bright as now.
>
> We every pray for thee with all our hearts,
> That strength be given thee to do thy part,

> To guide and counsel us from day to day,
> To shed a holy light around our way.
>
> We ever pray for thee with fervent love;
> And as the children's prayer is heard above,
> Thou shalt be ever blest, and God will give
> All that is meet and best while thou shalt live.

Stephens' three-part setting for ladies' voices has appeared in Latter-day Saint hymnals since. A four-part setting for congregation was added to the 1985 hymnal.

President Woodruff's final year was marked by declining health. On July 9, 1897, he recorded the following:

> I feel some better this morning at home all day. Brothers Nuttall [personal secretary to the First Presidency] and Joseph E. Taylor called this evening. I requested the brethren to sing "God Moves in a Mysterious Way" after which Brother Taylor prayed. I then asked the brethren to administer to me.[24]

In August of 1898, Wilford Woodruff, accompanied by a few close friends, went to San Francisco where he thought a change of climate would be good for him. On the morning of September 2, the beloved Prophet passed away peacefully in his sleep. Funeral services were held in the Salt Lake Tabernacle on September 8, during which the Tabernacle Choir sang his favorite hymn, "God Moves in a Mysterious Way." The motto, "The glory of God is intelligence," framed by a circle of cut flowers, hung near the casket. Also displayed was a large harp of flowers, a gift from the Tabernacle Choir as a reminder of the "divine harmony of President Woodruff's life."[25] The choir sang another of Wilford Woodruff's favorite hymns, "O My Father."

Three bands—Held's Brass Band, the Ogden Band, and the First Regimental Band of the Utah National Guard—accompanied his body to its final resting place in the Salt Lake City Cemetery.

1 Wilford Woodruff: Journal, Volume 9, p. 484.
2 Matthias F. Cowley: *Wilford Woodruff, History of His Life and Labors* (Salt Lake City, Deseret News, 1916) p. 14.
3 Ibid, p. 33.
4 Ibid, p. 33.
5 Leonard Arrington: *The Presidents of the Church* (Salt Lake City: Deseret Book, 1986) p. 126.
6 Matthias Cowley: *Wilford Woodruff*, p. 55, see p. 132.
7 Ibid, p. 55.
8 Ibid, p. 55-56.
9 Preston Nibley: *The Presidents of the Church* (Salt Lake City: Deseret Book, 1941), p. 140.
10 James B. Allen: *Men with a Mission* (Salt lake City: Deseret Book, Co., 1992) pp. 247-248.
11 Matthias Cowley: p. 116.
12 Ibid. p. 117.
13 Kenneth Godfrey: *Women's Voices An Untold History of the Latter-day Saints, 1830-1900* (Salt Lake City: Deseret Book Co., 1982) pp. 34-36.
14 A somewhat simpler version by Darwin Wolford was written for the dedication of the Tokyo Temple in 1985 and has been sung at each temple dedication since.
15 Matthais Cowley, p. 583.
16 Op. cit (Salt Lake City: Deseret Book, 1958), pp. 65-66.
17 Ibid., p. 66-67.
18 Ibid, p. 68.
19 Wilford Woodruff, Journal, Volume 9, p. 486, June 11, 1897.
20 *Church News*, August 28, 1983.
21 Wilford Woodruff, Journal, Volume 9, p. 485, June 11, 1897.
22 Matthais Cowley: p. 600.
23 Ibid., p. 600.
24 Wilford Woodruff, Journal, p. 490.
25 Matthais Cowley, p. 640.

LORENZO SNOW

LORENZO SNOW
(1814-1901)

*"Among the sublime display of the
Creator's works, we sang the praises of
His eternal name, and implored those
gifts which our circumstances required."*[1]

Oliver and Rosetta Snow moved with their family of four girls to Mantua, Ohio in 1806, from New England. There, their fifth child and first son, Lorenzo, was born.

The children were taught "habits of industry, economy, and strict morality, and extended to them the best facilities for scholastic education the country at that time afforded."[2] Eliza, Lorenzo's older sister by ten years, wrote of the religious atmosphere in their home:

> In their religious faith our parents were by profession Baptists, but not of the rigid, iron-bedstead order; their house was a resort for the good and intelligent of all denominations, and their hospitality of all denominations, and their hospitality was proverbial. Thus, as their children grew up they had ample opportunities for forming acquaintances with the erudite of all religious persuasions.[3]

Living in the near vicinity of Kirtland, the Snows were easily discovered by the Mormon missionaries. Lorenzo's mother and sister, Lenora, were baptized in 1831. Eliza became a member in April, 1835. In the fall of that year she moved to near-by Kirtland to live with the family of Joseph Smith and become a teacher for the Smith "family school."

In the meantime, Lorenzo, now twenty-one, decided to attend Oberlin Collegiate Institute (now known as Oberlin College). While enroute to Oberlin, he met David W. Patten, a man who would change his life forever. Only seven months before, this articulate gentleman had become one of the original Twelve Apostles. He awakened Lorenzo's mind to the things of eternity and prepared him for later conversion by his sister, Eliza. Three years later, David Patten was shot to death at the infamous battle of Crooked River, becoming the "first apostolic martyr of the restored Church."[4]

Though Oberlin College at that time was a Presbyterian institution, Lorenzo felt the religious teachings he was exposed to were "sorely lacking," and did not measure up to what he had learned from Elder Patten about God, man, and man's eternal relationship to God.

Eliza urged Lorenzo to leave Oberlin and come to Kirtland where he could study Hebrew at the School of the Prophets. He needed little persuasion. Upon hearing the Prophet Joseph Smith speak for the first time, he said:

> Joseph Smith was not what would be called a fluent speaker. He simply bore his testimony to what the Lord had manifested to him.... As I looked upon him and listened, I thought to myself that a man bearing such a wonderful testimony as he did and having such a countenance as he possessed could hardly be a false prophet.[5]

Lorenzo Snow was baptized by Apostle John F. Boynton, who earlier had baptized Eliza.

After his baptism and confirmation, Lorenzo had not yet felt the presence of the Holy Ghost as he was promised.

> Some two or three weeks after I was baptized...I began to reflect upon the fact that I had not obtained a *knowledge* of the truth of the work—that I had not realized the fulfillment of the promise "he that doeth my will shall know of the doctrine," and I began to feel uneasy. I laid aside my books, left the house, and wandered around through the field under the oppressive influence of a gloomy, disconsolate spirit, while an indescribable cloud of darkness seemed to envelop me. I had been accustomed, at the close of day, to retire for secret prayer, to a grove a short distance from my lodgings....

> I had no sooner opened my lips in an effort to pray, than I heard
> a sound, just above my head, like the rustling of silken robes, and
> immediately the Spirit of God descended upon me, completely
> enveloping my whole person, filling me, from the crown of my head
> to the soles of my feet, and O, the joy and happiness I felt! No lan-
> guage can describe the almost instantaneous transition from a dense
> cloud of mental and spiritual darkness into a refulgence of light and
> knowledge, as it was at the time imparted to my understanding. I
> then received a perfect knowledge that God lives, that Jesus Christ
> is the Son of God, and of the restoration of the holy Priesthood, and
> the fullness of the Gospel.[6]

The same experience was repeated for several nights in a
row.

Early in 1837, the Snow family left Kirtland for Far West
with other members of the Church who hoped to escape the
persecution of the Saints in that area. Lorenzo served a mission
in Ohio, the first of his many missions.

In early 1840, Lorenzo rejoined his family who, by this
time, had been driven from the state of Ohio and settled near
Nauvoo, Illinois. While discussing a passage of scripture with
Elder H. G. Sherwood

> and while [he was] endeavoring to give an explanation, the
> Spirit of God fell upon me to a marked extent, and the Lord revealed
> to me, just as plainly as the sun at noonday, this principle, which I
> put in a couplet:
>
> > As man is, God once was;
> > As God now is, man may become.[7]

Though, at first, Lorenzo was reluctant to share this revelation with anyone, Joseph Smith later confirmed this as "true
gospel doctrine."[8]

This far-reaching concept impressed Eliza deeply, and may
well have been the initial inspiration for her insightful hymn,
"O My Father."[9] Written sometime after June 29, 1884 when
Eliza became a plural wife to Joseph Smith, this tender hymn
presents a panorama of man's existence from his spiritual

birth, to his return from this "frail existence" to our Heavenly Father *and* Mother.

> O my Father, thou that dwellest
> In the high and glorious place,
> When shall I regain thy presence
> And again behold thy face?
> In thy holy habitation,
> Did my spirit once reside?
> In my first primeval childhood,
> Was I nurtured near thy side?
>
> For a wise and glorious purpose
> Thou hast placed me here on earth
> And withheld the recollection
> Of my former friends and birth;
> Yet oft-times a secret something
> Whispered, "You're a stranger here,"
> And I felt that I had wandered
> From a more exalted sphere.
>
> I had learned to call thee Father,
> Thru thy Spirit from on high,
> But, until the key of knowledge
> Was restored, I knew not why.
> In the heav'ns are parents single?
> No the thought makes reason stare!
> Truth is reason; truth eternal
> Tells me I've a mother there.
>
> When I leave this frail existence,
> When I lay this mortal by,
> Father, Mother, may I meet you
> In your royal courts on high?
> Then, at length, when I've completed
> All you sent me forth to do,
> With your mutual approbation
> Let me come and dwell with you.

"O My Father" has been a favorite of all of the presidents of the Church, as well as members of the Church around the world. This hymn is unique among all of the hymns of Zion: Though the doctrine of a Mother in Heaven is not articulated in any of the four standard works, it is considered to be as true as if it were. The hymn is a testimony of the greatness of Eliza R. Snow—her spiritual insights and of her great literary skills. It is also a tribute to her brother, Lorenzo Snow, as well.

In the spring of 1840, Lorenzo left for a three-year mission to Great Britain. During this time he worked with members of the Twelve who were laboring in England. He proved himself to be an effective missionary and administrator, and was appointed to the "superintendency" of the Church in London. One of his special projects in England was to organize a series of "tea meetings" that consisted of various "entertainments" to raise money for the Nauvoo temple. Organizing the programs with musical performances, as well as dramatic readings and poetry, was an activity in which Lorenzo engaged himself throughout his public-life.

Little is said of Lorenzo's singing ability. However, the *Millennial Star* published the minutes of a conference held in Manchester on May 5, 1842, which makes this point about Lorenzo's beautiful singing voice:

> Elder Snow then addressed the meeting, and stated the method they had adopted in the London Conference...of raising funds for the Temple, which was by holding tea meetings; at which time any person wishing to appropriate for this purpose, had the opportunity. *Elder Snow concluded his address by singing beautifully in tongues.*[10]

Lorenzo moved with the same grace and ease among all classes of people. His social graces were obviously recognized by Brigham Young, who, before leaving England, left two beautifully bound copies of the Book of Mormon for Lorenzo to give to the Queen. Lorenzo, indeed, presented the two copies of the Book of Mormon to Queen Victoria and Prince Albert, an occasion that prompted the writing of a twelve-verse poem by

Eliza: "Stanza on the Presentation of the Book of Mormon to Queen Victoria."

Lorenzo Snow was a remarkable man, a highly successful missionary who, like the missionaries of old, healed the sick and cast out devils. In 1843, Lorenzo returned from his mission to Illinois and accepted a teaching position at Lima with seventy "roughnecks." Nevertheless, he treated those ruffians with kindness and dignity. He gained their respect and created a well-mannered classroom.

Lorenzo Snow had heard of the doctrine of plural marriage through Eliza, but found the whole notion repugnant. In a private conversation, however, Joseph Smith explained the doctrine of celestial marriage, and pointed out his "duty in reference to the law." Finally, at twenty-nine and unmarried, Lorenzo was sealed to four women in the Nauvoo Temple. One of them was a mother of three sons by an earlier marriage.

Lorenzo was in Cincinnati campaigning for the presidency of Joseph Smith when he received the shattering news of the murder of both Joseph and Hyrum. He returned to Nauvoo, and by February, 1846, conditions there forced the Snow family and the other residents to leave. Like the others, the Snow family fled with little or no preparation.

In addition to caring for his own growing family, Lorenzo served as captain of one hundred saints as they traveled west. This was a heavy responsibility, considering sickness and death had struck most families. At Mt. Pisgah, the cemetery was teeming with the bodies of the faithful, and even Lorenzo had been dreadfully ill. Morale was low. Yet, making the most of a terrible situation, he planned activities to lighten the moods of the others. He wrote of one such "entertainment," as he referred to them:

> During the long winter months, I sought to keep up the spirits and courage of the Saints in Pisgah, not only by inaugurating meetings for religious worship and exercises, in different parts of the settlement, but also by making provision for, and encouraging proper

amusements of various kinds. These entertainments corresponded with our circumstances, and, of course, were of a very unpretentious and primitive character; their novel simplicity and unlikeness to anything before witnessed, added greatly to the enjoyment. They were exhibitions of ingenuity.

As a sample, I will attempt a description of one, which I improvised for the entertainment of as many as I could reasonably crowd together in my humble family mansion which was a one-story edifice, about fifteen by thirty, constructed of logs, with a dirt roof and ground floor, displaying at one end a chimney of modest height, made of turf cut from the bosom of Mother Earth. Expressly for the occasion we carpeted the floor with a thin coating of clean straw, and draped the walls with white sheets drawn from our featherless beds.

How to light our hall suitably for the coming event was a consideration of no small moment, and one which levied a generous contribution of our ingenuity. But we succeeded. From the pit where they were buried, we selected the largest and fairest turnips—scooped out the interior, and fixed short candles in them, placing them at intervals around the walls, suspending others to the ceiling above, which was formed of earth and cane. Those lights imparted a very peaceable, quiet, Quaker-like influence, and the light reflected through those turnip rinds imparted a very picturesque appearance....

The hours were enlivened, and happily passed, as we served up a dish of succotash, composed of short speeches, full of life and sentiment, spiced with enthusiasm, appropriate songs, recitations, toasts, conundrums[11] exhortations, etc. At the close, all seemed perfectly satisfied, and withdrew, feeling as happy as though they were not homeless.[12]

Even though he spent considerable time and exercised an amazing amount of creativity in his efforts to cheer others, Lorenzo was not without his own sorrow. His journal includes this poignant entry:

In Pisgah, Charlotte gave birth to a daughter (my firstborn), which we named Leonora, after my eldest sister....

Little Leonora was taken sick and died, and with deep sorrow we bore her remains to their silent resting place, to be left alone, far from her father and the mother who gave her birth.[13]

One year and a half later after the arrival of the Saints in the Salt Lake Valley, Lorenzo was called to a meeting with the First Presidency on February 12, 1849. Wondering what the purpose of such a meeting would be, he was "surprised" to learn of his call to the apostleship. He never aspired to that important calling, nor did he consider himself to be a candidate. At thirty-four, Lorenzo Snow was ordained an apostle by Heber C. Kimball.

Lorenzo's reputation for arranging successful programs for a variety of occasions put him in charge of the July 24, 1848 celebration in the Salt Lake Valley. The first anniversary of the arrival of the pioneers, and the first celebration, was a gala, all-day occasion that consisted of parades, brass bands, the ringing of the Nauvoo Bell, singing, banners, prancing steeds, "martial airs" and a performance of "Song of Liberty" by Lorenzo's sister, Eliza, by twenty-four young ladies, and still more music.[14]

At the October General Conference, 1849, three apostles were called to open new missions abroad: John Taylor was to go to France, Erastus Snow to Scandinavia, and Lorenzo Snow to Italy. Elder Joseph Toronto, of Italian lineage, accompanied Lorenzo Snow as his companion. The trio departed later that month for their assigned destinations.

Arriving at the Mormon community of Kanesville, the party was "met with shoutings, firing of cannons, *songs of rejoicing*, etc."[15] Lorenzo then passed through Mount Pisgah and Garden Grove, and there he wrote:

> I proceeded to Nauvoo-gazed upon her ruins...My heart sickened as I contemplated that once beautiful city, *filled with the songs of rejoicing.*[16]

After a two-month stop-over in England, Elders Snow and Toronto left for Italy, and arrived in Genoa in July, 1850. Lorenzo was struck with the sublime beauty of the Italian landscape, "where heaven and earth seem to meet," plus the abundant sense of history. But, at the same time, Elder Snow was overwhelmed by the almost impenetrable wall between the missionaries and the spirit of Catholicism that permeated the land. Lorenzo learned the Italian language well enough to converse effectively, and eventually to make the first translation of the Book of Mormon into Italian.

Lorenzo sent for Elder Jabez Woodard and Elder Margett of London to join him, Joseph Toronto and Elder Stenhouse. On the 18th of September—eleven months from the time he left Salt Lake City—the brethren climbed a high mountain to "organize the Church in Italy." Lorenzo wrote of the experience: "We ascended to a very high mountain, a little distance from LaTour, and having taken our position on a bold projecting rock, *we sang praises to the God of heaven.*"[17] Like a miniature general conference, the four men offered prayers, conducted various items of business, and sang "Praise to the Man" and other hymns not specifically mentioned by Elder Snow in his journal. Perhaps "For the Strength of the Hills" was sung then, as Lorenzo elsewhere acknowledged it to be a favorite.[18]

Two months later, Lorenzo and his companions returned to the same spot where Lorenzo "resolved to bestow upon them such blessings as they required in the discharge of their important duties." His journal entry reveals a man of God with an immense literary talent, who like an Old Testament prophet, sang praises to the Lord when his heart was full:

> We have here no temple—no building made by human hands, but the mountains tower around us—far above the edifices which Protestants and Papists use in this country.

> On Sunday, the twenty-fourth of November, we ascended one of these eminences which seem to occupy a position between earth and sky, and which, on a former occasion, we named "Mount Brigham." During our tedious ascent, the sun shone forth in all its brightness; but in such parts as were shaded, we found snow on the ground, and many a craggy peak and rocky summit on every side, were white with the snowy fleeces of winter.

Having reached the place we sought, we gazed with rapture on the enchanting scenes of surrounding nature. Before us was a plain so vast that it seemed as if immensity had become visible. All was level in the ocean of space, and yet no sameness appeared on its fertile bosom. Here towns and cities were environed by the resources from which their inhabitants had been fed for ages. Ancient and far-famed Italy, the scene of our mission, was spread out like a vision before our enchanted eyes. Light and shade produced their effect in that magnificent picture, in a surprising degree; for while the clouds flung their shadows on one part, another was illuminated with the most brilliant sunlight as far as the eye can reach.

But there was one hallowed reflection which threw all around a brighter lustre than the noontide firmament: it was in that place, two months before, that we organized the Church of Jesus Christ in Italy. If we had stood upon a pavement of gold and diamonds, it would not have produced an impression like the imperishable remembrance of that sacred scene.

Amid the sublime display of the Creator's works, we sang the praises of His eternal name, and implored those gifts which our circumstances required.[19]

Before returning to America, Elder Snow visited the island of Malta, where Apostle Paul had once labored. Though Elder Snow was prevented from going to India as he had planned, he called missionaries to both Malta and India. When Lorenzo returned to Salt Lake in the summer of 1858, he sadly discovered his beloved Charlotte had passed away during his absence.

A new assignment came to Lorenzo: he was called to preside over the Mormon settlement at Box Elder, some sixty miles north of Salt Lake. He called fifty families to move north with him and his family to join with the two hundred members who already resided there.

Lorenzo changed the name of Box Elder to Brigham City, to honor Brigham Young. Finding the settlement in a very "unprosperious condition," he conceived of a plan to divert water from the Bear River to irrigate the semi-arid environment of the area. He also admonished the settlers to "observe the regular fast on the first Thursday in the month and contribute the cost of the two meals to the poor."[20]

Lorenzo wrote, during the summer and fall:

> I succeeded in erecting a house, one story and a half in height,
> thirty by forth. It being impossible to obtain shingles, I covered the
> building with slabs, and for two winters the rattling of those slabs
> put in motion by the canyon breezes, *supplied us with music in the*
> *absence of organs and pianos.*[21]

Lorenzo developed a system of "cooperatives," through
which Brigham City developed into a thriving, prosperous
community. He also developed a school system, assessing a
one percent tax on property to support the schools. Biographer
Thomas C. Romney wrote of Lorenzo Snow's attitude about
the importance of education:

> He [Lorenzo]...was always a promoter of education and devoted
> a great amount of time and attention to the schools, 'endeavoring to
> secure good teachers and urging their patronage by the people.'[22]

Lorenzo Snow passionately felt that something should be
done "to raise the cultural level of the people." Previously in
Salt Lake City, he had organized what he called the
"Polysophical Society,"[23] which presented programs that con-
sisted of dramatic productions, reading of poetry and other lit-
erature, and various kinds of musical performances. In
Brigham City, Lorenzo once again organized the "Polysophical
Society."

In describing the Polysophical Society of Salt Lake, from
which the Brigham City Society was patterned, Henry W.
Naisbitt[24] wrote:

> This was the first nucleus of a varied intellectual character in
> the Church, and it speedily drew toward itself the lion's share of
> that latent talent which, through the gathering, gravitated to Salt
> Lake City.[25]

Thomas C. Romney draws further from remarks of Brother
Naisbitt:

> The programs...included productions in several languages such as English, French and Italian, as well as the Deseret Alphabet²⁶..anecdotes, narrations, and commentaries on various subjects. Orchestral instruments included *violins, piano, accordion, guitar, clarinets, flutes and scotch bagpipes.*[27]

An outgrowth of the Polysophical Society, the "Dramatic Association of Brigham City" first met in the basement of the courthouse, with Lorenzo Snow as president. After a vicious windstorm destroyed the partially completed courthouse, the Dramatic Association awaited the completion of the new Courthouse.

> The upper story of the building was used for worship, concerts, dancing and lectures until the large Tabernacle was completed. Theatricals were held in the basement of the new courthouse the first season, and then they were taken to the upper story where a stage was erected and furnished with scenery and other equipment required for the staging of first class shows. It was generally conceded that the Dramatic Association of Brigham City was the best in the Territory outside of Salt Lake City.[23]

Lorenzo Snow, like his sister, Eliza, had a life-long preoccupation with the expansion and refinement of the mind. Though he leaned particularly in the direction of literature and drama, his interests also included music. He knew, also, that diligent practice is necessary for success in life, as well as in the dramatic arts or music. In an address in the Salt Lake Tabernacle, he spoke the following:

> An individual undertaking to learn to play upon a flute at first finds a difficulty in making the notes, and in order to play a tune correctly there is a great deal of diligence and patience required. He has to go on, to pause, to turn back and commence afresh, but after a time he is enabled through a great deal of exertions, to master that tune. When called upon to play that tune afterwards, there is no necessity for remembering where to place the fingers, but he plays it naturally. It was not natural at the first; there had to be a great deal of patience and labor before it became natural to go through with the tune. It is just so in regard to matters that

pertain to the things of God. We have to exert ourselves and go from grace to grace, to get the law of action so incorporated in our systems, that it may be natural to do these things that are required of us.[29]

Elsewhere, Lorenzo Snow wrote the following:

Do not cease to persevere. I have noticed that many young ladies, and young men, too, start in to learn music, but get discouraged, and, failing to persevere, they do not succeed in accomplishing that which they undertook.[30]

In 1865, Lorenzo served a short-term mission to Hawaii, which at that time was known as the Sandwich Islands. Lorenzo and his party traveled to the west coast by stage. One evening as night was falling, the stage stopped for a change of horses and drivers:

One of our company remarked that our new driver had acquired the air and appearance of an intelligent gentleman, and we soon discovered that he possessed a wonderful musical talent, in the exercise of which he elicited our surprise and admiration. It really seemed to me that a sweeter, a more pathetic or melodious voice I had never heard. It is quite possible that the stillness of night and the wild scenery of nature around us had a tendency to enhance the effect and increase our appreciation of melodious accents; whatever it might be, I was charmed, delighted, and felt that I could embrace that man and call him brother.[31]

Francis Gibbons summarized the rest of this colorful story:

However, when the coach suddenly lurched, the serenade turned into an outburst of profanity. The driver, having drunk too much before the trip, lashed the team with his bullwhip, and the stage began a long downhill descent as the driver continued to whip his team violently. "Our coach swayed fearfully," wrote Lorenzo, "the wheels...striking fire as they whirled over the rocks, with a double span of horses upon a keen run, tossing us up and down, giving us a few hard strokes of the head against the cover of the coach." Foreseeing a serious accident unless the speed were reduced, Elder Benson rediscovered his tongue and 'in a tremulous yet powerful voice, demanded of the driver to moderate his speed. Heedless of his demand, seemingly angered by it, the driver responded 'by an increased and more furious lashing of the foaming, panting steeds.' The panic-stricken passengers were relieved of their terror only when they arrived at the next station, where another driver took over.[32]

Though Elder Snow easily responded to the beautiful singing, he learned on that occasion that sometimes drunks can sing rather beautifully!

In the company of Apostle George A. Smith and his sister, Eliza, Lorenzo left October 26, 1872 for a ten-month tour of Europe and Asia Minor. Their travels took them to Rome, Venice, Paris, Lyon, Antwerp, Amsterdam, Haarlem, Alexandria, Jaffy Damascus, the Holy Land and Athens. Lorenzo viewed Constantinople from the boat, and on the return visited Munich, Hamberg, and Berlin.

In Holland, Lorenzo recalls visiting the principal church in Haarlem, and hearing its famous organ:

> This church is renowned for its famous organ, which for a long time, has been considered the largest and most powerful in the world. It has four key boards, sixty-four stops, five thousand metal and two thousand wooden pipes; the largest of these pipes is thirty-two feet long, and fifteen inches in diameter. It is very beautiful—adorned with marble statuary, life size, and in attractive attitudes, representing personages playing on instruments of various descriptions. We employed the organist and three or four blowers to exhibit its merits. Imitations of different tones of the piano-forte, the trumpet, whistle, battle call, sacred music, closing with a tremendous thunder storm, all were executed with admirable accuracy, fully satisfying us as to its wonderful capabilities.[33]

While serving as President of the Box Elder Stake, Lorenzo was called to be one of seven counselors to Brigham Young. In 1885, he served a short-term mission to the Indians in the Northwest. He also served ten years as president of the Utah Territorial Legislative Council, and between 1886 and 1887,

Lorenzo served an eleven-month prison term on the charge of polygamy.

From his childhood, Lorenzo and Eliza shared an unusually close relationship. Eliza was Lorenzo's closest confidant. Each offered a special kind of inspiration to the other. Lorenzo's revelation about man's relationship with God—that we are the offspring of a Heavenly Father *and* Mother—was the seminal impetus behind Eliza's immortal hymn, "O My Father." Though the hymn bears her name, it is, nevertheless, linked to her brother. Of the ten hymns that remain in the current hymnbook, some inspiration, at least, could probably be traced back to Lorenzo Snow. No doubt, Lorenzo felt a special affection for such hymns as "O My Father," "How Great the Wisdom and the Love," "Though Deepening Trials," "In Our Lovely Deseret" and the other six hymns by Eliza that remain at the very heart of Mormonism.

This remarkable lady, "Zion's Poetess," passed away December 5, 1887. "O My Father" opened the funeral services held two days later in the Assembly Hall, in a performance by the Tabernacle Choir. The rest of the music for the services consisted of other hymns from her pen.

In 1889, at age seventy-five, Lorenzo Snow became the President of the Council of the Twelve, and served as President of the Salt Lake Temple when it opened in 1893. Already the life of Lorenzo Snow had been abundant; his accomplishments were brilliant and distinguished. Then at eighty-four, Lorenzo Snow became the fifth President of the Church.

While President Wilford Woodruff was yet alive, Lorenzo went into the Salt Lake Temple, alone, and prayed that the Lord might extend the life of the Prophet beyond his own, so that he would not have to bear the burden of the presidency. Then after Wilford's passing, Lorenzo went into the temple again to pour out his heart to the Lord. As he left the room where he had been praying, disappointed, he began walking through a hallway in the temple. Suddenly, the Savior of the world appeared to Lorenzo, standing just above the floor, and confirmed that he was to be Wilford Woodruff's successor.

When Lorenzo Snow was ordained President of the Church, he was frail, "only five feet six inches tall, and [weighed] barely 130 pounds."[34] The Church was heavily in debt because the Federal Government had been confiscating the Church's money; tithing revenues had decreased since the members did not want their tithing dollars going to the government. During his short three-year administration, the financial situation of the Church was reversed, partly due to the brilliance of President Snow's actions, and partly because of the renewed emphasis on paying a full tithing that resulted from a revelation that had come to him in St. George, Utah.

Throughout his illustrious life, the Saints prospered under his wise and inspired leadership. The missionary work spread in the world, and the Church increased in culture and refinement in all of the arts and humanities, including music, which Lorenzo Snow fostered with a special interest.

Eliza's great hymn, "O My Father," which he loved, was sung at his funeral held in the Tabernacle on Sunday, October 13, 1901. Lorenzo Snow was buried in the Brigham City Cemetery. He was the last prophet of this dispensation who knew Joseph Smith personally.

1 Eliza R. Snow Smith: *Biography and Family Record of Lorenzo Snow* (Salt Lake City: Deseret News Co., 1884) p. 174.

2 Ibid. p. 2.

3 Ibid. p. 2.

4 James B. Allen: *The Story of the Latter-day Saints* (Salt Lake City: Deseret Book Co., 1992) p. 136.

5 Leonard Arrington: *The Presidents of the Church* (Salt Lake City: Deseret Book Co., 1986) pp. 148-149.

6 Eliza R. Snow Smith, pp. 7-8.

7 Clyde J. Williams: *The Teachings of Lorenzo Snow* (Salt Lake City: Bookcraft, 1984) p. 2.

8 Francis W. Gibbons: *Lorenzo Snow: Spiritual Giant, Prophet of God* (Salt Lake City, Deseret Book Co., 1982) p. 29.

9 Number 292 in the current 1985 hymnal.

10 Eliza R. Snow Smith, p. 62.

11 A conundrums is a riddle.

12 Ibid., pp. 91-92.

13 Ibid., p. 93.

14 Ibid., p. 96.

15 Ibid., p. 112.

16 Ibid., p. 112.

17 Ibid., p. 130.

18 Ibid., p. 170.

19 Ibid., p. 173-174.

20 Thomas C. Romney: *The Life of Lorenzo Snow* (Salt Lake City: Deseret Book Co., 1955 p. 172.

21 Ibid., p. 168.

22 Ibid., p. 172.

23 The term "polysophical" was coined by Lorenzo Snow to indicate the many facets of one's intellectual development.

24 Henry W. Naisbitt is the author of "This House We Dedicate to Thee," No. 245 in the current 1985 Hymnal.

25 Ibid., p. 159.

26 The Deseret Alphabet, invented by George D. Watt and others, grew out of the Polysophical Society in Salt Lake City.

27 Ibid., p. 159.

28 Ibid., p. 174.

29 Gibbons, p. 85.

30 *Deseret Weekly*: Volume 54, p. 483.

31 Eliza R. Snow Smith, pp. 273-274.

32 Gibbons, pp. 90-91.

33 Eliza R. Snow Smith, pp. 503-504.

34 *Church History in the Fullness of Times* (Salt Lake City: Salt Lake City, Church of Jesus Christ of Latter-day Saints, 1989) p. 451.

JOSEPH F. SMITH

M Withers '94

JOSEPH F. SMITH
(1838-1918)

*"Good music is gracious praise of
God,...and it is one of our most acceptable
methods of worshipping God.*[1]

Mary Fielding, age thirty-three left England for Canada in 1834 in hopes of finding a brighter future. In Canada, she joined a religious study group led by John Taylor that consisted of former Methodists looking for answers to the deeper questions of life that their former church could not answer. Apostle Parley P. Pratt arrived in Toronto as a missionary in 1836 and discovered these good people who were searching for the truth. After hearing the message of the Restored Gospel, most of them followed John Taylor into the waters of baptism, including Mary Fielding, her brother, Joseph, and her sister, Mercy Rachel.

As soon as circumstances permitted, Mary Fielding—and other members of the study group—left Canada to join the Saints in Kirtland. It was in Kirtland where Mary met Hyrum Smith, brother of the Prophet, whose wife, Jerusha, had died two months before from complications giving birth to her sixth child. Hyrum and Mary fell in love and were married on Christmas Eve, 1837.

> Mary was cultured, refined, educated, a splendid companion for Hyrum, and fully able and qualified to take care of his motherless children.[2]

Suddenly, Mary found herself encompassed about by the swirling events in the darkest, ugliest period in Church history. While caring for five step children—one of Hyrum and

Jerusha's six children had died—in the most dire of circum-stances, Mary became pregnant with her first child.

Not long after the marriage, Hyrum, Mary and the children moved from Kirtland to Far West, Missouri. Governor Lilburn Boggs had issued the infamous extermination order against the Mormons. Nineteen Mormons were murdered in cold blood by angry mobsters at Haun's Mill—with twelve others seriously wounded. Two days later, Joseph and Hyrum were arrested for "treason, murder, and other crimes," and were taken away. General Alexander Doniphan was ordered to execute them in a public square, but he refused to carry out the ludicrous order. Amid this turmoil, Mary gave birth to a son—Joseph Fielding Smith—on November 13, 1838 at Far West.

Years later, Joseph F. Smith—as he came to be known—related this incident that occurred soon after his birth:

> After my father's imprisonment by the mob, my mother was taken ill and continued so for several months. In January, 1839, she was taken in a wagon, on her sickbed, to see her husband, who was confined by the mob, a prisoner in Liberty Jail, for no other reason than that he was a Latter-day Saint, and while in this condition of health, and her husband in jail, a company of men led by a Methodist preacher named Bogart, entered her house, searching it, broke open a trunk and carried away papers and valuable belongings to my father. I, being an infant, and lying on the bed, another bed being on the floor, was entirely overlooked by the family (my moth-er being very sick, the care of me devolved upon my Aunt Mercy and others of the family, during the fright and excitement). So when the mob entered the room where I was, the bed on the floor was thrown on the other, completely smothering me up, and here I was permitted to remain until after the excitement subsided. When thought of, and discovered, my existence was supposed to have come to an end; but subsequent events have proved their supposi-tions were wrong, however well-founded.[3]

Historian, Preston Nibley, continued the tragic story:

> Somehow, during February or March of 1839, Mary Smith, still confined to her bed, was carried out of Missouri in a sleigh or wagon

and taken to Quincy, Illinois, where some of the Saints had made temporary headquarters. Here she and her child remained until joined by their husband and father, Hyrum Smith, on April 22, after his escape from the Missouri officers. In a few weeks Hyrum removed his family to Commerce, later named Nauvoo, and here they remained until the great migration westward.[4]

An unfriendlier, less hospitable environment for which an infant to come into this world can not be imagined. Yet, Joseph F. later recalled:

> I can remember when I was a little boy, hearing my father sing. I do not know how much of a singer he was, for at that time I was not capable of judging as to the quality of his singing, but the hymns he sang became familiar to me, even in the days of my childhood. I believe that I can sing them still, although I am not much of a singer.[5]

When Joseph F. was only five years old, his father Hyrum and his uncle Joseph were brutally murdered in Carthage jail. Preston Nibley wrote of Joseph F.'s last memory of seeing his father alive:

> Of Joseph F. Smith's childhood years, which were spent in Nauvoo, I have some knowledge, as I was fortunate in being a member of his party when he visited that abandoned city in 1906. His memory was vivid regarding many interesting events. He pointed out to us the place in the raid where he had stood as he watched his father and "Uncle Joseph" ride away to Carthage on that fateful day in June, 1844. "This is the exact spot," he said, "where I stood when the brethren came riding up on their way to Carthage. Without getting off his horse father leaned over in his saddle and picked me up off the ground. He kissed me goodbye and put me down again and I saw him ride away." The child never saw his father again, except in death. "I remember the night of the murder," he continued, "when one of the brethren came from Carthage and knocked on our window after dark and called to my mother, "Sister Smith, your husband has been killed." He remembered his mother's scream on hearing the dreadful news, and her moans and cries throughout the night.
> When we went to the old home of the Prophet Joseph Smith, the President said, as we stood in the kitchen, "In this room the

bodies of the martyrs lay in their coffins, after they had been brought from Carthage and dressed for burial. I remember my mother lifting me up to look upon the faces of my father and the Prophet, for the last time."

Outside, as we stood on the bank of the Mississippi River, President Smith pointed out to us where he had stood as he watched the Saints leave Nauvoo in the early months of 1846. "Many of them crossed on the ice," he said, "the river being completely frozen over at times during that winter."[6]

Before leaving Nauvoo, Mary sold her property—for what she could—to buy provisions. Besides Joseph and the five stepchildren, the "family" consisted of three others Hyrum had taken in while he was alive: George Mills, an eccentric, old man who was not a member of the Church; an older woman, Hannal Grinnel, whom the children called "Aunty;" and a younger, somewhat disabled woman whose name was Jane Wilson.

Though "Old George" and Aunty Grinnel were quite helpful to Mary, the full responsibility of moving six children and four adults across America—with wagons, cattle and horses—was hers. At only seven years of age, Joseph was responsible for driving their ox team and caring for the other animals.

Between the fall of 1846 and the spring of 1848, they lived at Winter Quarters. By the time of their departure from Utah, several of the oxen had died. Consequently some of the seven wagons had to be hooked up to cows and calves, making the journey even more difficult. At least twice, one of their oxen became ill. With unshakable faith, Mary asked some of the brethren to anoint and administer to the ox—she could *not* afford to lose one more of her oxen. After each administration, the animal recovered instantly, rose to its feet and continued the journey!

At Winter Quarters, Mary's family was assigned to the company of Cornelius Lott, who did *not* want the added burden of caring for a widow and her family, saying, "I will have to carry you along the way." But Mary, showing her spunk, replied to the captain, "I will beat you to the valley and will ask no help from you either."[7] In spite of Captain Lott's pettiness towards her during the entire exodus, Mary and her family drove into the Salt Lake Valley ahead of the arrogant Mr. Lott.

Even though Joseph was only five years old when his father, Hyrum, and Uncle Joseph were assassinated, his father's singing had made a lasting impression on the child. No doubt, Joseph's sensitive nature made him responsive to the frequent singing of "All Is Well" by the pioneers during their massive, arduous exodus. Since Mary Fielding had come from an English environment of culture and refinement, where *Bible reading and hymn singing* were part of the daily routine[8], she would have provided similarly for Joseph and the other children under normal circumstances. But the life of Mary Fielding, from her baptism in Toronto until her death in Salt Lake City in 1852, was a saga of suffering and sorrow. It was an exercise in survival. But Mary planted deep in the hearts of her children an appreciation of beauty and an abiding faith in the gospel of Jesus Christ.

When Mary Fielding Smith—widow of Hyrum Smith—died at her home in Salt Lake City September 21, 1852, Joseph was thirteen.

At fifteen, Joseph Fielding began his ecclestical career with a mission to the Sandwich Islands, known today as Hawaii.

As Hyrum Smith son and the Prophet Joseph's nephew, Joseph F. Smith's reputation preceded him.

> As we landed at the wharf in Honolulu, the native Saints were out in great numbers with their wreaths of leis, beautiful flowers of every variety and hue. We were loaded with them, [Elder Smith], of course, more than anyone else. The noted Hawaiian band was there playing welcome, as it often does to incoming steamship companies. But on this occasion the band had been instructed by the mayor to go up to the Mormon meetinghouse and there play selections during the festivities which the natives had arranged for. It was a beautiful

sight to see the deep-seated love, the even tearful affection, that
these people had for him.[9]

The warm affection shown Joseph and the other Elders
with the colorful flowers, their enthusiastic singing and stirring selections by the bands became very familiar to the fifteen-year-old Elder Smith.

Possessing a natural gift for learning the native language of
the Islands, Elder Smith said, after three months, "I could say
anything in the Hawaiian language, and took my turn with
[Elder] Pake in preaching." Pake was a "full-blooded native,
and a good speaker."[10]

One hundred days after his arrival in Honolulu, Elder
Smith spoke the native tongue well enough that

> Elder Reddick N. Allred, one of the old missionaries on the
> island of Maui, declared that he spoke the language well enough to
> do missionary work wherever he was called to labor. At the next
> meeting, over which Elder Allred presided, Joseph F. Smith was
> called on to take charge. He gave out the hymn, opened the meeting
> with prayer, and before it closed spoke fluently, all in the native
> tongue.[11]

No doubt, Elder Smith was as comfortable singing the
hymns in Hawaiian as he was in praying or preaching.

Joseph returned to Salt Lake City in February, 1858—nearly
four years after going to Hawaii. Turning his attentions to
more domestic matters, he became interested in Levira Smith,
the sixteen-year-old daughter of Samuel H. Smith, one of the
younger brothers of Joseph Smith. Their friendship blossomed
into romance, and they were married April 5, 1859.

Once again, while sitting in general conference, Joseph
learned of another mission call, this time to Great Britain. At
twenty-one, Joseph F. Smith left his bride with relatives and
departed for England—the homeland of his beloved mother,
Mary Fielding Smith. One of his traveling companions was
Levira's brother, Samual Smith. Joseph F. Smith arrived in

England in 1860—at age twenty-two—to begin his second full-time mission; and before long he was installed as president of the Sheffield Conference.

Elder Smith became acquainted with Brother William Fowler, an Australian living in England who had previously joined the Church. In the extensive biography of his father, Joseph Fielding Smith wrote of his father's friendship with William Fowler:

> Joseph F. Smith often referred to his acquaintance with William Fowler, who was employed in the cutlery works in Sheffield as a grinder and polisher of cutlery. At the time he joined the Church he had a good position, but after he became a member, persecution set in against him and his employment was taken from him.[12]

His enthusiasm for the Gospel far out-weighed whatever persecution that he may have come to him since joining the Church.

Brother Fowler presented a hymn he had written to Elder Smith entitled, "We Thank Thee, O God, for a Prophet," which he had coupled with a tune by Caroline Sheridan Norton, "The Officer's Funeral March." Joseph Fielding Smith was impressed with the humble musical and poetic offering presented to him, and arranged to have it sung in the small branch. Little did Elder Smith, Brother Fowler, or the members of that small branch in Sheffield realize that his hymn would one day be universally known and loved by members of the Church world-wide:

> We thank thee, O God, for a prophet
> To guide us in these latter days.
> We thank thee for sending the gospel
> To lighten our minds with its rays.
> We Thank thee for every blessing
> Bestowed by thy bounteous hand.
> We feel it a pleasure to serve thee,
> And love to obey thy command.

When dark clouds of trouble hang o'er us
And threaten our peace to destroy,
There is hope smiling brightly before us,
And we know that deliv'rance is nigh.
We doubt not the Lord nor his goodness.
We've proved him in days that are past.
The wicked who fight against Zion
Will surely be smitten at last.

We'll sing of his goodness and mercy.
We'll praise him by day and by night,
Rejoice in his glorious gospel,
And bask in its life-giving light.
Thus on to eternal perfection
The honest and faithful will go,
While they who reject this glad message
Shall never such happiness know.[13]

Caroline Sheridan Norton, composer of the simple tune to which the words of William Fowler have become permanently attached, was not a Mormon. She, however, was known in England as a writer of romantic poetry in the style of Lord Byron. William Fowler eventually emigrated to America with his family, and established a home in Manti, Utah.[14]

While in Great Britain, Joseph discovered there were, among the English, people "who acted as much like spoiled children as it was possible for the benighted Hawaiians to act and be."

On one occasion, while presiding in Leeds, he rebuked a local Elder publicly from the stand, saying: "I wish those who are in the habit of drinking liquor to keep off the stand on the Sabbath, when their breath smells." After the meeting and before the day was through, he received a communication from one offended member who returned his "Elder's license," stating, *"I have burn't up my hymnbook and all other works that I have, and will burn the Book of Mormon as soon as I can find it."*[15]

Apparently, the adversary's contempt for the hymns of Zion is the same as his contempt for the Holy Scriptures; and when one entertains the spirit of contention, he shares Satan's attitudes toward both.

A serious problem had been developing in Hawaii while Joseph F. was still in England. A charismatic missionary in the Islands, Walter Murray Gibson, had transferred all church property to his own name, and had begun charging the members a fee for all ordinations and blessings. While creating new callings with new, lofty titles, he charged the members increasingly more for each higher office. At the same time, he began to mix the teachings and practices of the Church with native superstitions.

Deeply concerned about the gravity of the developing situation with Walter Gibson and his following of Hawaiian Saints, Brigham Young determined it was necessary for two apostles to go to Hawaii to deal with it. Elders Ezra T. Benson and Lorenzo Snow were assigned to go, but since neither of them spoke Hawaiian, Joseph F. Smith, along with Alma L. Smith and William W. Cluff who had labored on the islands there and knew the language well—were asked to accompany the apostles.

Five months after Joseph F.'s return from Great Britain, he left for this special assignment. There the brethren discovered in Mr. Gibson the object of a kind of cult worship, a man who deftly nourished the veneration of the Hawaiian Saints and padded his pockets at the same time.

At the meeting called by Apostles Benson and Snow, Mr. Gibson took pains to ignore their presiding authority.

> Just before they reached the door, Mr Gibson made an excuse and said he would have to return for something he had forgotten. The brethren continued on, entering the building and taking seats on the stand. They were received very coldly by the assembled natives who looked upon them with suspicion. After the brethren were seated Mr.Gibson entered, when with one accord every person in the building, except the missionaries, suddenly arose to his feet and did homage to Mr. Gibson. His excuse in delaying his entrance

was for this very purpose, and to show to the brethren the esteem in which he was held by the native members of the Church. After the congregation was seated, at a gesture from Mr.Gibson that they could take their seats, he ignored the brethren on the stand, and *gave out the hymn which the congregation sang.* When Brother Benson saw the turn things had taken, and how willfully and purposely the brethren had been ignored and the authority of the Priesthood set aside, he called on Elder Lorenzo Snow to pray, not leaving time for Mr. Gibson to make the second move. There was determination on Mr. Gibson's part, however, for immediately after the close of the prayer he announced the second hymn, without giving time for any consultation. As the hymn was brought to a close Mr. Gibson immediately commenced to address the congregation....

As soon as Mr. Gibson was seated, Elder Benson called upon Elder Joseph F. Smith to speak rather intimating that it would be well for him to speak on general principles and that he need not feel bound to notice all that Mr. Gibson had said.[16]

Elder Smith, fluent in Hawaiian and speaking with great power, drew attention to Mr. Gibson's apostasy and the need to adhere to the teachings of the apostles and prophets. As mesmerized as the congregation seemed to be by Mr. Gibson, Elder Smith's message penetrated their hearts. At a later session, a court was held and Mr. Gibson was stripped of his membership. For some time, he continued to sputter around among the people, but gradually his influence among the Saints faded away.

Joseph F. Smith did not embrace the principle of plural marriage with any degree of enthusiasm. But finally, President Young convinced him that this was a responsibility he should not avoid. In 1866—after obtaining the full approval of Levira—Joseph married Julina Lambson. Perhaps, this became for Joseph a test of obedience, because later in the year he was ordained an apostle by Brigham Young and was set apart as one of his counselors in the First Presidency. Curiously, however, his ordination and setting apart were not made public for one year.

Joseph later married Sara Ellen Richards, Edna Lambson and Alice Ann Kimball, all of whom he loved deeply. But after ten years of marriage, Levira Clark filed for a legal separation and moved to California. Apparently the strain of her husband's long absences from home, and her inability to have a child, exacted a great toll emotionally upon her. Their eventual divorce was a source of great sadness to Joseph throughout his life.

Joseph F. Smith served as counselors in the First Presidency under John Taylor, Wilford Woodruff and Lorenzo Snow. If any future prophet had suffered the refiner's fire, surely it was Joseph F. Smith. At the death of Lorenzo Snow on October 10, 1901, Joseph F. Smith became the sixth President of the Church. He was ordained and set apart to that high calling October 17, 1901 at the age of sixty-two.

President Smith had developed a responsiveness to music—in particular the hymns of Zion—when he was a child and heard his father sing. On his two missions to Hawaii, he learned to love the lusty, enthusiastic singing of the islanders.

President Smith encouraged his children to study musical instruments and took pleasure in hearing them perform.[17] President Smith expressed concern about dancing, however, in the *Juvenile Instructor* of March 1, 1904.

> Home parties, concerts that develop the talents of youth, and public amusements that bring together both young and old, are preferable to the excessive practice of dancing....
>
> Our amusements should be consistent with our religious spirit of fraternity and religious devotion. In too many instances the ball room is devoid of our supplication for Divine protection. Our dancing should be, as far as possible, under the supervision of some Church organizations, and we should be scrupulously careful to open the dance by prayer.... The question of amusements is one of such far-reaching importance to the welfare of the Saints that the presiding authorities of every ward should give it their most careful attention and consideration.[18]

Joseph F. Smith came by his interest in Church history naturally, a nephew to the Prophet Joseph Smith and son of the Patriarch, Hyrum Smith, and a personal witness to much of the persecution of the pioneers. His interest in the history of the Church was kindled further while working in the Church Historian's Office in his mid-twenties.

On the centennial anniversary of the Prophet Joseph's birthday, President Joseph F. Smith dedicated the Joseph Smith Monument at his birthplace in Sharon, Vermont on December 23, 1905. The impressive granite shaft stands 38½ feet tall, one foot for every year of the Prophet's life. After the dedicatory prayer by President Smith, the congregation sang "Praise to the Man," after which the massive monument was unveiled.

The unveiled monument revealed this commemorative inscription carved into its south face:

> "Sacred to the Memory of Joseph Smith the Prophet. Born here 23d December, 1805, Martyred Carthage, Illinois 27th June 1844." And on its north face was etched the Prophet's "Testimony," which included this sentence, identifying him with the martyred Patriarch and thereby fulfilling, to a degree, the plan of jointly memorializing Joseph and Hyrum: "In his ministry he was constantly supported by his brother Hyrum Smith, who suffered martyrdom with him."[19]

The First Presidency, other dignitaries and representative of the Smith family proceeded to Palmyra, New York, where they visited the Smith farm and home, the Sacred Grove and the Hill Cumorah.

> The spirituality of the occasion was richly enhanced by a moving prayer offered by President Smith atop the Hill Cumorah, following, as it did, the singing of the hymns "An Angel from on High."[20]

The party then traveled to Kirtland where they visited the home in which President Smith's parents—Hyrum and Mary Fielding—began their marriage. Next they visited the Kirtland

Temple, where so many great heavenly manifestations had taken place before the persecutors of the Saints defiled it.

> President Joseph F. Smith was both annoyed and amused to read the inscription on the front of the temple: "House of the Lord, Built by the Church of Jesus Christ of Latter-day Saints, 1834, Reorganized Church of Jesus Christ of Latter-day Saints in Succession By decision of the Court February, 1880." After reading these words and reflecting on them, Joseph F. said aloud to the group standing with him in front of the building, "No order of the court could transmit the succession of the Holy Priesthood or the Spirit and power and religious rights of the Church established by revelation from God."[21]

In the once holy house, Joseph F. Smith had no desire to speak, pray or sing. President Smith led his party to Carthage, Illinois, where the infamous jail is located.

> While inspecting the jail where his father and uncle were murdered, he was gloomy and depressed. "Charley, I despise this place," he said to Bishop [Charles] Nibley. "It harrows up feelings to come here."[22]

This, too, was not a place that inspired the Prophet to pray or sing.

Joseph F. Smith took pride in the members of the Church who were developing their talents in singing.

> It delights my heart to see our little children learning to sing, and to see the people, our people everywhere, improving their talents as good singers. Everywhere we go among our people, we find sweet voices and talent for music. I believe that this is a manifestation to us of the purpose of the Lord in this direction toward our people, that they will excel in these things, as they should excel in every other good thing.
>
> When young men go out into the world to preach the gospel, they will find it very beneficial for them to know how to sing the songs of Zion. I repeat the admonition and request by Brother McMurrin, who has recently returned from a lengthy mission to Europe, that the young men who are eligible to preach the gospel,

and who are likely to be called in to the missionary field, begin at once to improve their talent to sing, and do not think it beneath their dignity to join the choirs of the wards in which they live and learn how to sing.[23]

President Smith loved the Tabernacle Choir, and felt that choral music in our services is a fitting method of worshipping the Lord. He said in October Conference, 1899:

> When we listen to this choir, under the leadership of Brother Evan Stephens, we listen to music, and music is truth. Good music is gracious praise of God. It is delightsome to the ear, and it is one of our most acceptable methods of worshipping God. And those who sing in the choir and in all the choirs of the Saints should sing with the spirit and with the understanding. They should not sing merely because it is a profession, or because they have a good voice; but they should sing also because they have the spirit of it, and can enter into the spirit of prayer and praise to God who gave them their sweet voices. My soul is always lifted up, and my spirit cheered and comforted, when I hear good music. I rejoice in it very much indeed.[24]

As President of the Church, Joseph F. Smith ordained two of his sons to the apostleship: Hyrum Mack Smith on October 24, 1901—the year he became the President—and nine years later, Joseph Fielding Smith on April 7, 1909, later becoming the tenth President of the Church.

Under Joseph F. Smith's administration, missions were opened in Switzerland and Germany, Japan, Sweden, Denmark, and Norway, France, Tonga and the Middle States. Under his direction, a magazine for the children of the Church was created and first published. The *Children's Friend* began its sixty-nine-year life, becoming *The Friend* in 1971. Joseph F. Smith became the first president of the Church to visit Europe as president, touring the missions of Europe in 1906. The Church seminary program was begun in 1912. Under his direction, in 1915, the *Relief Society Magazine* began publishing, and the home evening program was inaugurated.

The sermons of President Smith—covering a wide array of gospel subjects—were articulate and persuasive. Many of them were combined with other writings to form the book, *Gospel Doctrine*, which has served as a classic resource in the Church for many years.

Evan Stephens, conductor of the Tabernacle Choir, was deeply moved on one occasion by a sermon delivered by Joseph F. Smith on the subject of "The Third and Fourth Generations."

At the close of the service Professor Stephens strolled alone up City Creek Canyon pondering the inspired words of the President. Suddenly the music came upon him and seated upon a rock which was standing firm under the pressure of the rushing water and happily symbolic of his theme, he wrote with a pencil the words of "True to the Faith" and with roughly drawn staves composed the music.[25]

The hymn, when introduced to the Church, became a favorite, and to this day remains one of the core of standards among our LDS hymns. It appears as Hymn #254 in the 1985 hymnal:

> Shall the youth of Zion falter
> In defending truth and right?
> While the enemy assaileth,
> Shall we shrink or shun the fight? No!
>
> *Chorus:*
> True to the faith that our parents have cherished,
> True to the truth for which martyrs have perished,
> To God's command, Soul heart, and hand,
> Faithful and true we will ever stand.
>
> While we know the pow'rs of darkness
> Seek to thwart the work of God,
> Shall the children of the promise
> Cease to grasp the iron rod? No!
>
> *Chorus*

We will work out our salvation;
We will cleave unto the truth;
We will watch and pray and labor
With the fervent zeal of youth. Yes!

Chorus

We will strive to be found worthy
Of the kingdom of our Lord,
With the faithful ones redeemed
Who have loved and kept his word. Yes!

Chorus

As a climax to his fifty-one-years as an apostle, his distinguished service as a counselor to presidents Brigham Young, John Taylor, Wilford Woodruff and Lorenzo Snow *and* the eighteen years as the Prophet of God on earth, on October 3, 1918—six weeks before his death—Joseph F. Smith received the great vision of the redemption of the dead. The account of this vision was presented to and accepted by his counselors—Anthon H. Lund and Charles W. Penrose—and the Quorum of the Twelve. On April 3, 1976 it was accepted by the Church as scripture.

Joseph F. Smith described—in what is now Section 138 of the Doctrine and Covenants—seeing the Savior minister to the spirits of the departed during the time his body lay in the tomb. Spirits of the righteous were organized in a way that they might teach "those who had died in their sins, without a knowledge of the truth." (v. 32).

Section 138 records:

[A]mong the righteous there was peace;
And the saints rejoiced in their redemption, and bowed the knee and acknowledged the Son of God as their Redeemer and Deliverer from death and the chains of hell.
Their countenances shone, and the radiance from the presence of the Lord rested upon them, and *they sang praises unto his holy name.*

Among the many truths regarding the state of the departed is this: *the righteous will continue to sing their praises to the Lord in the Spirit World just as they have done on earth!*

Within weeks of his marvelous vision, Joseph F. Smith suffered an attach of pleurisy that soon developed into pneumonia. On November 19, 1918—at eighty—the Prophet passed away peacefully.

A raging epidemic of influenza had prevented the customary public service in the Tabernacle. Instead, the casket carrying his body was taken directly from the Beehive House to the cemetery in a cortege that passed thousands of onlookers who lined the streets to pay their last respects to the venerable leader. These included the thoughtful priests of the Catholic Church who stood in front of the Cathedral of the Madeline on East South Temple and ordered the tolling of the cathedral's mournful bells as the cortege passed.[26]

The brief graveside services included prayers by George Albert Smith and Charles W.Penrose, and remarks by Anthon H. Lund and Bishop Charles W Nibley. With no funeral service, sadly, the only music to honor him was the tolling of bells that sounded from the towers of the Cathedral of the Madeleine.

1 Joseph F. Smith: *Gospel Doctrine* (Salt Lake City: Deseret Book Co., 1975, p. 259.
2 Preston Nibley: *The Presidents of the Church* (Salt Lake City: Deseret Book Co, 1968) p. 227.
3 Ibid., p. 182.
4 Ibid., p. 183.
5 Joseph F. Smith: *Gospel Doctrine* (Salt Lake City; Deseret Book Co. 1975) pp. 258-259.
6 Preston Nibley: pp. 228-229.
7 Leonard Arrington: *The Presidents of the Church* (Salt Lake City: Deseret Book Co, 1986) p. 182.
8 Francis M. Gibbons: *Joseph F. Smith, Patriarch and Preacher, Prophet of God* (Salt Lake City: Deseret book, 1984) p. 34.
9 Joseph Fielding Smith: *Life of Joseph F. Smith* (Salt Lake City: The Deseret News Press, 1938) p. 173.
10 Gibbons p. 36.
11 Joseph Fielding Smith p. 173.
12 Ibid., p. 199.
13 Hymn No. 19 in current 1985 hymnal.
14 Karen Lynn Davidson: *Our Latter-day Hymns* (Salt Lake City: Deseret Book, 1988) pp. 47-48.
15 Joseph Fielding Smith, p. 200.
16 Ibid., pp. 219-220.
17 Recorded in Joseph F. Smith's Journals in the Church Archives, as reported by a grand-daughter Amelia Smith McConkie.
18 Joseph F. Smith: *Gospel Ideals*, p. 321.
19 Francis M. Gibbons: pp. 226-227.
20 Ibid., p. 229.
21 Ibid., p.230.
22 Preston Nibley, p. 254.
23 Joseph F. Smith: *Gospel Doctrine* p. 258.
24 Ibid., p. 259.
25 J. Spencer Cornwall: *Stories of Our Mormon Hymns* (Salt Lake City: Deseret Book Co., 1971) pp. 173-174.
26 Francis Gibbons: p. 329-330.

HEBER J. GRANT

M Withers '94

HEBER J. GRANT
(1856-1951)

"I recommend to the youth of Zion, that they go to work with determination and learn to sing,... because, next to familiarity with the scriptures, the ability to sing will assist them, when they are called to the nations of the earth to preach the gospel."[1]

Jedediah M. Grant, was one of the faithful Mormon pioneers who followed Brigham Young to the Valley of the Great Salt Lake. He was ordained an apostle by Brigham Young and served as his second counselor. Besides his ecclesiastical responsibilities, Jedediah M. Grant was a General in Utah's Territorial Nauvoo Legion and became Salt Lake City's first mayor. To Rachael Ridgeway Ivins, his second wife, was born Heber Jeddy Grant on November 22, 1856. Nine days later, typhoid fever and pneumonia claimed the life of Jedediah M. Grant. Heber never knew his father.

Rachael and the other wives of Jedediah continued to live on Main Street not far from the home of Brigham Young. As a young boy, Heber was invited to join the Young family for their nightly ritual of singing and family prayer.[2] In that setting, Heber learned of prayer, and developed a love for singing, especially the songs of Zion. An incident in Heber's boyhood illustrates one of the fundamental characteristics for which he became so well known.

Heber and several of his boyhood friends were playing marbles. Heber's concentration was interrupted when one of his playmates, pointing to a prosperous-looking man on the other side of the street, said, "Hebe, you see that long fellow across the road? He is working in Wells Fargo Bank, and gets $150 a month." Heber was duly impressed by this bit of knowledge, and it immediately set his analytical mind to work. At that time his main source of income came from shining shoes of his mother's borders for five cents a pair. He quickly calculated that this man made six dollars a day, which would be the equivalent of 240 shoes. "As I saw in my mind's eye 240 shoes to be shined to get six dollars," Heber later mused, "I decided that I would learn penmanship and bookkeeping, and some day, keep books in the Wells Fargo Bank."[3]

Later in life, Heber J. Grant was fond of recalling the words of Lord Bulwer Lytton which had been a shaping influence throughout his life:

> What a man wants is not talent, it is purpose; not power to achieve, but the will to labor.[4]

Heber's penmanship had been described as "lightning striking an ink bottle," but he labored unceasingly until the beauty of his penmanship became legendary. Later on, in his struggling years, Heber supplemented his income,

> especially near holidays, inscribing greeting and calling cards, for which he occasionally received more compensation than from his regular employment.[5]

One day, his self-prophecy was fulfilled when he became an employee of the esteemed Wells Fargo Bank.

> When Heber began to play baseball with his friends, his awkwardness made him the laughing stock of the neighborhood. Though he was among the taller players, he was usually delegated to the third team with the younger and smaller boys.
>
> He declared to his mother that he would play on the team that would win the championship of the Territory of Utah. Having made that prediction, he took immediate steps to put a foundation under it. "I shined forty shoes and I got a baseball," he reported. Then, with a tenacity almost frightening in its proportions, he commenced the laborious process of acquiring the skill necessary to fulfill his prediction. Reflecting on that process, he recorded: I stood up behind my mother's home and threw a ball night after

night, week after week, and month after month at Bishop Woolley's barn![6]

Eventually, Heber played on the baseball team that one day won the territorial championship.

Edwin D. Woolley's served as bishop of the Thirteenth Ward for thirty years where Rachael Grant and her son, Heber, lived. Considered one of the most progressive bishops in the Salt Lake Valley, Bishop Woolley organized the first modern Sunday School in the Church.

> Typically, the children met at [one of] the Assembly Rooms, where as a group they *listened to short talks and sang, and recited inspirational prose and poetry.* Leaders would also "catechize" the children with questions drawn from the Bible, Book of Mormon, or LDS history, giving prizes for correct answers and proper conduct.[7]

Heber won prizes for learning answers from John Jaques' *Catechism* and the revelation on the Word of Wisdom. He worked at memorization, and even mastered the Deseret Alphabet. Anthony C. Ivans offered a pair of buckskin gloves to his own son, or fourteen-year-old Heber, whoever would be first to read the Book of Mormon from start to finish.

> After the first day, Heber's hopes were virtually dashed. Young Ivins stayed up most of the night to read 150 pages, while Heber, hoping to read the scriptures thoughtfully, amassed only 25 pages. The incident, however had a "Tortoise and the Hare" ending. "When I finished the book, Heber remembered, "I not only got a testimony [of it] but...the gloves as well." After a fast start, his cousin never read another page. [8]

Goal setting and dogged determination to accomplish them were part of the fundamental fabric of Heber's soul. Learning to sing for Heber—"who couldn't carry a tune in a bucket"— was more difficult than acquiring fine penmanship, becoming a competent baseball player, or memorizing scripture. He recalled his early struggles in leaning to "carry a tune."

My mother tried to teach me when a small child to sing, but failed because of my inability to carry a tune. Upon joining a singing class taught by Professor Charles J. Thomas, he tried and tried in vain to teach me when ten years of age to run the scale or carry a simple tune, and finally gave up in despair. He said that I could never, in this world, learn to sing. Perhaps he thought I might learn the divine art in another world. Ever since this attempt, I have frequently tried to sing when riding alone many miles from anyone who might hear me, but on such occasions could never succeed in carrying the tune of one of our familiar hymns for a single verse, and quite frequently not for a single line.[9]

Heber persevered, however, in spite of a poor voice, the lack of a musical ear and a certain lack of encouragement. When about twenty-five years of age, I had my character read by Professor Sims, the renowned physiognomist[10], and he informed me that I could sing, but added, "I would like to be at least forty miles away while you are doing it."[11]

To his other accomplishments may be added learning to dance:

Undeterred...by the fact that his tone deafness handicapped him in learning to dance with grace, Heber persisted in dancing and taking dancing lessons until he had attained a desired proficiency. "I determined to learn to dance," he wrote," so I joined a dancing school, and paid lessons to a dancing master by the name of Sheldon...I had about as hard work learning to dance as I did leaning to play marbles and write, but "I finally mastered it and became a pretty good dancer." In the process, Heber acquired a great liking for this diversion, and was later to say that he "would sooner waltz than eat."

In time, so-called round dancing became the favorite diversion of Heber's social group; it was such a rage that President Young decreed that there were to be only two or three round dances in an evening, with the balance of the program being taken up with the more conventional and less daring square dances....

Too often these dances, with their lengthy intermissions and extended programming, carried on into early hours of the morning. This was especially hard on active young men like Heber who had to be at the top of their form at the office or in the classroom the next morning. To avoid this, while preserving the delightful aspects of the dance, Heber and his friends organized what was later to be known as the Wasatch Literary Association, which, among other things, operated its dances on the Cinderella principle. These dances always ended at five minutes before midnight to get home at a reasonable hour.[12]

Historian Ronald Walker details the activities of the Wasatch Literary Association:

> With its sixty members drawn from the ablest young people in the city, the society met each Wednesday evening for cultural exercises. These might include declamations, lectures, debates, readings, musical renditions, and even small-scale theatrical productions. In reality, "Wasatchers" often used culture as an excuse for good natured fun.[13]

Among the "Wasatchers" were Emily Wells—whom Heber later married as a plural wife—and Lucy Stringham—a neighbor and fellow Thirteenth Ward member. Before long, the relationship of Heber and Lucy went beyond the dances and musical renditions. In 1877—the year President Brigham Young died—Heber married Lucy in the St. George Temple. Marriage for eternity meant more to the young couple than inconvenience, and so Heber and Lucy made a trip by rail to Utah County and by wagon the rest of the way to St. George, requiring several days traveling each way.

As a child, Heber had been promised in a patriarchal blessing that he would be "called to the ministry in his youth." Heber had not received a mission call before his marriage, and he began to doubt the validity of that blessing. However, the promise by his patriarch was to be *literally* fulfilled, but in a most unexpected way. At twenty-three, Heber was called by the first presidency to move to Tooele—some forty miles west of Salt Lake City—to become the stake president. He was installed as President of the Tooele Stake on October 30, 1880, the youngest stake president in the Church. Present were President John Taylor and his counselors, George Q. Cannon and Joseph F. Smith, as well as Francis M. Lyman—former President of the Tooele Stake and recently called as a member of the Quorum of the Twelve—and Edwin D. Woolley, Bishop of the Thirteenth Ward, who wanted to "assure the local Saints that they were 'getting a man and not a boy.'" The new stake president gave a seven-and a half minute speech that "told everything I could think of...and part of it I told twice."[14]

The second daughter of Heber and Lucy, who was named after her mother—but was called Luty—spoke of her mother's artistic talents:

> Mother was artistic and loved beautiful things. She did some pen and ink sketches which Father had framed, and they were in our house for years. I am sure if she had the opportunity for even a little instruction she would have excelled in some of the fine arts.[15]

Heber was determined that there be music in the home. He purchased a Steinway piano and promised to pay for lessons for the children, with one stipulation:

> When the Steinway piano arrived, we were old enough to take lessons. Father said he would pay for the lessons if we play for him whenever he asked us. This seemed a reasonable request, but occasionally when he had company, he would call us to play before we thought we were well enough prepared. I remember I would get Mother to put my hair up in rags, that was the way we made curls in those days, so I could be presentable when asked to come into the parlor to play.[16]

Lucy did not enjoy good health and was bedfast for months at a time. She bore six children in the thirteen years of their marriage. She died on January 3, 1892, at age thirty-two, sixteen years after her marriage to Heber J. Grant, and a little more than one year before the completion of the Salt Lake Temple. The long journey to the St. George Temple was a small price for an eternal marriage, which would not have been possible had they married civilly while waiting for the completion of the Salt Lake Temple.

Embracing the principle of plural marriage, Heber married Agusta Winters and Emily Wells. Agusta had only one child—a daughter—but cared for the six children of Lucy Grant after their mother's death. Emily was the mother of four girls.

The Tooele Stake extended as far as Oakley, Idaho, a settlement north and west of the Great Salt Lake. But by wagon—which was the only mode of transportation available—the round-about trip required two or three weeks. After becoming an apostle, Heber quickly proposed transferring Oakley to the Box Elder Stake which was half as far for a stake president to travel!

> It was on one of his trips to Oakley from Tooele that Heber was first imbued with the desire to learn to sing. On this particular trip, Elder Francis M. Lyman's son relinquished his seat in his father's white-top [buggy] to Heber. In the course of the day Elder Lyman sang a number of songs for his guest, including the old favorite, "Let Each Man Learn to Know Himself," whose chief message is condensed at the end of the last stanza: "So first improve yourself today and then improve your friends tomorrow."
>
> So impressed was Heber by this song that he persuaded Elder Lyman to sing it again as they gathered around the campfire that evening. As he did so, Heber wrote down the words and committed them to memory. When he later learned to sing, persevering in spite of his tone deafness, this song became one of the mainstays of his repertoire. Of it he was to write: "I have repeated this song from one end of the church to the other—from Canada on the north to Mexico on the south, in the Hawaiian Islands and over to Japan and in different parts of Europe and have asked missionaries at home and abroad to learn it off by heart."[17]

Heber proved to the members of the Tooele Stake that he was a capable leader and administrator, and could if necessary, preach a long sermon. Apparently, he also proved this to the authorities as well. Two years later he was called by President John Taylor to fill a vacancy in the Quorum of the Twelve Apostles. He was set apart to that calling October 16, 1882 at the tender age of twenty-five. He ably served as an apostle for sixty-three years, including twenty-seven years as the

President of the Church. In the history of the Church, only David O. McKay served longer as a general authority; and only Brigham Young served longer as the President of the Church.

In 1901, Elder Grant was assigned by the First Presidency to go to the Orient where he would open the Japanese Mission. On July 24, he left with three men, whom he "hand picked" to accompany him on this challenging mission: Horace S. Ensign, Alma O. Taylor and Louis B. Kelsh. Brother Ensign, who succeeded Elder Grant as the Mission President, had a beautiful baritone voice and later served as soloist with the Tabernacle Choir as well as its assistant conductor under Evan Stephens. Alma O. Taylor was just eighteen years of age at the time. He remained in Japan for nine years, succeeding Horace Ensign as mission President and made the first translation of the Book of Mormon into Japanese. Elder Kelsh accepted the assignment to go to Japan with Heber J. Grant, even though he had already served ten years in the mission field.

The four brethren left by train for Vancouver, British Columbia. Francis Gibbons relates what happened once the train had pulled out:

> Within minutes after [the train's] departure, Heber assembled his companion in the drawing room of the sleeping car, where they sang three favorite hymns whose lyrics aptly expressed basic Mormon doctrines and whose tunes, sung with volume and gusto, assured the passengers that this was not to be a dull trip. As the strains of "Truth Reflects Upon Our Senses," "Do What Is Right," and "God Moves in a Mysterious Way" floated through the car, the erstwhile sleepers likely had alternate feelings of the enjoyment, amusement, and annoyance at this nocturnal serenade.[18]

> Shortly after their arrival in Yokohama, the four brethren, on a Sunday Morning, selected a secluded spot in the woods near the city to dedicate the land for the preaching of the Gospel.

Elder Taylor wrote of the proceedings:

> After the four prayers [by each of the brethren] had been offered up we knelt again in a circle and brother Grant offered up the dedi-

catory prayer. His tongue was loosened and the spirit rested mighti-
ly upon him; so much so that we felt that the angels of God were
near for our hearts burned within us as the words fell from his lips. I
have never experienced such a peaceful influence or heard such powerful prayer before; every word penetrated into my very bones and I
could have wept with joy.[19]

"After the dedicatory prayer," wrote Francis Gibbons,

the brethren sang "O My Father," then bore their testimonies,
each one in his turn. "More than once while the brethren were
speaking," Heber wrote, "tears of gratitude filled my eyes for the
rich outpouring of the Good Spirit which I felt in our midst."[20]

The mission was difficult, the success was meager. But "the
Japanese Quartet"[21]—as they were called—sang together often.
At least three of the four sang rather well together; the fourth
made up in enthusiasm what he may have lacked in beauty.

Heber J. Grant had succeeded Francis M. Lyman as the
President of the Tooele Stake, and had followed him into the
Quorum of the Twelve. In General Conference, October 6,
1903, President Joseph F. Smith announced that Heber J. Grant
would succeed Elder Francis M. Lyman as president of the
European Mission.

For this mission, Elder Grant received permission for his
third wife, Emily Wells Grant, and their six daughters to
accompany him. This would be Emily's second trip to
England—the headquarters of the European Mission—as she
had accompanied her father, Daniel H. Wells, who previously
had served as the mission president years before.

Elder Grant was given permission to buy a new mission
home, one that would better meet their needs. Francis Gibbons
describes their new headquarters at 10 Holly Road:

A red brick, mansion-type building, surrounded by an impressive wrought-iron picket fence, the main floor, which doubled as a
chapel for the Saints in Liverpool; a mezzanine with living quarters
for the elders; a spacious second floor that comprised the private

apartment for the Grant family; an attic; and a spacious basement in which the print shop was installed, including the press that had published the first *Millennial Star*. The first editor of this famous early Church publication, Parley P. Pratt, had included a copy of his poem "The Morning Breaks, the Shadows Flee" on the front of the first issue of the *Star* in Manchester, England, more than sixty years before. The sentiment seemed to typify Heber's feelings as he faced this new day in his apostolic career.[22]

In Salt Lake City, Augusta's father, Oscar Winters, visited the Grants in their home on one occasion. In discussing the hymn, "Come, Come, Ye Saints," Brother Winters said this to the apostle and son-in-law:

> Brother Grant, I do not believe that the young people today fully appreciate what a marvelous inspiration it was to the Saints in crossing the plains to sing, almost daily, the hymn "Come, Come, Ye Saints." If the young people of the Church today understood all that it meant to the early Pioneers, while crossing the plains, to sing this hymn nearly every night around the campfires, I do not believe they would be guilty of singing only three verses. I have never yet heard a choir sing more than three verses, and yet to my mind the fourth verse is the climax to its splendid prayer.[23]

Brother Winters continued by relating this now-famous story:

> One night, as we were making camp, we noticed one of our brethren had not arrived. A volunteer party was immediately organized to return and see if anything had happened to him. Just as we were about to start, we saw the mission brother coming in the distance. When he arrived, he said he had been quite sick. So some of us unyoked his oxen and attended to his part of the camp duties.
>
> After supper, he sat down before the campfire on a large rock, and sang, in a very faint but plaintive and sweet voice, the hymn, "Come, Come, Ye Saints."[24]

It had become a standing rule among the pioneers, when anyone began singing "Come, Come, Ye Saints"—which was a source of great strength, encouragement and comfort—the other

Saints joined in the singing. But this night, for whatever reason, the brother sang the entire hymn alone. His singing created a spirit in which "there was not a single dry eye in the camp." He passed away during the night, and the men who did his chores the night before buried him in a shallow grave, and rolled the stone—the same stone on which he sat while singing "Come, Come, Ye Saint" the night before—at the head of the grave.

Continuing with the visit with Oscar Winters, Elder Grant wrote:

> I noticed tears in my father-in-law's eyes when he finished relating this incident. And I imagined the reason he did not relate to me another far more touching incident to him was the fear that he might break down
>
> I subsequently learned that after he had been located for some time in Pleasant Grove, he came to Salt Lake with his team with a cheerful heart to meet his mother [who had come with a later company], and learned that she, too, had died before her journey's end and was sleeping in an unknown grave on the vast plains between here and the Missouri River.
>
> [In 1902, fifty years after her death,] when engineers of the Burlington Railroad were surveying the route in Nebraska, they ran across a piece of wagon tire sticking in the ground with the word "Winters" chiseled upon it. They immediately surmised, knowing that they were on the old Mormon Pioneer trail, that this piece of wagon tire must mark the grave of one of the Pioneers. So they very considerately went back several miles and changed the line of the road so as to miss the grave. The railroad company [has] since built a neat little fence around the grave, and the Winters' family has erected a little monument of temple granite on which is chiseled the fourth verse of "Come, Come, Ye Saints."[25]

> And should we die before our journey's through,
> Happy day! all is well!
> We then are free from toil and sorrow too;
> With the just we shall dwell.
> But if our lives are spared again
> To see the Saints their rest obtain,
> O how we'll make this chorus swell-
> All is well! All is Well![26]

Though Heber had struggled unsuccessfully as a youngster to learn to sing—probably his only unsuccessful endeavor—he continued to harbor an intense desire to sing well.

In the August, 1890, issue of the *Improvement Era*, Heber J. Grant chronicles his most famous attainment:

Nearly ten months ago, while listening to Brother Horace S. Ensign sing, I remarked that I would gladly give two or three months of my spare time if by so doing it would result in my being able to sing one or two hymns. He answered that any person could learn to sing who had a reasonably good voice, and who possessed perseverance, and was willing to do plenty of practicing. My response was that I had an abundance of voice, and considerable perseverance. He was in my employ at the time, and I jokingly remarked that while he had not been hired as a music teacher, however, right now I would take my first music lesson of two hours upon the hymn, "O My Father." Much to my surprise, at the end of four or five days, I was able to sing this hymn with Brother Ensign without any mistakes. At the end of two weeks, I could sing it alone, with the exception of being a little flat on some of the high notes. My ear not being cultivated musically, did not detect this, and the only way I knew of it was by having Brother Ensign and other friends tell me of the error.

One of the leading Church officials, upon hearing me sing, when I first started to practice, remarked that my singing reminded him very much of the late Apostle Orson Pratt's poetry. He said Brother Pratt wrote only one piece of poetry, and this looked like it had been sawed out of boards, and sawed off straight.

Once, while practicing in Brother Ensign's office in the Templeton Building, (his were next to the dentist's) some of the students of the Latter-day Saints College who were in the hall, remarked that it sounded like somebody was having his teeth pulled....

One Sunday, at the close of a meeting in the Thirteenth Ward, upon telling Professor Charles J. Thomas that Brother Ensign informed me that I could sing, he said: "Didn't you tell him I said no?" I answered, "Yes." He said, "Why you can't even run the scale." I said, "I am aware of that fact, having tried for half an hour this morning and failed." My voice at ten years of age, must have made a very deep impression upon Brother Thomas, seeing that he had remembered it for thirty-three years. Noticing that he seemed quite skeptical, I asked him to walk over with me into the corner of the building, so as not to disturb the people who had not yet left the meetinghouse, when I sang to him in a low voice, "God Moves in a Mysterious Way." At the close he said: "That's all right."

At the end of two or three months, I was able to sing not only, "O My Father," but God Moves in a Mysterious Way," "Come, Come, Ye Saints," and two or three other hymns. Shortly after this, while taking a trip south, I sang one or more hymns in each of the Arizona stakes, and in Juarez, Mexico. Upon my return to Salt Lake City, I attempted to sing "O My Father," in the big Tabernacle, hoping to give an object lesson to the young people, and to encourage them to learn to sing. I made a failure, getting off key in nearly every verse, and instead of my effort encouraging the young people, I feel that it tended to discourage them.

When first starting to practice, if some person would join in and sing bass, tenor, or alto, I could not carry the tune. Neither could I sing, if anyone accompanied me on the piano or organ, as the variety of sounds confused me.

I am pleased to be able to say that I can now sing with piano or organ accompaniment, and can also sing the lead in "God Moves in a Mysterious Way," in a duet, a trio or quartet. I have learned quite a number of songs, and have been assured by Brother Ensign, and several others well versed in music, to whom I have sung within the past few weeks, that I succeeded without making a mistake in a single note, which I fear would not be the case, were the attempt to be made in public. However, I intend to continue trying to sing the Hymn, "O My Father," in the Assembly Hall or the big Tabernacle until such time as I can sing it without an error.

How did I succeed so far? Brother Ensign adopted the plan of having me sing a line over and over again, trying to imitate his voice...It required a vast amount of practice to learn, and my first hymn was sung many hundreds of times before I succeeded in getting it right.

Upon my recent trip to Arizona, I asked Elders Rudger Clawson and J. Golden Kimball [who traveled with me] if they had any objections to my singing one hundred hymns that day. They took it as a joke, and assured me that they would be delighted. We were on the way from Hollbrook to St. Johns, a distance of about sixty miles. After I had sung about forty times, they assured me that if I sang the remaining sixty they would be sure to have nervous prostration. I paid no attention whatever to their appeal, but held them to their bargain and sang the full one hundred. One hundred and fifteen songs in one day and four hundred in four days, is the largest amount of practicing I ever did.

Today my musical deafness is disappearing, and by sitting down to a piano and playing the lead notes, I can learn a song in less than one-tenth the time required when I first commenced to practice. Where a person has a low voice—as in my case—he should ask some kind friend, who understands music, to transpose his songs to a lower key. It is impossible for me to sing a majority of our hymns in the keys in which they are written in our psalmody. The above points are mentioned for the benefit of my musically deaf friends who desire to be cured, and are willing to do a goodly amount of hard work in order to accomplish that very pleasant result.[27]

Elder Richard L. Evans comments on the quote made famous by Heber J. Grant which was adapted from Ralph Waldo Emerson.

How many times this people have heard from this pulpit the words of Ralph Waldo Emerson so often uttered in the ringing voice of President Grant: "That which we persist in doing becomes easier for us to do; not that the nature of the thing itself has changed, but that our power to do is increased," although President Grant, as I remember quoted them just a bit differently from the above.[28]

Heber J. Grant—for whom herculean struggles were required to learn to sing—offers living proof that persistence pays off. The obsession of a future prophet of God to learn to sing well, and the seemingly unending toil to accomplish this goal, speaks volumes about the Lord's regard for singing, especially for those good people who are *not* tone deaf.

Referring to his singing, Heber J. Grant preached a sermon on persistence and determination in April Conference, 1901 in the Tabernacle:

I propose to sing the "Holy City" in the big tabernacle before I get through with it, and I propose to sing it without a mistake. I do not say this boastingly, because I believe what Alma of old said, in the twenty-ninth chapter of his book, that "God granteth unto men according to their desires, whether they be for good or evil, for joy or remorse of conscience." I desire to sing, and I expect to work at it and stay right with it until I learn.... There are a great many people who can learn to sing very easily. When I started to learn to sing, it took me four months to learn a couple of simple hymns, and recently I learned one in three hours by the watch and then sang it without a mistake.

"*That which we persist in doing becomes easier for us to do; not that the nature of the thing itself is changed, but that our power to do is increased.*" I propose to keep at it until my power to do is increased to the extent that I can sing the songs of Zion. Nobody knows the joy I have taken in standing up in the tabernacle and other places and joining in the singing, because it used to be a perfect annoyance to me to try and to fail, besides annoying those around me, *because I loved the words of the songs of Zion, and would sing.*

I am very sorry now for having persecuted people as I used to. In our meetings in the temple the brethren would say, "That is as impossible as it is for Brother Grant to carry a tune," and that settled it. Everybody acknowledged that was one of the impossibilities.

I believe what the Lord says: "For my soul delighteth in the song of the heart; yea, the song of the righteous is a prayer unto me, and it shall be answered with a blessing upon their heads" (D&C 25:12). *I desire to serve the Lord and pray unto him in the songs of Zion; and I know that it produces a good influence.*[29]

Heber J. Grant relished the joy of singing, but he also loved the gospel messages and the sentiments expressed in the hymns. Repeatedly, he referred to the familiar quotation in the Doctrine and Covenants that "the song of the righteous is a prayer unto me" (D&C 25:12). Moreover, this great apostle understood the power of music in preaching the gospel, and its importance in missionary work:

President Brigham Young once remarked, that the Spirit of the Lord would do more to convert people than the eloquence of man. The same is true of singing. It is not always the ability that a missionary has to sing in a creditable and entertaining way that will aid him most in his missionary work; but on the contrary, *if he can sing some of our beautiful hymns with the spirit in which they were written, he will be able to carry conviction to the hearts of his hearers as to the truths of the Gospel.* As an example of this: Elders J.

Golden Kimball and Charles A. Welch, neither of whom claim to sing well, while on a mission in the Southern States, were about to baptize some converts; a mob had assembled, and the brethren were given to understand that if they carried out their intentions of baptizing that the mob would throw them into the river. The brethren determined to go ahead no matter what the result might be. Before doing so, however, they sang a song. The song seemed to have an effect upon the mob that they were almost transfixed. The brethren proceeded with their baptisms, and then went some distance to attend to confirming the baptized. A message came from the mob asking them to come and sing that song again, and the request was complied with. The leader of the mob, Joseph Jarvis, afterwards joined the Church, and he stated to Elder Kimball that the sentiments of the hymn, and the inspiration attending the singing, as above related, converted him to the Gospel. Brother Kimball's recollection is that the hymn was "Truth Reflects Upon Our Senses."[30]

Elder Grant recalled another incident among the mission experiences of J. Golden Kimball:

Calling at a home while in the Southern States, the people informed him and his associates that they were from Missouri, and immediately commenced making attacks upon the "Mormon" people. Brother Kimball and his companions energetically defended our people, refuting many of the islanders which were advanced. The arguments became quite heated, when the head of the house said, "Daughter, play us a piece, and sing us a song to drive the evil spirit away." After some music and singing, he remarked to brother Kimball that he believed they could now proceed with their argument with a much better spirit. Elder Kimball assures me that he had never forgotten this incident and that it was a lesson to him which has ever since been of great value.[31]

"I am confident that the hymns of Zion," stated Heber J. Grant," [will] aid in the preaching of the gospel of Jesus Christ." The high priority of music for the prospective missionary is shown in this statement by Elder Grant:

I recommend to the youth of Zion , that they go to work with determination and learn to sing. Particularly is this recommendation made to the young men, because, *next to a familiarity with the scriptures, the ability to sing will assist them when they are called to the nations of the earth to preach the gospel.* It will insure them many a friend, furnish them many a meal and bed, which they would otherwise go without.[32]

Music, Heber J. Grant felt, is not a mere adornment of our church services like a bouquet of flowers at the pulpit as some would suppose, but provides a vehicle for the gospel message to penetrate the heart. The spirit of our hymns, also, promotes a feeling of spirituality.

> *The singing of our sacred hymns, written by the servants of God, has a powerful effect in converting people to the principles of the gospel and in promoting peace and spiritual growth....*

> Let us not forget our hymns when we go to the house of worship. Let the congregation sing; and by all means let the choir members become familiar with the beautiful sentiments that are contained in our hymns. And so shall our Father in Heaven delight in the songs of our hearts...and...He will graciously answer with blessings upon our heads.[33]

Heber J. Grant was anxious for the truths of the restored Gospel to be expressed in our own poetry and music.

> I wish that as far as possible we would get into the habit of singing our own music, that is, music composed by our own people. There are an inspiration and spirit which accompany the music of George Careless, Evan Stephens, Joseph J. Daynes, and other of our own faith.
> I am free to confess that when I go out into the country district and hear sung certain anthems, I wonder why the people do not show preference for the home-made article. I think that Evan Stephens and these other men were inspired of the Lord to write music for us. I do not want to reflect on any of the magnificent things that have been written by others, but I have gone to many a conference where I have listened to anthems when I would rather have heard a good Latter-day Saint hymn sung.
> *The more beautiful the music by which false doctrine is sung, the more dangerous it becomes. I appeal to all Latter-day Saints, and especially to our choirs, never to sing the words of a song, no*

matter how beautiful and inspiring the music may be, where the teachings are not in perfect accord with the truths of the gospel.[34]

Music, Heber J. Grant felt, brings a feeling of peace into our homes, and draws the family members closer to the Lord and to each other.

I so feel that there is a great deal lost in the homes of the people by not having the songs of Zion sung therein....

I am confident that the hymns of Zion, when sung with the proper spirit, bring a peaceful and heavenly influence into our homes, and also aid in preaching the gospel of Jesus Christ.[35]

Apostle Grant spoke of using music as part of our daily family worship:

There is nothing more pleasing and inspiring than music in the home, and since I learned to sing, we generally have a hymn at our house each morning before family prayer. There certainly is a delightful influence which attends the singing of the songs of Zion, and it is my opinion that the Saints should make singing part of their family worship.[36]

Soon after returning to Utah from Great Britain, Emily was diagnosed with stomach cancer. Apparently, it was not the will of the Lord that the blessings and prayers should spare her life. As Emily's health worsened, her mother, Martha Harris Wells passed away. The funeral was held in the Grant home, so that Emily could be present. Within a month, Emily passed away. The funeral for Heber's second wife to be taken was held on May 27, 1908—the twenty-fourth anniversary of Heber and Emily. His deep sadness is shown in these lines:

Her sickness and death [have] been very sad indeed, in fact, pathetic. To have our loved ones dying month after month, and not to be able to do anything for their relief or for their restoration, is hard to endure, in fact beyond one's expression to tell...To my mind, the sad-dest of all deaths is to have a mother taken away from her children, just at the time when they seem to need most her counsel and advice...However, I feel to say in the language of Job, "The Lord giveth and the Lord taketh away. Blessed be the name of the Lord."[37]

Upon the death of Francis M. Lyman on November 18, 1916, Heber J. Grant became the President of the Council of the Twelve. Then, two years later, President Joseph F. Smith passed away on November 19, 1918. Four days later, the Twelve met together in the Salt Lake Temple where they sustained and ordained Heber J. Grant as the seventh president of the Church. This remarkable servant of the Lord led the Church for twenty-seven years—longer than any other president in Church history.

Two years into his presidency, a wealthy couple, Brother and Sister Alfred W. McCune met with President Grant with a very interesting proposal: they offered to make a gift of their property and mansion to the Church to be used as a private residence for the living prophet. On behalf of the Church, President Heber J. Grant was happy to accept their generous offer, but suggested, instead, that the mansion could be better used as a conservatory of music. And thus was born the McCune School of Music and Art.[38]

With B. Cecil Gates appointed as director, the McCune School assembled a large faculty of very illustrious musicians, artists and dance instructors. Among those who taught there were Tabernacle organists Edward P. Kimball and John J. McClellan; future Tabernacle organists Tracy Y. Cannon and Frank W. Asper; Richard P. Condie, who served many years as assistant conductor of the Tabernacle Choir as well as the conductor; soprano Margaret Summerhayes; such gifted and accomplished pianists and teachers: Frederic Dixon, Mable Borg Jenkins, Becky Almond and Helen Budge Folland; orchestra director Reginald Beal; Beverly Decker Adams, brilliant organist, pianist and authority on art and music history; and Virginia Tanner, whose work with children's dancing attracted national attention.

With such an illustrious faculty, the McCune School of Music attracted many hundred of serious music students during its twenty-five years of operation. Among the former students at the McCune School is a world renowned pianist; professors of piano at the University of Utah, Brigham Young University, Ricks College and Southern Utah University; members of the Utah Symphony; Herbert Klopfer and G. William Richards who both served on the Executive Committee for the publication of the Church's 1985 hymnbook; and Lilas Stefan who became a distinguished teacher of piano in southern California, and was a major contributor to the large Ruffatti organ at Ricks College.

It would be impossible to measure the rippling effect upon the music of the Church—still continuing today—that began with President Heber J. Grant's urging Brother and Sister McCune to allow the church to establish a school of music for the benifit of the church as well as state.

With commercial broadcast in its infancy, President Heber J. Grant saw the potential of radio in the spreading of the Gospel. The Church acquired a station in 1922, KZN. President Grant dedicated the station on May 6 and,

> for the first time in the Church's history, delivered a message over the airways. In his talk, the Church president bore his testimony that Joseph Smith was a prophet of the true and living God. Two years later the station began broadcasting sessions of general conference. Thousands of Church members as well as nonmembers were able to hear the inspired messages of the General Authorities. During the summer of 1924 the station's call letters were changed to KSL.[39]

As an enthusiast of radio, Heber J. Grant wrote:

> It is very marvelous and wonderful how the gospel is being heard and proclaimed for thousands of miles in all directions over the radio. I often used to wonder how it would be possible for every ear to hear. But the wonderment had disappeared since the days of radio. I was reading one day a short time ago of a song, every note of

which and every word of which was heard for nine thousand miles...in all directions...It is almost beyond the comprehension of mortal man to understand how anything of this kind can happen. I rejoice in this invention.[40]

July 15, 1929, was a most auspicious day in Church history, one that, no doubt, excited and pleased President Heber J. Grant: The Tabernacle Choir made its first nationwide broadcast over KSL radio, under the baton of Anthony C. Lund, with Edward P. Kimball and Tracy Y. Cannon at the organ. Ted Kimball, son of the Tabernacle organist, announced the program. Previously, the choir had been heard locally over KSL.

J. Spencer Cornwall, who became the choir's director after Anthony Lund's death in 1935, wrote of the "mechanics" of getting the choir on the air:

> The first broadcast of the choir, a local one, was made with one microphone, borrowed from the local radio station KSL. A boy on a stepladder placed in front of the choir, held the microphone at arm's length above his head. The picture resembled somewhat the Statue of Liberty. (KSL had only one microphone and since the station was a block away from the Tabernacle, it had to close down temporarily while the microphone was in transit between the Tabernacle and the broadcasting studio).[41]

This NBC radio performance was broadcast on a Monday afternoon between 3:00 and 3:30. The choir sang choruses from *Die Meistersinger* and *Tannhauser* by Richard Wagner, plus the great restoration hymn by Parley P. Pratt and George Careless, "The Morning Breaks," and the Finale from Mendelssohn's *Elijah*. Edward P. Kimball played the first movement from the "Sonata in B Flat Minor" by Boslip.

In September, 1932, KSL became an affiliate of CBS[42], and at some point, Richard L. Evans, an employee of KSL, became the choir's narrator and fashioned the "Spoken Word" into the program's format. Thus was born the longest, continually running radio program in American history.

The weekly editions of Richard L. Evans' "Spoken Word" were generally acclaimed as masterpieces of beauty, substance and brevity. He was sustained to the First Council of the Seventy in 1938 at the age of thirty-two, and became an apostle on October 8, 1953. He was the "Voice of the Tabernacle Choir" until his unexpected death on November 1, 1971.

President Grant loved fine choirs, and was especially fond of the Tabernacle Choir, to which he often attested:

> Singing is a very splendid part of the worship of the latter-day Saints, and all are proud of the record which Utah's two great musical organizations, the Salt Lake and the Ogden Tabernacle choirs, have made at home and abroad. There are also hundreds of other excellent choirs, from Canada on the north to Mexico on the south, whose singing to the ordinary lay member, like myself, is an inspiration.
>
> I have listened in Stockholm, Copenhagen, Christiania, Zurick, and Rotterdam to our Mormon choirs. Their singing had been the equal in its inspiring and uplifting character to any that I have heard in the stakes of Zion.
>
> I rejoice in our wonderful tabernacle Choir. I rejoice in the fine management of this choir and our fine organists. I rejoice in our having such fine groups of singers in different parts of Utah that we can bring here to sing for us. I do not think there is another people in the world of the same number that can begin to compare with our people as congregational singers.[43]
>
> I say God bless our individual singers and the members of our musical organizations. I know of no more self-sacrificing and loyal people than those who constitute our choirs, and who are constantly singing at funerals and in our meetings for the benefit of the Saints. Their talents are given freely, and almost without exception without financial reward. I wish them God-speed, and there is no blessing too good for these faithful workers. From the bottom of my heart, I pray that the choicest may constantly grow and improve in their art, and that they may also advance in a knowledge of the gospel of Jesus Christ.[44]

The importance Heber J. Grant placed on music is reflected in the creation of the General Music Committee in 1920. Tracy Y. Cannon, a grandson of Brigham Young, became its chairman. In 1948, that committee—under the direction of the First Presidency—published a new hymnbook for the church. One of the members of that committee was Frances Marion Grant Bennett, Heber J. Grant's daughter.

Charles W. Penrose, a counselor to President Grant is the author of four hymns that are included in the 1985 edition of the hymnbook: "O Ye Mountains High," "God of Our Fathers, We Come unto Thee," "Up, Awake, Ye Defenders of Zion," and "School Thy Feelings."

Heber J. Grant—whose lifetime included the handcart and the airplane, pony express and television—guided the Church through the Great Depression and into its second century. His administration witnessed the horrendous second World War and the ignoble reign of Adolph Hitler. Church membership went from a half million to nearly one million. Missions were opened around the world. Heber J. Grant dedicated temples in Hawaii, Canada, and Mesa, Arizona. What is known today as the Welfare Program began under his direction, and the first Institute of Religion was established in Moscow, Idaho.

His practical, homespun sermons covered such subjects as the word of wisdom, education, economic prosperity and tithing, government and public affairs, marriage, special needs for our youth, fundamentals of Mormonism and living the Gospel, and, of course, music. It was not uncommon in a stake conference for him to preach and sing a solo besides.

Before the end of his years as President of the Church, Heber J. Grant called, by revelation, two stake presidents to fill vacancies in the Quorum of the Twelve; Spencer W. Kimball and Ezra Taft Benson. After a series of strokes, Heber J. Grant passed away peacefully on May 14, 1945. He was buried in the Salt Lake City Cemetery next to his father, whom he had never known.

1 Heber J. Grant: *Gospel Standards* (Salt Lake City, The *Improvement Era*, 1969), p. 171.

2 Leonard J. Arrington: *The Presidents of the Church* (Salt Lake City, Deseret Book Co., 1986) p. 218; and Clarissa Young Spencer: *Brigham Young at Home* (Salt Lake City, Deseret Book Co., 1963) pp. 32-33.

3 Francis M. Gibbons: Heber J. Grant: *Man of Steel, Prophet of God* (Salt Lake City, Deseret Book Co., 1979) pp.16-17.

4 Preston Nibley: *The Presidents of the Church* (Salt Lake City, 1968) p. 276.

5 Francis Gibbons: p. 18.

6 Ibid., p. 19.

7 Leonard J. Arrington: p. 222.

8 Ibid., pp. 223-224.

9 Heber J. Grant: "Learning to Sing," *The Improvement Era*, August, 1990, p. 886.

10 One who alleges to "read" character and personality traits from physical features, particulary the face and head.

11 Ibid., pp. 886-887.

12 Francis Gibbons: pp. 29-30.

13 Leonard J. Arrington: pp. 226-227.

14 Ibid., p. 230.

15 Bryant S. Hinckley: *Heber J. Grant, Highlights in the Life of a Great Leader* (Salt Lake City: Deseret Book, 1951) p. 79.

16 Ibid., p. 82.

17 Francis Gibbons: p. 42.

18 Ibid., p. 115.

19 Ibid., pp. 116-117.

20 Ibid., p. 118.

21 Matthew C. Godfrey: "The Beginning of the Church in Asia," *Mormon Heritage* Magazine, September/October 1994, Volume # 14, pp. 17-18.

22 Francis Gibbons: p. 137.

23 *Gospel Standards* pp. 277-278.

24 Ibid., p. 278.

25 Ibid., p. 278.

26 Hymn No. 30 in the current 1985 hymnal.

27 Heber J. Grant: "Learning to Sing," *The Improvement Era*, August, 1900, pp. 886-890.

28 *Conference Report*, April, 1963, p.22.

29 *Conference Report*, April, 1901, pp. 63-64; also found in Leon Hartshorn: Classic Stories from the lives of the Prophets (Salt Lake City, Deseret Book, 1988) p. 207-208.

30 Heber J. Grant: "Learning to Sing," *The Improvement Era*, August, 1900, Ibid., p. 891.

31 Heber J. Grant: "Learning to sing," *The Improvement Era*, etc. p. 891.

32 Heber J. Grant: *Gospel Standards* (Salt Lake City, *The Improvement Era*, 1969) p. 171.

33 Ibid., p. 168.

34 Ibid., p. 167-170.

35 Ibid., p. 170.

36 Heber J. Grant: "Learning to Sing," *The Improvement Era*, Etc. p. 892.

37 Francis Gibbons: p. 148.

38 Conrad B. Harrison: *Five Thousand Concerts, A Commemorative History of the Utah Symphony* (Salt Lake City, Utah Symphony Society, 1986) p. 47.

39 *Church History in the Fullness of Times* (Salt Lake City, The Church of Jesus Christ of Latter-day Saints, 1989) p. 506.

40 Francis Gibbons: p. 189.

41 J. Spencer Cornwall: *A century of Singing, The Salt Lake Tabernacle Choir* (Salt Lake City, Deseret Book., 1958) p. 224.

42 The Choirs relationship with CBS lasted 63 years. In 1995, KSL returned to NBC.

43 Heber J. Grant: *Gospel Standards*, pp. 168-169.

44 Ibid., p. 171.

George Albert Smith

GEORGE ALBERT SMITH
(1870-1951)

"[O]ur Heavenly Father has given a reve-
lation, teaching us that it is our privilege,
yea our blessing, to sing, and that our
songs should be sung in righteousness."[1]

George Albert Smith's grandfather, George A. Smith, was a cousin to the Prophet Joseph Smith, and, at twenty-one, became the youngest apostle of this dispensation. He also served as a counselor to Brigham Young. John Henry Smith, George Albert Smith's father, was ordained an apostle at thirty-two, and served as a counselor to President Joseph F. Smith.

Just twenty-three years after the Saints arrived in the Salt Lake Valley, George Albert Smith was born on April 4, 1870. He was the second child of a family of eleven.

George Albert developed a keen sense of humor, which no doubt was helpful to him in growing up in a large family with very limited resources. He learned to sing and play the guitar, banjo, harmonica and Jew's harp. As early as ten years of age, he combined his "love of music and funny stories" to produce amateur minstrel shows in his backyard for the neighborhood children, earning laughs and a few pennies.[2]

As George grew up, he continued to play his guitar (sometimes a banjo, harmonica, or Jew's harp) and to act the part of a comedian, garbed in a homespun checkered suit and a big western hat. About the suit, he used to say, "long after they couldn't see it any more they could still hear it." With a few wry gestures and jokes, he could provide a torrent of giggling.

Accompanied by strumming and illustrative gestures, the following song was a sure trigger to merriment:

I'm not very handsome, I know that I'm not.
I'm as ugly as sin, and ought to be shot.
My mouth is a feature that can't be forgot—
If you travel east, west, north or south.

Chorus:
Shut it! Shut it! Don't open it quite so wide.
Shut it! O Shut it! I don't want to get inside.[3]

George Albert obtained a job at the ZCMI clothing factory "punching buttonholes in overalls at two dollars and fifty cents a week."[4] Later on, he worked up to the position of traveling wholesale grocery salesman, working between Salt Lake City and St. George.

The young salesman was assigned to work with Jim Poulton, who "took orders for shoes and clothing."

The pair, fitted up with a rickety covered wagon loaded with food, bedding, personal effects, and samples, pulled by two unlikely nags, went on their way rejoicing.

With his personal effects, George Albert threw in his guitar, harmonica, and Jew's harp, along with a loud checkered suit, a garish bow tie, and a wide brimmed hat. These were part of a comic act he had worked up over the years with which he entertained his friends. Jim brought along his flute, and George Albert had a set of dumbbells and Indian clubs that he used mainly to help stay trim; but he had become so expert with the Indian clubs that he occasionally gave exhibitions with them. Added to these things was George's fine baritone voice and a repertoire of funny songs he had learned.

This pair was undoubtedly a welcome addition to the groups of travelers, mostly salesmen, who congregated in the evening at small hotels or rooming houses along the way. "Held a concert," George wrote on May 28, 1890. "Maynes singing; Jim singing and flute; I played guitar and harmonica." This entry was made in the little town of Holden, Utah, just a week after George Albert and his companion had started on their annual swing south... On the day they left Salt Lake City, May 21, they were delayed three hours when the wagon broke down. But they made it to American Fork, where, in the evening, they teamed up in a guitar-flute duet. In the days that followed, George sold "bills of goods" at American Fork, Pleasant Grove, Provo, and Springville; and on May 28, when the impromptu concert was held in Holden, he had "sold two nice bills" at Scipio and Holden.

The journey became a wearisome yet fascinating succession of small Mormon villages, where they sold their wares, made new friends, and *broke the monotony with almost daily musical sessions.*[5]

George Albert attended the University of Deseret, now known as the University of Utah, for one year. But because he needed the income, he accepted a job working for the Denver and Rio Grande (D&RG) railroad on a surveying crew. This experience proved tragic for George Albert: the burning desert sun caused permanent damage to his eyes, causing pain and weakness all of his life.

Since his youth—when he entertained the neighborhood children with his backyard minstrel shows—George Albert had shown an aptitude for getting along well with young people. When he was twenty-one, he received an unusual call from the First Presidency to work in several central Utah stakes "to activate and motivate the young people in these stakes who were members of the Young Men's and Young Women's Mutual Improvement Associations." Called to be his companion was William B. Dougall, one of the grandsons of Brigham Young.

> Because it was not a proselyting mission, these elders used devices unknown to conventional missionary work. George had taken along his outrageous checkered suit, and occasionally when the young people gathered in a social setting, he would put it on and accompanying himself on the guitar, sing funny songs. A favorite was "Shut It." The young people at Beaver, Utah, were an especially appreciative audience, whose applause after George Albert had sung this song was "quite enough to take the roof off if it hadn't been fastened."
>
> The comic quality in George Albert Smith's makeup, which was largely muted in later years, was occasionally exhibited off stage. "After supper at Brother Paxman's," he wrote on November 11, 1891, "I got a funny streak and the folks nearly died laughing at me. Sister Paxman nearly fainted and I had to stop."[6]

Long before this, George Albert had developed romantic interests with Lucy Woodruff, a granddaughter of Wilford

Woodruff, who had lived with her grandparents since her mother's death. After completing his mission for the MIA, George Albert married Lucy on May 25, 1892. Their marital bliss was interrupted one month later with George's mission call to the Southern States Mission. Happily, however, while George labored in Chattanooga, Tennessee, Lucy received a call to join her husband in missionary work.

George Albert arrived in Tennessee a little more than twenty years after the end of the bitterly fought Civil War, and not all of the Southern people openly accepted strangers in their midst. While the missionaries visited with a family of investigators on a hot summer day,

> refreshment were served, and the missionaries were invited to sit on the porch and sing their hymns. Meanwhile an anti-Mormon who had seen their approach had assembled a group of armed horsemen in the woods on a hill overlooking the little house. Unaware of their danger, the young men sang with fervor and conviction. One of their numbers was "Do What Is Right."
>
> A light breeze wafted the music to the concealed horseman. As the singing went on, the men put up their guns and dismounted. "We have made a mistake," the leader said. "These are not the kind of men we thought they were. Wicked men can't sing like angels and these men sing like angels." The horsemen dispersed without making their presence known. Impressed by what he had heard, their leader began to investigate the Mormon message and was later baptized.[7]

The missionary couple was released in June, 1894, and after a three-day journey by train they returned to Salt Lake City to set up housekeeping. George Albert continued to be plagued by "eye problems" and a generally frail constitution. A "nervous condition"—for which he often had to go to bed for a day or two—was a constant impediment throughout his life. Eventually, the couple was blessed with three children: Emily was born in 1895; Edith came four years later. George Albert Jr. was born in 1905.

On October 6, 1903, the Tabernacle was crowded during the afternoon session of General Conference. Rather than dealing with the crowd, George went home. From others, he learned of the announcement that he had been sustained as the newest member of the Quorum of the Twelve! Two days later, on October 8, George Albert was ordained and set apart in the upper room of the Temple, joining his father, John Henry Smith, who had been an apostle for more than twenty years.

> His father, John Henry Smith, was asked to give the customary apostolic charge, which underscored the historical significance of the fact that never before had a father and son served simultaneously in this quorum, nor has it occurred since.[8]

George Albert was a deeply spiritual man, and he also had a genuine love for people, *all people*. He loved the company of little children, as well as the elderly and the infirm. And since the days he had entertained the neighborhood children in his backyard, he loved to interact with others. Simple acts of kindness—directed toward the young or the old, or total strangers— became a trademark of his apostolic career.

In his travels as a special witness for Christ in the world, Elder Smith went with his pockets stuffed with missionary tracts. Invariably, he would take a seat by a single passenger on a train—and years later, a plane. Before long, he would pull out one of the tracts and begin talking about the Gospel. He usually recorded the name and address of his new friend in his little book, and carried on a correspondence with him or her thereafter. He loved to travel and see the new sights, but mostly he loved to visit and make friends. Besides the visiting and the gospel discussions, he often sang the hymns of Zion, or other old songs that dated well into the past.

> Elder Smith continued a life-long affair with young people. While in England as an apostle, he had become acquainted with Lord Baden-Powell, founder of the Boy Scout movement. President Smith, George Q. Morris and Oscar A. Kirkham were responsible for bringing the Boy Scout program to the Church. President Smith was proud of that association and served on the National executive

Board of the Boy Scouts. He loved to dress in full Scout regalia and often attended official functions to honor young men advancing in the Scouting program.[9]

George Albert Smith took an active interest in the establishment of the Primary Children's Hospital that was dedicated in 1922. He served as head of the Young Men's Mutual Improvement Association as one of his areas of stewardship as an apostle.

George Albert loved America, and with many of his forebears fighting in the Revolutionary War, he had a lifelong love affair with America. He saw the American Revolution and the creation of the United States as an unfolding of divine purpose. He became involved in an organization that called itself the American Flag Association, and served on its board of directors. He was enthusiastic in any activity that would create "a sentiment of respect and reverence for our flag."[10] George Albert, also, throughout his adult life was an active member of the Sons of the American Revolution, serving as an officer on both state, regional and national levels.

With his ancestry among the members of the Joseph Smith family during the very beginnings of the Church, and among the Saints who crossed the plains, George Albert Smith had a keen awareness and interest in Church history. In 1907, he began negotiations to acquire for the church both the Joseph Smith farm and the Hill Cumorah. The Smith farm was purchased without a lot of difficulty for $20,000, but for the acquisition of the Hill Cumorah—so rich in history—George Albert Smith had to negotiate for more than twenty years!

After several smaller pageants that were staged on the hillside, a script for a pageant in grand proportions was written by H. Wayne Driggs; *America's Witness for Christ* was first produced in 1917. Then in 1957, a musical score by Mormon composer Crawford Gates became a permanent part of the production. The work was recorded in the Salt Lake Tabernacle by the Utah Symphony and the Brigham Young a cappella choir, under the direction of the composer. The taped performance was heard in a new, elaborately designed sound system created for the Hill Cumorah pageant by Harvey Fletcher. A leading acoustical engineer in America and an active member of the Church, Harvey Fletcher is considered the "Father of stereophonic sound." That for which he was famous—the principle of stereophonic sound—was actually developed for the Hill Cumorah pageant.

In 1988, a new enlarged production of *America's Witness for Christ* was created with a script by Orson Scott Card and a new musical score composed by Crawford Gates. With a recorded performance by the Utah Symphony, the Tabernacle Choir and the Salt Lake Children's Choir, this opulent score in not merely incidental music to the production. It provides one hour and fourteen minutes of continuous music for the sweeping panorama of ten major stories of the Book of Mormon, climaxed by the appearance of Jesus Christ to the ancient Americans.

With a cast of 600 and a technical staff of 100, *America's Witness for Christ* is the largest outdoor religious pageant in the nation. Between 50,000 and 60,000 witness this penetrating, grand dramatic and musical event each year, many of whom are non-members. Though some baptisms are directly attributal to the pageant, it is impossible to calculate the conversions for which this pageant is, at least, contributing factor.[11]

Though the Hill Cumorah Pageant is a far cry from the backyard minstrel shows of ten-year-old George Albert Smith, *America's Witness for Christ* would not be possible today, nor would the conversion of thousands that result from it, if the Hill Cumorah were not in possession of the Church, which George Albert Smith made possible.

No pursuit in life gave George Albert Smith greater pleasure than tracing the pioneer trails across America, and establishing historical markers and monuments along the way.

> Probably no man in the United States has officiated at more
> unveiling exercises of historic monuments and markers over such a
> wide area than had President George Albert Smith. More than one
> hundred monuments and markers, ranging in cost from $50.00 to
> $45,000.00 have been sponsored by the group he headed, [Utah trails
> and Landmarks Association], and with very few exceptions he offici-
> ated at the dedicatory programs.[12]

The pinnacle of his markers and monuments career was
the dedication of the *This is the Place Monument* at the
mouth of Emigration Canyon as it opens up into the Salt
Lake Valley. The initial idea for such a monument was born
in the mind of George Albert Smith as early as 1934. Property
on which the monument stands had to be acquired, along
with easements, and a 177 acre tract that had to be rescued
from developers to become the *This is the Place State Park*.
All of this was a result of years of activity by George Albert
Smith.

This imposing granite structure contains scenes sculpted
by Mahonri M. Young, grandson of President Brigham Young,
commemorating not only "the arrival of the Mormon pioneers
in the valley but also the Indians, explorers, trappers, and
Catholic fathers who had preceded them."[13]

The ecumenical nature of the unveiling and dedication ceremonies reflected the wishes of President Smith, who served
as master of ceremonies for the occasion and also offered the
dedicatory prayer:

> Remarks were made by the Most Reverend Duane G. Hunt
> (Catholic), Right Reverend Arthur W. Moulton (Episcopalian), and
> Rabbi Alvin S. Luchs (Jewish).... Remarks were given by President
> McKay who was the chairman of the Utah Centennial Commission;
> President Clark, and Governor Maw. The governor also dedicated
> the *This is the Place State Park* in which the monument is located.
>
> John D. Giles directed the unveiling of the great shaft and its
> tableaux depicting the hardships and heroism of the pioneer journey.
> *The United States Marine Band and the vast audience swelled the
> strains of "Come, Come, Ye Saints"—the emotional paean of*

courage that had swept a whole people across the Desert—and [Elder] George Q. Morris...pronounced the benediction.[14]

Biographer Francis Gibbons describes another "George Albert Smith touch" to the dedication ceremonies:

> For weeks in advance, near the hour of the dedication, seeds had been scattered around the base of the monument each morning to attract seagulls. By whatever means of communication birds use, word had spread throughout the seagull community that breakfast would be served each morning at the base of that interesting new structure near the mouth of Emigration Canyon. So on the day of the dedication, the air was filled with dozens of seagulls, circling for the daily handout they had come to expect.[15]

As a member of the Quorum of the Twelve, Elder Smith traveled extensively throughout the world. He loved traveling, and seeing new places. He was an enthusiastic flier, and with his penchant for writing letters, he wrote often to Western Airlines offering "little suggestions" for improving their service. This eventually yielded George Albert Smith a position on the board of directors of Western Airlines!

In visiting the members of the Church in the Mormon Colonies in Mexico, he was pleased to find

> the same spirit and attitude that characterized similar Latter-day Saint communities north of the border, *where the members sang the same hymns, used the same instructional manuals, taught the same doctrine, and practiced the same religious rituals.*[16]

In 1937, George Albert traveled to Aukland, New Zealand with Matthew Cowley where Elder Cowley was installed as the mission president. Then, while traveling by boat to Australia,

> [a]t the request of the captain, George Albert and Rufus K. Hardy conducted religious services on Sunday. *A string trio provided the music, the congregation sang Episcopalian hymns, and George Albert preached.* He was intrigued by the attendance of cir-

cus people on the voyage, including a woman said to weigh 740 pounds and a man whose face was half white and half black.[17]

In Tonga, Elder Smith was received with great warmth, fanfare and enthusiastic singing.

One morning, a baptismal service was scheduled for the pre-dawn hours:

> As they approached the beach, they could hear the roar of the sea. And drawing near, they saw the tide pounding on the coral reef, sending salt spray shooting high into the air, then cascading down into a sheltered lagoon where the baptisms were to be performed.
>
> Almost two hundred people were found sitting quietly on the sandy beach facing the lagoon, "with a beautiful forest of trees behind them, with coconut palms pushing high in the sky from the depths of the woods." It was now daylight, "and the rays of the approaching sun tinted a few fleecy clouds on the horizon with a golden glow, and soon the glory of the sunrise [appeared]; and it was beautiful." The idyllic scene became perfect when "at a signal all arose and sang "The Day Dawn is Breaking." There was more singing sandwiched between the baptisms. And, at the end, Elder Smith addressed the assembled Saints, conferring on them an apostolic blessing none would ever forget.[18]

In earlier years, while the children were still at home, frequently, "he would call his family together for the singing of hymns and religious instruction."[19] Later on,

> many of his evenings were devoted to meetings, public dinners, and other functions, but he liked to reminisce and tell stories. On rare occasions, when spending the evening with members of the family or a close friend, he would sing some of the songs from the distant days of his youth.[20]

George Albert was especially sensitive to the needs of the disadvantaged. It was he who directed Spencer W. Kimball to assume the responsibility for the care and encouragement of the Indian people. He was active in promoting the cause of the sightless in Utah. In March, 1941, he arranged for the distinguished blind and deaf woman, Helen Keller, to visit Salt Lake

City and to speak in the Tabernacle. He not only wanted to point to the "plight of the blind," but also their potential.

Throughout his apostolic years, Elder Smith reached out to other religious denominations—Protestants, Catholics, and the Reorganized Mormons—to dispel, where possible, misunderstanding and distrust. In southern Utah, he gave permission for the Catholics to use the St. George Tabernacle for mass.[21]

On another occasion:

> George Albert was perturbed by a leaflet distributed by Catholic zealots showing Utah as a "black spot in the nation" and calling for greater efforts to overcome difficulties Catholics experience in this area. He called in John F. Fitzpatrick of the *Salt Lake Tribune* [a non-member] and asked if he could throw any light on this tactic. Fitzpatrick said he would discuss the matter with Bishop Hunt. Later he reported that the pamphlet had been put out while Bishop Hunt was in Rome and that the Bishop denied any knowledge of it. Incidentally, Fitzpatrick and George Albert were close friends and frequently worked together to counteract friction between Mormon and non-Mormon groups in the community.
>
> The archbishop of York, the Most Reverence and Right Honorable Cyril Foster Garbett, visited President Smith in September [1949] and addressed a large audience in the Tabernacle. *President Smith welcomed the Archbishop, and the Tabernacle Choir provided the music; the Episcopal clergy was in charge and presented its own program.*[22]

Lucy shared her husband's interests, and, when possible, accompanied him in his travels. But, after forty-five years of marriage, Lucy developed a number of infirmities, and for a period of several months, her health gradually deteriorated. On November 5, 1937, George Albert kissed her goodbye and whispered his love for her. Leaving her in the care of her nurse, he went to the Yale Ward to speak at a funeral. As he concluded his talk, "eulogizing his friend and speaking words of comfort to the family, he was handed a note saying he was needed at home immediately."[23] Arriving home a few minutes later, he found that his companion had—moments before—passed away.

Six years later, on July 1, 1943, George Albert Smith was sustained as President of the Quorum of the Twelve. And, at the age of seventy-five, George Albert Smith was ordained and set apart as the President of the Church on May 21, 1945. He served as the Lord's spokesman and prophet for six years. He never married again.

> On Monday, May 21, 1945, fourteen apostles, including David O. McKay and J. Reuben Clark, Jr., who resumed their places in the Quorum after long service in the First Presidency met in the Council room in the temple, fasting, to choose a new president. *After singing a hymn*, they dressed in temple robes and prayed at the altar. With his customary humility, George Albert expressed the feelings in his heart and asked each man present, beginning with the newest member, Mark E. Petersen, to respond. Tears flowed freely as everyone expressed confidence in George Albert and agreed that the president of the quorum should become president of the church, its prophet, seer and revelator.
>
> The motion to reorganize the First Presidency was made by George F. Richards, the second apostle, and seconded by David O. McKay. The voting on both his motion and the motion that George Albert Smith should be the new president was unanimous. Thirteen apostles then laid their hands upon his head and George F. Richards was mouth in ordaining the new president and invoking the blessings of the Lord upon his leadership.[24]

In 1950, at age eight-one, President Smith participated in the dedication of two monuments honoring Brigham Young—the first in Whittingham, Vermont, the birthplace of the great prophet and colonizer; the second was the unveiling of the statue of Brigham Young in Statuary Hall in the Capitol in Washington.

> The ceremony in the rotunda of the Capitol turned out to be very impressive. Music was furnished by the United States Marine Band, the Utah Centennial Chorus, and the Manhattan [Stake] Choir. The speakers were Senator Elbert D. Thomas, Governor Lee, and Vice-President Alben W. Barkley. The statue of the pioneer leader was unveiled by his daughter, Mrs. Mabel Young Sanborn; Mahonri Young, grandson of Brigham and sculptor of the statue; and

Orson Whitney Young, a great-grandson. President Smith delivered a beautiful dedicatory prayer.[25]

Throughout his life, George Albert Smith enjoyed singing. He enjoyed humorous songs that he learned as a boy, and he certainly loved the songs of Zion. He spoke of the good influence the hymns had been in his life:

> I am thinking of one of the things in Sunday School that influenced me as a child. I was not a very good singer, but I enjoyed music, and I remember some of the hymns that influenced my life. I have jotted a few of them down and I would like to read them to you:
>
> > *Abide With Me*
> > *Angry Words, Oh let Them Never*
> > *We Are Sowing, Daily Sowing, Countless Seeds of*
> > > *Good or Ill*
> > *Beautiful Words of Love*
> > *Haste to the Sunday School*
>
> (I think that was the way I got my idea of punctuality, because when I was a boy we dared not go into class late.)
>
> > *Catch the Sunshine*
> > *Ere the Sun Goes Down*
> > *Did You Think to Pray*
>
> I ask the audience, "Ere you left your room this morning, did you think to pray? Did you sue for loving favor as a shield today? Then,
>
> > *Hope of Israel, Zion's Army*
> > *Kind Words Are Sweet Tones of the Heart*
> > *Improve the Shining Moments*
> > *Scatter Seeds of Sunshine*
> > *Let Us All Press On in the Work of the Lord*
> > *Never Be Late to the Sunday Class*
>
> And one I shall always remember was
>
> > *Joseph Smith's First Prayer*
>
> Also,

*In Our Lovely Deseret, Where the Saints of God
    Have Met*

and

Today While the Sun Shines, Work With a Will

I remember George Goddard and William Willis, two dear old
brethren who used to come to the Sunday School in the Seventeenth
Ward when I was there and lead us in singing "I Am A Mormon
Boy," and other hymns. All these things have come to my mind
today, and *I feel that the hymns that have been taught the sons and
daughters of the Latter-day Saints in the Sunday School are a continuous sermon of righteousness.* I am sure that they have inspired
many of us to do the things that the Lord would like us to do.[26]

George Albert Smith was always appreciative of those who
provided music for conference, and was eager to express his
appreciation. He also pointed out that *it is a blessing to sing
praises to our Heavenly Father, and that we ought to sing
those praises in righteousness.*

I wonder sometimes if we realize the importance of music. I
wonder if we know that the Lord himself is concerned about it. He
has given us the information that the song of praise is a prayer unto
him. In our day he has given revelation ABOUT MUSIC. He gave
instruction that Emma Smith was to gather the hymns that were to
be sung in the Church. He said to her: "And verily I say unto thee,
thou shalt lay aside the things of this world, and seek for things of a
better. And it shall be given thee also, to make a selection of sacred
hymns, as it shall be given thee, which is pleasing unto me to be had
in my Church. *For my soul delighteth in the song of the heart, yea
the song of the righteous is a prayer unto me, and it shall be
answered with a blessing upon their heads*" (D&C 25: 10-12).

So to this fine chorus, the choir and these other musicians, I
would like to call attention to the fact that in our day our Heavenly
Father has given a revelation, teaching us that *it is our privilege,
yea, our blessing to sing, and that our songs should be sung in righteousness.*[27]

George Albert Smith suffered from a frail disposition throughout his life, and though a chronology of his activities would indicate otherwise, he found it necessary to go home each afternoon to rest "an hour or two," and often had to go to bed for a few days at a time to recuperate from exhaustion or some other malady. Because of his very poor eyesight, he rarely wrote a talk, or even an outline. He often admonished others to fill their mind with scriptures and good ideas, and then "give the Lord a chance" to inspire them from the pulpit.

During the fall and early winter of 1950, he suffered from increasing weakness and was confined to his home.

> Numerous relatives, church officials, and others came to see him. Arthur Haycock [his private secretary] brought the mail from the office every day, and Presidents Clark and McKay came into discuss important policy matters.

> As Christmas approached, Emily, Edith and Arthur began working on an unusual greeting from the president. This year, instead of a card, it was to be a record. George Albert dictated a message based on Luke's account of the birth of the Savior, and this was blended in with Christmas carols played as background music by Alexander Schreiner on the Tabernacle organ. It was, indeed, a much prized greeting, but George Albert was somewhat reluctant about it. "I am afraid," he wrote in his journal, "it may be considered by some to be a little bit egotistical, but Arthur and the girls seem to be quite thrilled about it, and are working very hard on it."[28]

President George Albert Smith passed from this life and returned to his Lord on April 4, 1951. As the Saints were assembling for general conference, some of the sessions had to be rearranged to accommodate his funeral service that was held on Saturday, April 7. Among his mourners was Israel A. Smith, president of the Reorganized Church, with whom he had maintained a close personal friendship for years.

One of his biographers, Merlo J. Pusey, wrote:

Some of his associates used to wonder if he lived on love. What he ate was meager, and his sense of well being seemed to be closely associated with the flow of good will and affection that came from his contacts with people. *Love was the most welcome reward as well as the coin that he spent most freely.*[29]

One of George Albert Smith's close non-member friends said this about this humble prophet:

He was not a poet or a great financier, nor was he as fine an orator as his father, but if ever a man walked the streets of this world who was fit to walk and talk with God, it was George Albert Smith.[30]

1 Church section, *Deseret News*, February 16, 1946.
2 Merlo J. Pusey, *Builders of the Kingdom: George Albert Smith, Henry Smith and George Albert Smith* (Provo, Utah: Brigham Young University Press, 1981) p. 204-205.
3 Ibid., P. 205.
4 Francis M. Gibbons: *George Albert Smith: Kind and Caring Christian, Prophet of God* (Salt Lake City, Deseret Book, 1990) p. 8.
5 Ibid., pp. 12-13.
6 Ibid., pp. 18-19.
7 Merlo J. Pusey: p. 218; also *Conference Report*, October, 1945, p. 115.
8 Gibbons: p. 45.
9 Heidi Swinton: *In the Company of Prophets* (Salt Lake City, Deseret Book, 1993) p. 35.
10 Gibbons: p.120.
11 From a conversation with Jerold Argetsinger, director of the Hill Cumorah Pageant since 1990, September 19, 1994.
12 George Q. Morris: "Markers and Monuments," *Improvement Era*, April, 1950, p. 284.
13 Gibbons: p. 145.
14 Pusey: p. 334.
15 Gibbons: p. 147.
16 Ibid., p. 247.
17 Pusey: pp. 294-295.
18 Gibbons: p. 184.
19 Pusey: p. 240.
20 Ibid., p. 342.
21 Ibid., p. 325.
22 Ibid., p. 347.
23 Gibbons: p. 163.
24 Pusey: p. 314.
25 Ibid., p. 352.
26 *Instructor*, November, 1946, pp. 163-164.
27 Church Section, *Deseret News*, February 16, 1946.
28 Pusey: p. 356.
29 Ibid., p. 336.
30 Ibid., p. 361.

DAVID O. MCKAY

M Withers '94

DAVID O. MCKAY
(1873-1970)

"The most wonderful story that was ever given to the world was proclaimed by an angel, accompanied by a choir."[1]

Ordained an Apostle at thirty-two, spending sixty-four years as a General Authority, including seventeen years as a counselor in the First Presidency and nineteen years as the President of the Church, David O. Mckay was known and loved throughout the world by members and non-members alike.

A constant theme in the sermons of this venerable Prophet was the sanctity of the home and the family. Yet, perhaps more than any other prophet, David O. Mckay is responsible for creating a favorable image of the church nationally and internationally. This great man was tall and handsome with flowing, white hair like an Old Testament prophet. His charm and affable personality were infectious, and he moved as easily and naturally among the kings and presidents of the world as he did with the blacksmith or a plumber. As the first President of the Church to be seen and heard on television, his persona was extended to millions unseen. All of this, coupled with his longevity as a General Authority, make David Oman Mckay one of the most remarkable prophets in the history of the Church.

The year was 1859. Fifteen-year-old David Mckay arrived in the Upper Ogden Valley with his family. The McKay family had heard the message of the Restored Gospel in Scotland, joined the Church and emigrated to Utah. There, David McKay met for the first time Jennette Evans, a ten-year-old who had come to Utah with her convert family from South Wales. Eight years later, Jennette Evans had blossomed into a beautiful, young lady. David, at twenty-three, proposed marriage to her and sought permission from her parents. Jennette and David Mckay were married by Wilford Woodruff, of the Quorum of the Twelve, in the Endowment House on April 9, 1867.

The young couple established their home in Huntsville, Utah, where David joined his brother, Isaac, in a farming and ranching partnership. To that idyllic marriage were born ten children. Their third child and oldest son, David Oman Mckay, was born on September 9, 1873.

The innocent, care-free childhood of "David O.," as he came to be known, was rather short. When he was seven, both Ellena and Margaret, his older sisters, died of diphtheria, and one year later, his father received a mission call to serve in the British Mission. Just ten days after his departure, Jennette gave birth to their sixth child. David O., at eight, was now the "man of the family," doing much of the farm work and helping his mother at home.

He worked without complaining. He loved caring for the animals, especially the horses. In addition to the hours he spent working, David O. developed a love for reading, swimming, dancing, singing and playing the piano.

A conference was held in Huntsville when David O. was a deacon, and one of the conference visitors who spoke was Eliza R. Snow. The deacons quorum sang a song that they had prepared for the occasion, which obviously impressed Sister Snow. She said in her address:

> I can see in that group of boys bishops of wards, presidents of stakes, apostles, and some of you will live to see [the] Savior.[2]

Perhaps the prophecy of Sister Eliza R. Snow on that occasion was literally fulfilled, years later, as David O. Mckay became an Apostle and a Special Witness of the Savior to the world, and eventually the Prophet of the Lord!

The future prophet became part of the musical life of Huntsville:

> David O. played on the piano for Huntsville's band, an ensemble that enlivened things at town dances. And its talents were occasionally exported to Eden and other neighboring communities. Members of the band, who, in addition to the pianist, included a cornet player and a fiddler, took their turns dancing with the exuberant, shapely, fresh-faced ladies around the valley.[3]

Graduating from high school, David attended the University of Utah where he was well-known on campus as a member of the football team and a writer for *The Chronicle*, the student newspaper. Increasing his visibility on campus, David played the piano frequently on programs, for church, and for his own pleasure. David O. Mckay was a well-rounded, well-liked student who excelled academically, athletically and musically. He served as a student-body officer and was chosen valedictorian for his class.

In the fall of 1897, David O. left to serve in the British Mission. When he arrived in Liverpool, the new missionary from Huntsville and three others were quickly assigned to the Glasgow (Scotland) Conference. He was excited, first of all, to serve in the same mission as his father, and also, to go to the land of his ancestral roots.

> [His going to Scotland] aroused feelings to inspect the quaint, ancient village and the humble cottage where some of the missionary's progenitors had lived and to visit with neighbors who had known his grandparents and who remembered his father when he had served in Scotland.[4]

While in Scotland, David O. was able to go to Cardiff, Wales, to attend the International Eisteddfor Music Festival. As the "official representative of the Church," he took with him a letter of introduction from Tabernacle Choir Director Evan Stephens, a Welsh convert who directed the Tabernacle

Choir when they performed at the International Eisteddfor when it was held in conjunction with the World's Fair in Chicago in 1893. The letter was presented to Dr. Parry, the administrator of the festival.

The Welsh are a talented people. Their love for singing, and especially choral singing, is legendary.

> Here for the first time Jennette Even's son was introduced to the rich cultural inheritance from his Welsh ancestry. The haunting melodies and lively tunes of the choirs and solo vocalists: the energetic numbers played by the instrumentalists, the harpists, the crowders,[5] and the pipers; the displays of the painters and sculptors; and the poetic, prosaic, and dramatic competitions enjoyed there would have given David O. McKay important insights into the ancestral origins of some of his innate characteristics—his love for music, literature, and beautiful decor.[6]

Years later as an Apostle, Elder Mckay was fond of recounting experiences of his mission in Scotland. He described

> his attempts to sing on street corners with the elders of Glasgow to attract an audience for a street meeting. He demonstrated his repertoire: "Israel, Israel, God Is Calling," "O My Father," and "What Was Witnessed in the Heavens"—all sung to the tune of "Israel, Israel, God Is Calling." The repetition "made no difference," he pointed out, "because we didn't have the same audience at the conclusion that we had at the beginning."[7]

David O. returned from Scotland to a position at the Weber Stake Academy teaching pedagogy and literature. Beginning her teaching career at the Madison School in Ogden that year was Emma Ray Riggs, whom David had known prior to his mission. Like David, she was a graduate of the University of Utah. A fine pianist, Ray had also studied at the Cincinnati College of Music. She, too, loved good literature, drama and the arts, including music. David and Ray became the first couple to be married in the Salt Lake Temple in the 20th century. They were married on January 2, 1901.

In 1901, David became the principal of Weber Stake Academy. As an administrator, he often had to "fill in" where there was a need. Besides his other duties, David headed up the music department, and even directed the band, though that was certainly not his strongest asset. In his book, *My Father, David O. Mckay,* David Lawrence Mckay writes of his father's less-than-successful efforts at directing the band:

> He was leading the band one day when Ernest W. Nichols, the father of famous band leader "Red" Nichols was walking by the school under the open windows. Wincing, Mr. Nichols entered the building, sought our Father, and announced, "You need a band leader!" Father hired him on the spot.[8]

David and Ray become the parents of seven children. In 1912, three-year-old Royale Riggs—their fourth child—passed away, their "first sorrow in parenthood,"[9] as David O. referred to the tragic event. Lawrence wrote of his mother's grief, and how she could not bear to listen to Royale's favorite song:

> Father had earlier recorded finding "Ray in inconsolable grief. She had attempted to sing Rowland [Aunt Nettie's son] to sleep, but the memory of little Royale emphasized keenly her loss, and she could only weep and sob for comfort—and poor comfort too. O this yearning of the heart for our baby boy!" I remember that Royale's favorite song, had been a little gramophone record about Santa Claus's workshop which he would listen to over and over again. Mother put it away. She couldn't bear to hear Royale's music again.[10]

Music can store both memories and feelings in the mind, to be easily awakened. Sometimes, unfortunately, those memories may be painful.

Singing and the playing of musical instruments were part of the experience of growing up in the Mckay home. In his beautiful and sensitive biography of his father, David Lawrence Mckay wrote of music in the Mckay family:

Music was an important part of life in our home. Father and Mother *both* played the piano. Father had played for priesthood meeting and dances in Huntsville, held on the second floor above the village mercantile store. Sometimes he'd sit down and play hymns at home, but he did not have time to maintain his proficiency with the instrument in a serious way. Mother, however, kept up her music. She could transpose and play by ear. But as soon as Lou Jean began to play, Mother quietly turned aside invitations to accompany our singing or performances by saying, "I'd rather hear Lou Jean play." We know she loved music, but only later did we realize that she did this to encourage Lou Jean.

Father was anxious for all of us children to have music. By the time Lou Jean played the piano, Llewelyn the clarinet, and I the violin, we were able to produce passable trio music. Father's favorite was "Believe Me, If All Those Endearing Young Charms." I suspect that it was a bit of a special love song between Father and Mother, although she would always make a mock-wry face when we got to the line about the "dear ruin." We played selections from the operas, popular songs, trio arrangements from the classics. The high point of our joint career was being invited to perform over KSL radio for one program.

I'd have to attribute whatever proficiency we gained to Mother's persistence. Her method was the direct approach: "Lawrence, have you practiced yet?" I don't recall her nagging, however, or following up on that question, and certainly there would be no bribes or threats. She simply assumed that we would know what was right and would do it.

For many years, our piano was an old Chickering [grand] that Mother's grandfather had brought across the plains by wagon [one of the first three to be brought by the pioneers].

Father, to surprise Mother, bought a new upright Chickering and had it delivered when she was at a Relief Society meeting. He installed it in the library the day before Christmas. I went in to look at it; but Father hustled right in after me and ushered me out again, explaining that if Mother saw the light on and came in to see what I was doing, the surprise would be spoiled. I can't remember now what subterfuge he used to send her into the library on Christmas morning, but I can still remember her cry of delight.

Mother and Father also enjoyed singing together and with us. We sometimes spent hours singing hymns and popular songs such as "After the Call."

Once, years later, when Mildred and I were driving Mother and Father to Huntsville, the topic turned to music and the songs they

enjoyed. They were both in their eighties, but they started singing the songs from their youth—"Just Tell Them That You Saw Me," "A Bicycle Built for Two," ballads, and other love songs. The duet lasted for the entire trip—
Father singing melody and Mother the harmony. How I longed for a tape recorder![11]

Llewlyn, who played the clarinet, described his father's pleasure in listening to the family trio:

One of Father's joys was to sit (sometimes for hours) and listen to the trio...It seemed to relax him to listen to strains of *Il Trovatore*, Schubert's "Barcarole," "Angel's Serenade" or the Sextet from *Lucia*.[12]

When younger, the children did not always hold their musical instruments with the highest esteem. On one occasion, wrote Lawrence:

Llewlyn and I were playing "sword fight," I with my violin bow and Llewlyn with a butcher knife. I got a bad cut on my hand and felt lucky that it wasn't worse.[13]

The McKays maintained the old home and family farm in Huntsville and often returned while living in Ogden, and later Salt Lake City. Caring for the animals was therapy for David O., especially his favorite horse, Sonny Boy, and he often spoke about the horses as though they were people, and occasionally drew lessons from their personalities and behavior for his talks.

Winters were a time for sledding parties in Huntsville. Even when the family was grown and married, the grandchildren returned with their parents to Huntsville for the traditional sledding parties. Lawrence writes more about the sleighriding in Huntsville:

[The] Christmas parties for the grandchildren were lots of fun. Into his eighties, every Christmas vacation he [David O. Mckay] took the children on a bob-sleigh ride, bells-a-jingle, Father driving in his long thick raccoon coat and big gloves, beaming from ear to ear.

Those sleigh-riding sessions sometimes ended with caroling around the piano, and they blend in my mind with our Christmas Eve parties where each grandchild performed on a family program. In the caroling that followed, Father would slip away and come back with the bells which he would shake merrily while we all sang a rousing chorus of "Jingle Bells." These evenings ended with "Love at Home."[14]

While in Salt Lake City for conference, David O. was called into the office of Francis M. Lyman, President of the Council of the Twelve. At that auspicious meeting, David O. McKay received a call to become an apostle. He was told not to tell anyone, and he didn't. Ray learned of her husband's appointment to the Twelve at the same time as everybody else—as his name was being announced at conference! David O. was generally not known in the church except in and around Ogden, and to some extent in Salt Lake City from his student days at the University of Utah. He had not been a bishop or a stake president. On April 9, 1906, David O. McKay was ordained a High Priest *and* an Apostle by President Joseph F. Smith. At thirty-two, David O. Mckay was the youngest member of the Quorum.

At the time of his ordination, church membership was a mere 330,000, with only fifty-five stakes in the Church. During the next sixty-four years while Elder Mckay served as an apostle and eventually the President of the Church, membership grew to just under three million in five hundred stakes. David O. Mckay played a key role in the dramatic growth of the Church worldwide, and in reshaping the image of the Church from an American institution to an international world-wide organization.

During the long years that he addressed the Saints from the Tabernacle pulpit, David O. Mckay treated every major principle of the gospel, considered practically every aspect of the Church's organization and procedure, and analyzed and commented on the roles of the church and its individual members in a changing world. He also defined the conditions for spiritual growth and material prosperity, elaborated the earthly and eternal blessings that derive from obedience to gospel principles, and admonished the saints about marital fidelity and domestic accord. He encouraged the disheartened, chided the arrogant, and instructed the ignorant.[15]

Drawing from his extensive literary background, Elder Mckay often quoted Shakespeare, Thomas Carlyle, William Wordsworth, Robert Browning, Charles Dickens, and the Scottish poet, Bobbie Burns. In France, he quoted Victor Hugo, and in the German-speaking countries, he quoted Goethe.

In 1920, President Heber J. Grant gave Elder Mckay the assignment to visit every mission in the world, "to become thoroughly familiar with actual conditions [there]."[16] His assigned companion for the thirteen-month, 62,000-mile tour was Hugh J. Cannon, editor of the *Improvement Era*. Particularly memorable were his visits to the missions in the South Pacific, where he was regularly greeted with singing, and, in one case, a band!

> Arriving by ship in the port of Upolu, in Samoa, "A party of men with red headbands and white shirts rowed [Elder Mckay] and Brother Cannon ashore, singing. The customs officials threw open the double gates usually kept locked and declined to inspect their luggage. "The streets were packed with people, and the Church school band from Sauniatu [the little village sixteen miles into the interior where the Church school is located], composed of native boys, played stirring strains.... Business in the town was at a standstill. Stores, banks and offices were closed and everybody was on the streets. All had heard of Apostles, but this was the first opportunity ever given most of these people to see one." At least fifteen hundred people were gathered on the grounds of the mission home for the ceremony of greeting.[17]

The Samoan singers performed songs for the Apostle that were newly composed for his visit, which Elder Mckay had "recorded in both Samoan and English."[18] He was also moved by the stirring music played by the Sauniatru brass band. He was saddened, however, to learn that the boys were playing on borrowed instruments. He later returned to the island and presented new instruments to the musicians of the band.[19]

In Tonga, Elder Mckay and Brother Cannon were also greeted with singing.

> Notwithstanding our sickness, sleepiness, and exposure, we held meetings from nine p.m. with 116 people in attendance. *The school children gave an impromptu concert after dismissal of meeting, and accompanied me to the house where I was to sleep, sang two more songs, and joined in evening prayer.*[20]

Similarly, enthusiastic singing provided a warm welcome in Hawaii, where David O. Mckay heard an all-Japanese choir of Saints sing, "For the Strength of the Hills," "Ye Who Are Called to Labor," and "We Thank Thee, O God, for a Prophet."[21]

In London, Elder Mckay attended a performance by the great pianist-composer, Sergei Rachmaninoff in September, 1924, and enjoyed two operas and two plays in Paris.[22] In our nation's capital he enjoyed "an organ recital and the theater."[23]

Lawrence, acting as a translator in the French-speaking countries, accompanied his father on his 1952 European tour as senior apostle. He wrote:

> In those few weeks, we heard "We Thank Thee, O God for a Prophet" sung in English—including Scots and Welsh accents—French, German, Finnish, Norwegian, Dutch, Danish, and Swedish.[24]

As President of the Church, David O. McKay returned to Europe in 1953 for the ground breaking ceremonies of the Swiss Temple. In his August 5, 1953 journal entry, Lawrence wrote—somewhat in jest, no doubt:

> There was a stand for the favored few to sit in the shade but about 300 people had to stand to listen to six people talk *and the cook sing.*[25]

In 1954, President and Sister McKay left the country to tour the missions in South Africa and South America. Emma Ray wrote in her journal on January 9, 1954 from Johannesburg:

> When we moved off [the plane], several newspaper cameras took our pictures with a little girl who held a large bouquet of flowers for us presented by the Relief Society.... A crowd of about 500...[sang] "We Thank Thee, O God, for a Prophet."[26]

Again on January 15, 1954, Emma Ray wrote:

> Went to a concert given by the Saints of Capetown. It was very good...*Dad was asked to talk and he gave an excellent one on music.* He is always equal to the occasion. We shook hands with people from East London who had driven 600 miles to come to meet the President.[27]

In a rather poignant letter to Ray from Montreal, dated June 3, 1929, David O. describes a meeting conducted by six elders for a group of unusual investigators:

> "But God hath chosen the foolish things of the world to confound the wise; and God hath chosen the weak things to confound the things which are mighty; and base things of the world and things which are despised, hath God chosen."
>
> This saying of Paul's came to my mind last Thursday night at the opening of our meeting in Amherst, Nova Scotia. There is not a member of the Church residing in that town. Excepting the six missionaries, there was not a member present at the meeting. A dingy, old stairway led us up one flight of stairs to an unattractive, low ceiling hall...[rented from a local organization].
>
> As we entered, a man was playing the piano. He was a stranger, but a friend to the Elders. I was surprised when he changed from a more difficult selection that he was playing to "An Angel from on High." Then I noticed that he had no music before him.
>
> *He was blind!*
>
> Just then two people came in—a man and his wife—The man was on crutches.
>
> *He had only one leg!*
>
> Later an old but intellectually alert woman took her seat in the small audience—

She was paralyzed in the right arm!
Near her on the same seat sat a young girl about 23 years of age.
She is the mother of two illegitimate children!
I did not become intimately acquainted with the other twenty-eight who had accepted the invitation of the Elders to attend that special meeting.

When I looked at the hall, and observed the good, honest, though unfortunate people in that humble audience, as I say I was reminded of I Corinthians 1: 26, also of the hymn we sing:

> Ye Elders of Israel, come go now with me,
> And search out the Righteous, where'er they may
> be...
> We'll go to the poor, like our Captain of old,
> And visit the weary, the hungry, and the cold;
> We'll Cheer up their hearts with the news that he
> bore
> And point them to Zion and life evermore.[28]

Lawrence and his wife, Mildred, planned to move to Washington in the fall of 1929, where Lawrence planned to start law school. With a shortage of money, it became necessary to make some difficult sacrifices. Though Lawrence loved his violin, he sold it, planning to buy another once he had finished school and was working. His father, saying nothing to Lawrence, bought back the violin—at a higher price. He wrote a hand written note to Lawrence saying, "Your old violin is on its way to Washington," and enclosed a typewritten poem:

> As I looked at your violin tonight,
> I heard sweet tunes that you played at sight.
>
> When you were a growing boy,
> I saw Lou Jean, Llewelyn and you
> Playing trios as you used to do—
> A memory of treasured joy!
> The thing I know isn't the best of its kind,
> But it's won a place in my heart and mind,
> Which no Stradivarious can fill;

So I've bought it again for counted joy,
And the tones it gave forth at the touch of your
    boy—
I recall them e'en now with a thrill.

So accept it, dear son, as a memory of youth
(For its purchase, you'll say, if you speak the real
    truth
Is not an example of thrift.)
But we're sending it not for its intrinsic worth
But for memories as precious as any on earth
With love, as a birthday gift.

O we love you as only fond parents can love
And invoke choicest blessings from Heaven above,
On Mildred and darling wee Dean;

May each coming year find you happier than last
With a rich store of memories of incidents past—
There's no greater blessings, I ween.

                    Affectionately,
                    Daddy and Mama Ray[29]

After receiving his recovered violin and the poem by his father, Lawrence wrote:

> When I opened the case containing that familiar old instrument, my vision blurred and my hands fumbled as I picked it up. I tuned it by touch, unable to speak past the lump in my throat. That night, I played everything I knew by heart—played for hours into the night with tears of joy and gratitude for my beloved parents streaming down my cheeks, and Mildred wept with me. No matter how straitened our circumstances in the years that followed, I never considered parting from it again, and it still has an honored place in our living room as one of my greatest treasures.[30]

About ten years before Utah and the Church were to commemorate the centennial anniversary of the arrival of the pioneers in the Salt Lake Valley, both the State of Utah and the Church began to make plans for the 1947 celebration. While serving as a member of the First Presidency, David O. McKay was selected, first, as a chairman of the Centennial Study Committee, and then the Centennial Commission.

Under the inspired direction of President McKay many commemorative events took place in Utah and the nation. Besides the parades, pageants, athletic and cultural events, the impressive *This is the Place Monument* was completed and dedicated during the centennial year, and the hit musical, *Promised Valley* by Crawford Gates received premier performances in the University of Utah stadium. At the time of his commission to compose *Promised Valley*—a pet project of President McKay's —Crawford Gates was an unbelievably young seventeen-year-old composer in the Church. Gates asked Arnold Sundgaard—who was not a member of the Church—to write the script.

Francis Gibbons wrote of President McKay's personal interest and involvement in the production of the musical:

> President McKay and members of his committee conferred with New York choreographer and dancer, Helen Tamaris, who was in the city holding auditions to select the dancing cast for "Promised Valley," which would be the showcase of the entertainment events. This production concerned the chairman [President McKay] more than any other thing about the Centennial. It was scheduled to run throughout the heart of the celebration and was expected to play to a larger audience than any other event. He knew, therefore, that in the public mind the success or failure of the entire Centennial would ride on this play. So although the staging of such a performance was foreign to President McKay's experience and inclinations, and although he relied on the professionals to provide the technical expertise, *he watched over every aspect of the production with the same care which he tended his fields and trained his horses....*
>
> Toward the end of the month [President McKay] again became involved in the technicalities of the "Promised Valley" production with C. Lowell Lees [long-time head of the drama department at the University of Utah] and Lorin Wheelwright [long-time dean of the College of Fine Arts at Brigham Young University] about the script. And later that threesome was joined by Crawford Gates, the com-

poser of the score for the production, of whom President McKay wrote: "Mr. Gates is a genius. The music he has written is superb."[31]

These meetings gave David O. a tremendous lift, providing an assurance that the play would be successful. The elation and sense of relief this produced are reflected in this joyful entry:

> "Things are beginning to shape out," he recorded on May 28. "I told President Smith and President Clark this morning I feel as though I am walking on air...that a big load seems to have been lifted."[32]

The audiences loved *Promised Valley!* Soon word-of-mouth reports made tickets more difficult to obtain, and when rain made it necessary to cancel two performances, many were unable to see the musical. But Brother Wheelwright and President McKay had a solution to the problem, which Lawrence details:

> Promised Valley turned out to be a smashing success, and word of mouth brought people streaming in from out of town to obtain tickets. Two performances had been rained out, and the play was scheduled to close after two weeks on a Saturday night. There was pressure to extend the performance on a Sunday night. Brother Wheelwright discussed the pros and cons with Father who, after a day's deliberation, authorized him to have a final performance on Sunday at 8:30 P.M., after sacrament meetings in the Valley wards would be over.
>
> Brother Wheelwright recorded: "No sooner is the word published than I receive a phone call from another high Church official who says, 'Brother Wheelwright, I see you are going to break the Sabbath and run that show.' "I respond by thanking my caller, and then observing, 'You flatter me to think that I possess the authority to make this decision alone. The fact is, it was made by our chairman, David O. McKay. His office is not far from yours. I suggest that you discuss the decision with him.' Then I call our beloved leader to report the conversation. Here is a sensitive problem, and I wonder how he will respond. After a moment's pause, he says simply, 'I have given this matter full consideration, and I am willing to face

my Maker on this decision.'" [33] The final performance took place Sunday evening at 8:30 p.m. in the spirit of the Sabbath.

President George Albert Smith passed away at conference time, April 4, 1951. Though David O. McKay was his second counselor, he was also the senior apostle. Thus, it was he who presided over and conducted General Conference that began Saturday morning, April 7. Funeral services for President Smith were held in the Tabernacle Saturday afternoon. Then on Sunday afternoon, the apostles met in the temple and ordained David Oman McKay the ninth President of the Church. To everyone's surprise, he selected J. Reuben Clark who had served as the first counselor to the two previous presidents, as his *second* counselor. Stephen L. Richards, senior to President Clark in the Quorum, became the first counselor.

Under the inspired leadership of David O. McKay, missionary work increased at home and abroad, making popular the expression "Every member a missionary." The missionary force increased from 2,000 when David O. McKay took over the reins of the Church to 12,000 when he died. There were 1.10 million members of the Church when David O. McKay became president; there were about three million when he died.

Under his administration, the first three non-English-speaking stakes were organized in the Hague, in the Netherlands, Mexico City, and Sao Paulo, Brazil. The first temples outside of the United States were dedicated in Switzerland, New Zealand, and England.

President David O. McKay dedicated the temple at Bern, Switzerland, on September 11, 1955—the first temple built on European soil. Accompanying the beloved Prophet were a number of other General Authorities and the Tabernacle Choir. "Blessed with a historic sense," wrote Francis Gibbons, "the Prophet had selected 'The Morning Breaks, the Shadows

Flee' as the opening [selection] to be sung by the Tabernacle Choir."[34]

Parley P. Pratt's great text no doubt appealed to President McKay, not only because of its poetic beauty and power, but because, symbolically, it was a proclamation to the Saints and the gentiles in Europe, "The dawning of a brighter day Majestic rises on the world."

> The morning breaks, the shadows flee;
> Lo Zion's standard unfurled!
> The dawning of a brighter day,
> Majestic rises on the world.
>
> The clouds of error disappear
> Before the rays of truth divine;
> The glory bursting from afar,
> Wide o'er the nations soon will shine.
>
> The gentile fullness now comes in,
> And Israel's blessings are at hand.
> Lo, Judah's remnant, cleansed from sin,
> Shall in their promised Canaan stand.
>
> Jehovah speaks! Let earth give ear,
> And Gentile nations turn and live.
> His mighty arm is making bare,
> His cov'nant people to receive.
>
> Angels from heav'n and truth from earth
> Have met, and both gave record borne;
> Thus Zion's light is bursting forth,
> To bring her ransomed children home.[35]*

A press conference was scheduled in Glasgow, the day before the choir's concert, for the President of the Church and representatives of "seven or eight of the major Glasgow newspapers." Outside of the United States, questions often arose about polygamy, but President McKay—whose charm could be very disarming—said to the group assembled: "I would like to introduce you to my wife," and after a well-timed pause, he added, "my only wife."[36]

Glasgow's great Kevin Hall holds 3500 people. For the choir's concert, every seat was taken. In Wales,

> the people shouted, whistled, and stamped in delight and appreciation. As in all other places, they wanted "Come, Come, Ye Saints" twice and would have liked it even more. They liked "Let the Mountains Shout for Joy."[37]
>
> The presence of the Tabernacle Choir and the President of the Church made the ground-breaking ceremonies for the London Temple an impressive occasion for the Saints in Great Britain.
>
> President McKay addressed over a thousand Latter-day Saints who had gathered to witness the commencement of work on their beloved temple. Here the Prophet gave emphasis to the sacred and eternal nature of the temple ceremonies, comprising the University of the Lord.[38]

Many awards were accorded President David O. McKay during his lifetime, including four honorary doctorate degrees. Buildings were named after him on the campuses of Ricks College and Brigham Young University. But one of the most unusual honors given this great man came to him in 1962, in his ninetieth year. Over four hundred business and civic leaders of Utah organized an impressive banquet in his honor at the Hotel Utah, at which he was presented with "a silver plaque and an organ to be installed in the chapel then being built in Merthyr Tydfil, in Wales, the birthplace of his mother."[39] Interestingly, *no member of the committee that planned and organized the event was a member of the Church.* In August of the following year, when the building was completed, Robert Cundick, "serving as organist at the Hyde Park chapel and future chief organist at the Salt Lake Tabernacle, came [to Wales] especially to inaugurate the organ."[40]

On May 15, 1966, the LDSSA (Latter-day Saint Student Association) at the University of Utah presented a special program in the Salt Lake Tabernacle in tribute to President David

O. McKay. Because of his frail health, he could not attend, but witnessed the event on television in his apartment adjacent to Temple Square.

On that occasion, prose selected from the writings of President McKay was read by Paul Engeman, with musical interludes composed and performed by Tabernacle organist, Robert Cundick. A choir of some two hundred voices and a full symphony orchestra composed of LDS students at the University of Utah performed two pieces appropriate for the occasion— an arrangement of one of President McKay's favorite hymns, "I Need Thee Every Hour," composed by Darwin Wolford, plus a dramatic work by Randall Thompson, entitled, "The Last Word of David." The text, written by King David of Old—with its beautiful, poetic imagery—characterizes the leadership qualities of David O. McKay:

> He that ruleth over men must be just, ruling in the fear of God.
>
> And he shall be as the light of the morning, when the sun riseth, even a morning without clouds; as the tender grass springing out of the earth by clear shining after rain (2 Samuel 23: 3-4).

Elder Paul H. Dunn spoke of David O. McKay in a talk he titled, "In the Presence of a Prophet."

Inspired by the life and teachings of David O. McKay, composer-in-residence at Brigham Young University, Merrill Bradshaw, composed his *Third Symphony*, with the subtitle: *A Tribute to a Great Leader.* The twenty-two minute work reflects president McKay's Scottish roots, the idyllic setting of his boyhood days in Huntsville, and the inspired, dynamic leadership, with which he led the international, world-wide Church. The dramatic work, reflecting both the tenderness and the strength of the Prophet, was first performed by the Brigham Young University Symphony Orchestra in 1967 under the baton of Ralph G. Laycock, and one year later by the Utah Symphony Orchestra, with Ralph G. Laycock, guest conductor.

During his sixty-four years as a General Authority, David O. McKay preached about all of the Gospel principles, and the need to share the message of the restored Gospel with all of the people of the world. He spoke incessantly of the Christian life and the sacred relationships within the family, as well as the need to nourish and protect those relationships. He believed in everything that would beautify or add meaning to our lives, including music.

The sermons and writings of David O. McKay are those of a highly cultured individual, and bespeak his lifelong love of poetry and literature. In one conference address, he said:

> Music is truly the universal language, and when it is excellently expressed how deeply it moves our souls![41]

On another occasion he said:

> The LDS life is an abundant life as it embraces all that is beautiful and worthwhile. Music, often referred to as the divine art, is a part of this abundance, bringing joy to all.[42]

Still on another occasion, President McKay said this about the "divine art":

> We do not have any thoughts that cannot be expressed either in words or gestures, but there are feelings in the human breast which cannot be expressed in any language or words; so we must provide ourselves with mediums of expression; for instance, music, art, architecture—the wonderful arts which do not belong to any nation, but which speak the language of the soul. Music is international. Although the words may be Latin or Italian, German or English, music is always understood by the soul. *Music is a divine art*. And the people who love music are not a bad people. But there is in music that which appeals also to the basic emotions of man. *Music can, as with love, be drawn down into the gutter*; but the music which these children sang this morning is the music which lifts us up and brings us to a nobler and better sphere, and I am glad that I belong to a church that from the beginning had held this divine art as an ideal.

In one of our revelations, the Lord had said that the song of the righteous is a prayer to our Father in Heaven; and I am reminded that just before the mob broke into Carthage jail, just before the bullet pierced the heart of Hyrum, the Patriarch, the beautiful hymn of Montgomery's had echoed through those barricaded halls. Music in praise of Christ and in thanksgiving was the last impression on the spirit of Joseph Smith and of his brother, Hyrum.

I say to you, *develop this art of divine melody further and better. Try so to live that good music will fill your heart.*

The most wonderful story that was ever given to the world was proclaimed by an angel, accompanied by a choir. I believe that it is not only the most glorious story, but also the most beautiful and sweetest story ever related. What did the choirs sing when Christ had His glorious birth? What message did they bring to the world which had resounded throughout the world for 2000 years and should find a place in the hearts of those who love the truth? First, every person should give the honor to the Father in heaven—give glory to God who was personified in the birth of the Savior at Bethlehem, who lives to glorify the Father, the Creator of all. Second, *peace, not passion, not even happiness—peace, the greatest blessing which a man can receive.* Third, good will toward men. Oh how large is this thought! Oh, how few are there who really welcome these three principles![43]

President McKay, moved by the performance of the Tabernacle Choir in a conference session, expressed gratitude to the singers for their sacrifice to provide beautiful music for conference. He could easily, however, have spoken of the ward choirs in the Church which struggle from week to week to lift and edify the souls of those who worship on our Sacrament Meetings:

We must not close the conference without expressing appreciation to the Tabernacle Choir, its leader, assistant, to the organists, and to every member. That singing group has attained, through merit, outstanding recognition as one of the great choral organizations in the world. It merits the gratitude on all members of this Church. I do not know of another choir in the world that gives so much time and means, financially, in their service, as the members of this choral group. In your behalf, I thank them with all our hearts for their unselfish devotion and continual attention to this great duty....

The Lord has said: "For my soul delighteth in the song of the heart; yea, the song of the righteous is a prayer unto me, and it shall be answered with a blessing on their heads (D & C 25: 12).

Your unison in song in the national broadcast this morning deeply impressed me—yours were truly songs of the heart. I pray that they will be visited with blessings upon your heads, and that this choir in rendering such a wonderful service to the Church, to the state, and to the nation may receive added blessings. I would that the same oneness, unity, and harmony manifested in that congregational singing might characterize every righteous endeavor of the Church.[44]

In his ninety-seventh year, after sixty-four years as a general authority, David Oman McKay passed away at his Hotel Utah apartment in the early, peaceful hours of a Sabbath morning on January 18, 1970. "David" is a biblical name meaning "beloved." And that he was. Bryant S. Hinckley, the father of Gordon B. Hinckley, said this of President McKay:

David O. McKay has done many good things and said many good things, but, somehow, he is finer than anything he has ever said or done."[45]

Lawrence wrote briefly of his mother's remaining months:

Mother lingered on, sweet and uncomplaining, for ten months. None of us ever heard her merry peal of laughter again after Father's death, although she always greeted us with her warm smile and loving caresses. When she slipped away on November 14, 1974, despite our heartache, none of us would have delayed that last, permanent reunion with her beloved sweetheart.[46]

1 David O. Mckay: *Pathways to Happiness* (Salt Lake City, Bookcraft, 1957) p. 185.
2 David Lawrence Mckay: *My Father David O. Mckay* (Salt Lake City, Deseret Book, 1989) p. 73.
3 Francis M. Gibbons: *David O. Mckay, Apostle to the World, Prophet of God* (Salt Lake City, Deseret Book, 1986) p. 22.
4 Ibid., p. 52.
5 Players of the *crowd*, an ancient string instrument resembling a violin that was used in Wales and Ireland.
6 Ibid., p. 52.
7 David Lawrence Mckay: p. 226.
8 Ibid., p. 36.
9 Ibid., p. 85.
10 Ibid., p. 86.
11 Ibid., p. 88-89.
12 Francis Gibbons: p. 63.
13 David Lawrence McKay: p. 103.
14 Ibid., pp. 70-71.
15 Francis Gibbons: p. 90.
16 *Church History in the Fullness of Times* (Salt Lake City, The Church of Jesus Christ of Latter-day Saints, 1989) p. 499.
17 David Lawrence Mckay: p. 132-133.
18 Ibid., p. 133.
19 Ibid., p. 143.
20 Ibid., p. 142.
21 Francis Gibbons: p. 199.
22 David Lawrence Mckay: p. 170.
23 Ibid., p. 198.
24 Ibid., p. 219.
25 Ibid., p. 242.
26 Ibid., p. 243.
27 Ibid., p. 244.
28 Ibid., p. 179-180.
29 Ibid., p. 182-183.
30 Ibid., 183.
31 When *Promised Valley* was actually performed, Crawford Gated was twenty-six. To have commissioned him—at seventeen—to compose such a large scale work, David O. McKay said he relied on inspiration and great faith.
32 Francis Gibbons: pp. 248-249.
33 David Lawrence McKay: p. 215.
34 Francis Gibbons: p. 355.

35This is the first hymn in our current, 1985 hymnbook.

36 David Lawrence McKay: p. 253.

37 Ibid., p. 251.

38 Gibbons: p. 354.

39 David Lawrence McKay: p. 261.

40 Ibid., p. 262.

41 *Conference Report*, April 1945, p. 119, or *Improvement Era*, May, 1945, p. 309.

42 *Church News*, August 28, 1983.

43 Llewelyn R. McKay: *Pathways to Happiness* (Salt Lake City, Bookcraft, 1957) pp. 184-185.

44 David O. McKay: *Gospel Ideals* (Salt Lake City, *The Improvement Era*, 1953) pp. 256-257; *Conference Report*, October 1951, p. 157, and *Conference Report* Octover, 1936, pp. 102-103.

45 Francis M. Gibbons: p. 136.

46 David Lawrence McKay: p. 266.

Joseph Fielding Smith

M Withers '94

JOSEPH FIELDING SMITH
(1876-1972)

"My soul is lifted up, and my spirit cheered and comforted, when I hear good music."[1]

Joseph F. Smith's first wife, Levira Clark, had no children. Though he had sons by his other wives, Joseph had planned for his first son by Julina Lamson—his second wife—to bear his name.

Julina's first son, Joseph Fielding Smith Jr., was born on July 19, 1876. The year was the centennial anniversary of the nation's birth. July 19th fell midway between the fourth and the twenty-fourth, the dates which marked the anniversaries of the founding of the nation and the pioneer's arrival in the Salt Lake Valley. All of his life Joseph Fielding loved to reflect upon the significance of the day of his birth, as well as the year.

In 1876, when Joseph Fielding was born, Brigham Young was President of the Church. Yet, Joseph Fielding's long life extended from the time of the pioneers into the space age.

> When Joseph Fielding Smith was born, his father had three wives and nine children. Joseph F. Smith would yet take two more wives; thirty-five children would be added to the family by birth and another five by adoption. Of a certainty, when it was necessary to do without, there were a lot to do it with. [2]

Joseph F. Smith recalled in his later years one sad Christmas in which "he had not so much as a single cent to buy anything for his children."

> I walked up and down Main Street, looking into shop windows—into Amussen's Jewelry store, into *every store*—and then

slunk out of sight of humanity and sat down and wept like a child,
until my poured-out grief relieved my aching heart; and after a while
returned home, as empty as when I left.[3]

Though Joseph grew up poor, he was surrounded by love
where the Gospel of Jesus Christ was taught and practiced.
Joseph was no stranger to hard work.

Joseph's mother became an experienced midwife, who was
called upon frequently to deliver a baby. Whenever she was
called to assist a woman in labor, it was Joseph's job to hook
up the horse and buggy, drive his mother to the woman's
home, then wait for the baby's birth to drive his mother home
again. "I wondered," he said, "why babies were so often born
in the middle of the night."[4]

But in spite of the poverty and hard times, young Joseph
was deeply spiritual and sensitive, and he seemed always to
thirst after a knowledge of gospel principles.

> I used to read the books that were prepared for the Primary chil-
> dren and for the Sunday School children in those days, and I usually
> had a book in my hands when I was home...One thing that I did
> from the time I learned to read and write was to study the gospel. I
> read and committed to memory the Children's Catechism and
> Primary books in the gospel. Later I read the History of the Church
> as recorded in the *Millennial Star*. I also read the Bible, the Book of
> Mormon, the Pearl of Great Price, the Doctrine and Covenants, and
> other literature that fell into my hands.[5]

Both of Joseph's parents loved the hymns of the Church and
sang them frequently with the children. Joseph's love for the
hymns of Zion began in his early childhood. From the pulpit in
the Tabernacle on October 5, 1969, Joseph Fielding Smith
echoed his own father's words which were spoken in October
Conference, 1899:

> I can remember as a young boy, hearing my father sing. I do not
> know how much of a singer he was, for at that time I was not capa-
> ble of judging as to the quality of his singing; but the hymns he sang

became familiar to me in the days of my childhood.[6]

Growing up in a polygamous home, young Joseph experienced firsthand the persecution against the Church for its doctrine of plural marriage. While politicians were busy augmenting the anti-polygamy legislation already on the books, federal marshals were hell-bent tracking down men who had multiple wives and families. They relished, whenever possible, the capture of any Church leader. The more visible their "catch," the greater delight in "bringing them to justice."

> Prosecution quickly turned to persecution, and from the time Joseph Fielding was baptized by his father until he was fifteen years of age, his father was in exile. President John Taylor had been especially concerned to have Joseph F. out of the way, because as an officiator and recorder in the Endowment House, he had a detailed knowledge of the plural marriages that had been performed. During this period, Joseph F. Smith filled a mission in Hawaii under the assumed name of J. F. Speight. He had hid right under the noses of those who were looking for him, serving a mission in Washington, D. C., under the alias of Jason Mach [his maternal great-grand uncle], where he labored for the admission of the Territory of Utah to statehood.
>
> Several times during this period, the Smith home was raided and searched by marshals looking for Joseph, Sr. When this happened, the children were interrogated and threatened, but they refused even to give their own names.[7]

These were difficult years for each of the children. Besides the frightening circumstances of growing up without his father at home, young Joseph—the oldest son—had to assume many of the fatherly duties of his family.

After the issuance of the Manifesto in 1890 by President Wilford Woodruff, the breach between the Church and the federal government began to heal. Life among the Mormons finally became more peaceful.

The acceptance of the Mormons by the nation was nowhere more ostensively visible than in 1893 when the Salt

Lake Tabernacle Choir was invited to perform at the World's Fair in Chicago. Traveling with the choir were all three members of the First Presidency: President Wilford Woodruff, and his counselors, George Q. Cannon and Joseph F. Smith. Some members of their families were privileged to accompany the brethren and the singers, including seventeen-year old Joseph Fielding Smith.

Joseph sensed the significance of the Tabernacle Choir's national exposure. Sixty years later, Joseph Fielding Smith reflected on this historic journey and the opportunity to travel with the President of the Church:

> I was well acquainted with President Woodruff and the members of his family. I had the privilege of accompanying my father and President Woodruff to the World's Fair in Chicago in 1893. We rode in a pullman car from Salt Lake City. I had the privilege of sitting in the State room that was given to President Woodruff, and listened to his counsel and advice.[8]

Enroute, the choir had scheduled a performance at Independence, Missouri, which, years before, had been enemy territory, and the Saints had been the object of an order of extermination.

In striking contrast of the treatment the Church received fifty years before, the Tabernacle Choir was given a special reception at Independence. The First Presidency and the Tabernacle were received by the mayor and the city council. At their request, remarks were given by President Woodruff and his first counselor, George Q. Cannon. After an enthusiastic reception, the choir and the First Presidency adjourned to the "handsome gray stone church of the Josephites, who numbered about eight hundred."

> The building was crammed to overflowing. The choir was singing, the audience applauding,...especially Easton's rendition of "O My Father."[9]

As sensitive and reflective as he was, Joseph Fielding was as moved by the singing of the choir in what was previously the scene of bitter persecution, as by the warmth and enthusiasm of the now-friendly mob!

The choir, the First Presidency and the family members who accompanied them, then went on to Chicago where the choir participated in the International Eisteddfod competition. This choir of nearly three hundred voices from the wilderness in the West claimed the second prize of $1,000.

As an apostle, Joseph Fielding recalled in a conference address in 1965:

> When I was a small boy, too young to hold the Aaronic Priesthood, my father placed a copy of the Book of Mormon in my hands with the request that I read it. I received this Nephite record with thanksgiving and applied myself to the task which had been assigned to me. There are certain passages that have been stamped upon my mind, and I have never forgotten them. One of these is in the twenty-seventh chapter of third Nephi, verses 19 and 20. It is the word of our Redeemer to the Nephites as he taught them after his resurrection. It is as follows:
>
> "And no unclean thing can enter into his kingdom; therefore nothing entereth into his rest save it be those who have washed their garments in my blood, because of their faith, and the repentance of all their sins, and their faithfulness unto the end.
>
> "Now this is the commandment: Repent, all ye ends of the earth, and come unto me and be baptized in my name, that he may be sanctified by the reception of the Holy Ghost, that he may stand spotless before me at the last day."[10]

No teenager took more seriously than Joseph Fielding Smith the admonition: "Seek ye out of the best book words of wisdom: seek learning, even by study and also by faith" (Doctrine and Covenants 88:118). Joseph was a voracious reader of good books of all kinds, but especially the scriptures. When his eyes tired of reading, he memorized favorite passages. Years later, he said that he could never preach a sermon without turning to the scriptures.

At eighteen, Joseph came home one afternoon, reflecting on some of the passages of the New Testament which he carried with him.

> As Joseph turned in at the gate of the Smith home, he suddenly became aware of the sound of piano music coming from the house, a favorite hymn, "Sweet Hour of Prayer." But who was playing it? He stopped and listened carefully a moment. There was a difference in the way individuals played and he had not heard the piano played this way before: a very fine, soft touch, whoever it was at the keyboard. Then he remembered something he had forgotten:

> Mama had mentioned that morning as he was leaving for work that this might be the day Louie Shurtliff, a young woman from Ogden, would be moving into their home, to stay there while attending school across the street at the University of Utah (now West High School.) Might that be she at the piano? [11]

During the three years Louie lived in their home, Louie and Joseph fell in love. He loved her beautiful piano playing, and he loved every other beautiful thing about her.

> Louie's last year as a boarder at the Smith home passed swiftly and pleasantly. We can imagine with what alacrity Joseph left the drudging work at the store [where he worked] and hurried home to clean up so he could spend time with Louie. He enjoyed listening to her play the piano. And occasionally she could coax him into singing a duet. They had little money and little spare time, so their courting consisted almost entirely of visiting in the family parlor in the evening, attending social events at their ward or at the university, and, when the weather was good, strolling. [12]

On April 26, 1898, Joseph Fielding and Louie Shurtliff were married by Joseph's father in the Salt Lake Temple. One year later, however, Joseph received a call to serve a mission in Great Britain.

With his young wife at home, Joseph Fielding arrived in London in May of 1899. His first field of labor was

Nottingham—Robinhood country. He arrived there on a Sunday evening after a three-hour train trip—tired and lonely.

> Through miscommunication, the missionaries in Nottingham had not been advised of Elder Smith's arrival, so no one came to the train station to meet him. Since he had been furnished with the address of the conference headquarters, Joseph collected his baggage and hired a cab to take him there. He found the missionary quarters locked and empty. The elders had gone to afternoon worship services at the branch. Putting his trunk and grip in the doorway, Joseph began walking back and forth in front of the building to stretch his legs and case the neighborhood. He was careful not to walk beyond the view of his gear, because many rough-looking boys were playing in the street. Joseph questioned their intentions, and they returned the favor. "[They] eyed me with curiosity," wrote the new missionary, "and sang a parody on one of our mountain hymns for my own personal benefit." Joseph found the serenade amusing. "Chase me, girls, to Salt Lake City, where the Mormons have no pity."[13]

In a time and place where "Mormonism" was synonymous with "polygamy," this little ditty—sung to some Mormon tune that was well known in Great Britain—must have added to Joseph's loneliness and bewilderment.

> "If I approached them, they would run from me," he wrote, "which amused me as much as I amused them." Such a reception the first day in his first field of labor boded ill for the future. The attitudes of derision and unfriendliness shown by these boys likely reflected attitudes they had learned at home, attitudes that would not be conducive to missionary work.[14]

Before his mission, Joseph enjoyed Louie's piano playing and her singing. And even though Louie had coaxed Joseph to sing duets with her, he seemed content to listen to her sing alone. She realized, however, that missionaries *must* sing while on their missions, and inquired how he was doing with his singing.

> "You want to know how I am getting on with my singing," he replied. "Well, I have no voice in the first place, and what I have in

its place is like a file. I would never be able to sing here if there was any sing in me. I am a singer after the order of Dr. James E. Talmage." But like many another missionary who thinks he cannot sing, Joseph eventually learned that you sing anyway. He and three other elders even organized a quartet known as "The Sagebrush Singers," to sing at street meetings. "After listening to us *sing*, people were glad to hear us *talk*!"[15]

Joseph Fielding completed his mission and returned home in July, 1901. By October, President Lorenzo Snow had become critically ill. Finally, on October 10, the eighty-seven-year old prophet passed away, and one week later, Joseph F. Smith—Joseph Fielding's father—became the new president of the Church.

Anthon H. Lund, a kindly apostle and counselor to Joseph's father, also served as the Church Historian. Elder Lund offered Joseph Fielding a position in the Church Historian's Office. With his keen interest in Church history, the new position became a source of great satisfaction to Joseph. In addition to his work in the Historian's office, Joseph assisted his father with his personal and official correspondence. So trusted was Joseph by his father, he frequently was asked to fill in for his father in speaking assignments.

> One notable example occurred when the Prophet, unable to fill a commitment to dedicate a chapel in Brigham City, Utah, sent Joseph Fielding as a substitute without telling the stake president, Oleen H. Stohl, of the change. President Stohl [said], "I could bawl. We were expecting the President of the Church and we get a boy instead." Flashing his wry sense of humor, Joseph...is reported to have answered, "I could bawl, too."[16]

Joseph advanced from clerk in the Historian's Office to Assistant Church Historian in 1906, and Church Historian in 1921. His deep interest in Church history resulted through the years in a number of published books, including—*Essentials in Church History*, the two-volume *Church History and Modern Revelation* and *Origin of the Reorganized Church and the Question of Succession*.

Among Joseph Fielding's many-faceted experiences in the Church is his service as treasurer of the Tabernacle Choir. His brother, George, had served in that capacity until he was called on a mission to Scandinavia in 1905.

> Already carrying a heavy load of church assignments, Joseph was asked to replace George as choir treasurer. Although he never did sing in the choir, Joseph for the next two years as treasurer attended rehearsals and performances of the choir. Thus it was that years before he ever met and married Jessie Evans, and years before she ever joined the choir and achieved notoriety as a soloist, *Joseph Fielding Smith was an officer in the famed Mormon Tabernacle Choir!*[17]

Louie and Joseph had become parents of two daughters: Josephine and Julina. Both were born with great travail, and additional problems arose during Louie's third pregnancy. After a period of intense suffering, Louie passed away on March 30, 1908. Suddenly Joseph was both father and a mother to his two little girls, age six and two.

Employed in the Church Historian's office was an eighteen-year-old girl, Ethel Georgina Reynolds, daughter of George C. Reynolds, a member of the Council of the Seventy.

> Ethel was beautiful, gracious, friendly, and talented. She was a good conversationalist, she played the piano well, she had been a ward organist at the age of 11, and she loved the gospel.[18]

A love affair soon developed between Joseph and Ethel, and between Ethel and Joseph's two beautiful, little girls. They were married in November in the Salt Lake Temple, with Joseph's father officiating.

President Joseph F. Smith's first counselor, John R. Winder passed away on March 27, 1910, leaving a vacancy in the Quorum of the Twelve. In the meeting in the upper room of the temple, the brethren met to discuss various candidates who might be called to that vacancy. There was no clear consensus, however, among the brethren about a candidate for the apostleship. Finally, President Smith excused himself to go into another room to pray about the matter. In the privacy of that room, the Lord revealed to His prophet that his own son, Joseph Fielding Smith should be called.

> But while the revelation was clear, it was not an easy step for the Prophet to take. His son Hyrum and a cousin, George Albert Smith were already members of the Twelve; and his son David A. was a member of the Presiding Bishopric; his brother, John Smith, was not his counselor. There had been furor when the other sons were called, and he knew an even greater hue and cry would be raised with the call of his namesake. Nevertheless, he presented the matter to his brethren, who unanimously approved.[19]

Joseph attended conference on April 6, 1910 and took the seat reserved for him as assistant Church Historian, with no inkling, whatsoever, about what would soon transpire. After the opening hymn, "We Thank Thee, O God, for a Prophet," the invocation by Brigham H. Roberts, and a special number by the Tabernacle Choir, "The Spirit of God Like a Fire is Burning," Heber J. Grant presented the names of the General Authorities for a sustaining vote. Suddenly, Joseph felt a strong impression that his name would be called, and it was. At the age of thirty-three, Joseph Fielding Smith then took his place on the stand with the Twelve Apostles.[20]

After the conference session, Joseph made this comment to his wife, reflecting his wry sense of humor: "I guess we'll have to sell the cow. I haven't time to take care of it anymore!"[21]

The next morning, April 7, Joseph joined the brethren in the upper room of the temple. After receiving the apostolic charge given by his father, the brethren gathered around him, placed their hands on his head, and President Joseph F. Smith ordained him an apostle and set him apart as a member of the Quorum of the Twelve Apostles. With that sacred ordinance, Joseph Fielding Smith received all of the keys and powers need-ed to serve as president of the Church, should that day ever come. And, as the Lord controls the succession of the Twelve by revelation when a call is given, and by the natural process of life and death, that responsibility did fall upon the shoulders of Joseph Fielding Smith sixty years later.

Pursuant to his new apostolic calling, Joseph Fielding Smith spent vast amounts of his time in travel.

> To Elder Smith the long, lonely, tedious hours of travel were perhaps the least desirable aspect of being an apostle. Nearly every month for several days he was gone from family and loved ones. Fortunately there were ways to help pass the time, such as preparing notes for the upcoming conference talks, writing letters home, reading, and for Joseph Fielding, writing poems.[22]

While riding on a train across the expansive Arizona landscape, Elder Smith penned these reflective lines:

> Does the journey seem long,
> The path rugged and steep?
> Are there briars and thorns on the way?
> Do sharp stones cut your feet
> As you struggle to rise
> To the heights through the heat of the day?
>
> Are you weighed down with grief,
> Is there pain in your breast,
> As you wearily journey along?
> Are you looking behind
> To the valley below?
> Do you wish you were back in the throng?
>
> Let your heart be not faint
> Now the journey's begun;
> There is One who still beckons to you.
> Look upward in gladness
> And take hold of his hand,
> He will lead you to heights that are new.
>
> A land holy and pure
> Where all trouble doth end,
> And your life shall be free from all sin,
> Where no tears shall be shed

For no sorrows remain;
Take his head and with him enter in.

A prominent Salt Lake City musician and civic leader, George D. Pyper, was impressed with the poem when he read it and asked Elder Smith for permission to set it to music. Four of the original five verses now appear as Hymn No. 127 in the Church's 1985 hymnbook.

In her splendid book, *Our Latter-Day Hymns*, Karen Lynn Davidson offers these comments about the hymn by Joseph Fielding Smith:

> Perhaps it was this train ride, as he saw miles of desert country passing by his window, that suggested to Joseph Fielding Smith the metaphor of the long journey. Or perhaps it was just the train ride that gave him some free time in his busy schedule to turn his thought to poetry.[23]

Two other hymn texts by Joseph Fielding Smith have been published in earlier hymnbooks of the Church, but are not included in the present hymnbook: "Come, Come, My Brother, Wake! Arise!" in a stirring setting by Evan Stephens, and "The Best is Not Too Good for Me" in a fine musical setting by Tabernacle Organist, Tracy Y. Cannon.

Tabernacle Organist, Alexander Schreiner, composed an anthem for choir and organ to these lines by Joseph Fielding Smith:

> We are watchmen on the towers of Zion
> Endowed with God's holy pow'r.
> We give our message to the world,
> The message of Christ and him crucified.
>
> We preach repentance and belief
> In redemption through the Son of God,
> Through the atonement of the Son of God,
> Whose blood was shed for the sins of the world.

May we walk in the paths of righteousness
For His name sake:
And thus glorify our Father in Heaven.

This anthem by Joseph Fielding Smith and Alexander Schreiner has had repeated performances by the Tabernacle Choir. "We Are Watchmen on the Towers of Zion" was performed by the Choir at the laying of the cornerstone of the Oakland Temple on May 25, 1963. Appropriately, the anthem characterizes the Oakland Temple which stands like a beacon high in the hills above Oakland overlooking the San Francisco Bay. On a clear day, it can be seen by ships that sail into the Bay under the Golden Gate Bridge.

President Joseph F. Smith, Joseph Fielding's father, received the now-famous "Vision of the Redemption of the Dead" on October 3, 1918, in which he saw the Savior appear to the righteous spirits who had died and were awaiting the resurrection. Joseph Fielding wrote the vision as his father dictated it to him, and two weeks later he read it—for his father—to his counselors for their acceptance.[24]

Ethel became the mother of nine children, which she cared for in addition to Josephine and Julina. An excellent pianist and organist, Ethel gave lessons to the daughters, and then encouraged them to move on to other teachers. Lewis took vocal lessons, and Joseph F. became a fine clarinetist. Other members of the family learned to play several other musical instruments.[25] A grandson, Joseph Fielding McConkie, describes the Smith home on Douglas Street:

[It was] a *house filled with books, good music, and activity.* President Smith delighted in gathering his family around him in the evening to tell them stories from the scriptures or the history of the Church.[26]

Ethel had suffered for many years from a disabling illness. Then, at forty-seven, she was released from her suffering on August 26, 1937. Though Joseph would not recall her from the grave, he grieved deeply. By this time, many of the children were married. Amelia was engaged to marry Bruce R. McConkie, and Lewis was about to go on a mission.

Joseph made these terse comments about the funeral in his journal on August 30:

> The funeral services for my beloved wife Ethel were held today. The speakers were Bishop T. Fred Hardy, Nettie D. Brandford, Samuel O Bennion, and President David O. McKay. Music by John Longdon, Harry Clark, and *Jessie Evans*. Organ: Sister Darrell Ensign.[27]

Joseph had not known Jessie Evans personally, though both he and Ethel knew her by reputation and loved her singing. Biographer Francis M. Gibbons describes Jessie Ella Evans as

> an attractive, vivacious woman of thirty-five who, through her talent and charm, had carved out a successful career in both music and politics. Endowed with a rich contralto voice, she had, through years of training, become a professional singer of note. However she gave up a promising operatic career because of the responsibility to care for her widowed mother and the lack of opportunity for professional employment in Salt Lake City where the family lived. The reputation she had gained as a singer had given Jessie Evans widespread recognition in Utah, and this coupled with her jovial, outgoing personality, made her a natural for politics. So, she had been elected to the office of Salt Lake County Recorder without difficulty. And her musical talent had earned her the role as a soloist with the Salt Lake Tabernacle Choir, whose performances were broadcast weekly over a national radio network.... Due to the circumstance of her age, talent, and reputation, Jessie Evans' prospects for marriage had almost dwindled to a point of extinction. She was simply overqualified as a potential wife. Most suitors would have been intimidated to approach her with matrimony in mind. Only someone with the stature and reputation of Joseph Fielding Smith would have had any reasonable prospect of winning her as a bride.[28]

Joseph wrote a warm note of appreciation to Miss Evans for singing at Ethel's funeral. She gave a cordial response. There were other notes...and then there were personal visits.

Joseph Fielding was twenty-six years older than Jessie Evans. He was an apostle; she was a well-known soloist with the Tabernacle Choir—known from the weekly CBS radio broadcasts, recordings and concert performances. Joseph Fielding was a quiet, reserved gentleman, known for the serious deliveries of rather weighty sermons. Jessie Evans was an extrovert and a humorist—a "character" with a totally disarming personality.

On New Year's day, 1938, Joseph wrote of Jessie in his journal:

> With the most lovely voice—to me—that I ever listened to, whose music and song have charmed thousands, but more especially me. Always willing and ready to bless others, never refusing to sing at funerals and entertainments, if at possible to accommodate all who make requests. I love her for her goodness, virtue and loveliness, her consideration and care of her mother, and because she loves me.[29]

The happy couple was married on April 12 by Heber J. Grant. Since both the bride and groom were very prominent, "their marriage...was one of Salt Lake City's top society stories of 1938."[30]

After the ceremony, Joseph and Jessie left for a honeymoon trip to the Hawaiian Islands. Upon their arrival, wrote Joseph:

> We were royally entertained by two groups of Hawaiian women who came with their ukuleles, guitars and bass viol and sang for us.[31]

Among a people who *love* to sing, Jessie and Joseph felt right at home.

> Their singing of Hawaiian songs was a delightful thing. Jessie joined in with them, learning one of their songs, and singing at their request. They were delighted with her singing and made arrangments for her to sing with them at the conference on Sunday.[32]

Through the many happy years that followed, Joseph Fielding went with Jessie and the Tabernacle Choir whenever she was to be a featured soloist. And Jessie went with Joseph Fielding on his conference assignments. Because he loved her singing, he usually arranged for her to sing whenever he was to speak. Before long, however, Jessie cajoled the apostle to join her in singing a *duet,* with Jessie sitting at the piano providing the accompaniment. No doubt he enjoyed joining her in song, but he maintained that he only did so because of her strong urging: "She told me to DO-IT; and I DID IT!" And for thirty years, congregations of the Saints around the world loved it!

> While her husband was the principal speaker, and together they sang, often Jessie spoke, too.
> Once in awhile they would sing one of the songs that he had written. One of the songs they sang most frequently together was "If I Knew You and You Knew Me." They thoroughly enjoyed singing together, and spent many a pleasant hour at home practicing and singing for their own amusement, as well as singing in public.[33]

In 1941, the Tabernacle Choir planned a concert tour of California. Joseph Fielding could not go with Jessie and the choir. But, with tongue in cheek, Elder Smith wrote a letter to his fellow apostle and official "voice of the choir" to millions of radio and television audiences, Richard L. Evans:

> You are hereby authorized, appointed, chosen, designated, named, commanded, assigned, ordained, and otherwise notified, informed, advised and instructed, to wit...to see that the said Mrs. Jessie Evans Smith is permitted to travel in safety, comfort, ease, without molestation and that she is to be returned again to her happy home and loving husband and family in the beautiful and peaceful State of Utah and to her anxious and numerous kindred.[34]

Catching the spirit of the letter, Richard L. Evans replied:

> Your masterful document of August 15 has cost me a good deal of brow-wrinkling and excruciating concentration. I think without question it will go down in history with the Bill of Rights and the

Magna Charta. The remarkable thing about it is, as my legal staff and I have studied it over, that it conveys to me no privileges that I did not already feel free to take and imposes on me no responsibilities that it was not already my pleasure and intention to assume. However, it is a good idea, as many man can testify, to have the consent of a husband before traveling two thousand miles with his wife.[35]

During his years as an apostle, Joseph Fielding Smith authored some twenty-five books, many of them dealing with Church doctrine. Among his legacy of doctrinal books are the three-volume *Doctrines of Salvation*, a several-volume set entitled *Answers to Gospel Questions*, *The Way to Perfection* and *The Origin and Destiny of Man*.

His son-in-law, Bruce R. McConkie said of him:

Joseph Fielding Smith is the greatest doctrinal teacher of this generation. Few men in this dispensation have approached him in gospel knowledge or surpassed him in spiritual insight. His is the faith and the knowledge of his father, President Joseph F. Smith, and his grandfather, the Patriarch Hyrum Smith.[36]

For each of the twenty-five books that bear his name, Joseph Fielding did his own typing. "I have written them all with these two hands," he said.[37] A self-taught typist, he called his style of typing the "scriptural method—Seek and ye shall find."[38] A regular part of his daily routine included several hours in research and writing, which continued throughout his long life.

Besides his apostolic duties, his research and writing projects, Joseph Fielding Smith served for many years as the Church Historian, and as president of the Genealogical Society. Between the years of 1944 and 1949, he served as the president of the Salt Lake Temple.

In 1939, Heber J. Grant assigned Joseph Fielding Smith and his wife to tour the missions in Europe. Their itinerary would include England, Switzerland, Italy, Austria, Czechoslovakia, Germany, Denmark, Norway, and Sweden.

The political climate throughout Europe at this time was tense. Nazi troops seemed to be everywhere, and Italy's dictator, Mussolini, was flexing his military muscle at every opportunity. Talk of war was in the air.

On July 24—Utah's Pioneer Day—the Smiths arrived in Berlin from Czechoslovakia. In Berlin,

> Jessie was invited to sing on Germany's largest radio station, and was paid for it. Agents of the Nazi party kept watch on their movement but did not interfere with them. In Danzig, the quaint city on the Baltic shore of Poland, the Smiths...attended an open air night staging of Richard Wagner's opera, "Siegfried."
>
> The following Sunday, July 30, the Smiths attended LDS services in Berlin, and as they entered the chapel 650 German saints sang "We Thank Thee O God for a Prophet" at Sevvin. In nearby Chemnitz later that day the hymn was repeated by 900 German saints. At each service Joseph Fielding and Jessie both spoke and sang duets to the appreciative congregations.
>
> From May through October, 1939, Joseph Fielding and Jessie Evans Smith toured Europe, England, Scotland, Belgium, France, Switzerland, Italy, Czechoslovakia, Austria, Germany, Sweden, Norway, Holland, and Denmark, visiting the missions of the Church, preaching and singing and conferring.[39]

While the Smiths began their tour with the objective of strengthening the mission, as the clamor of war increased, their attention shifted to evacuating at least 200 missionaries from the war-threatened countries.

In a letter to his son, Lewis, serving in the Swiss-German mission, Joseph Fielding wrote:

> We have preached the gospel as the Lord has commanded us to do and have borne witness to these nations for over one hundred years of the restoration of the gospel. We have tried to convince them that the Lord has again spoken from the heavens and that he has sent his servants forth with the message of salvation as it has again been revealed in this dispensation of the fullness of times, but they do not want our message and will not heed the warning. We have been crying repentance among the nations for all these years as the Lord commanded us to do, but steadily and persistently the

nations have been growing more corrupt and more ungodly year by year.... The Lord has decreed that the wicked shall slay the wicked, and this will go on until eventually the earth will be cleansed of its evil and wickedness when Christ shall come in glory to take vengeance upon the ungodly who shall be as stubble and burned. That day is not far away.[40]

As history would have it, Elder Lewis Warren Smith was one of the missionaries to return to the United States with his father and "Aunt Jessie."

Joseph Fielding made this terse entry in his journal on March 4, 1942, the day his son was inducted into the U.S. Army:

This condition brought sadness to us all. It is a shame that the clean and the righteous are forced into a conflict of world proportions, because of the wickedness of men. [41]

Joseph Fielding was optimistic that Lewis would return from the war. But on January 2, 1945, he received a telegram form the War Department: "We regret to inform you..." Lewis had been killed in the service of his country. Ironically, the same day, a card arrived from Lewis which he had sent from the Holy Land. Stunned, Joseph opened his journal and wrote:

My son Lewis W. was killed [December 29, 1945] in the service of his country. He was returning from an appointment which took him to India. He spent Christmas day in Bethlehem and, from all we know, was on his way back to his base somewhere in Western Africa when the plane crashed.[42]

President Heber J. Grant died on May 14, 1945, one week after the surrender of Germany. Then, three months later— August 14—Japan surrendered, marking the end of World War II.

With the passing of Elder George F. Richards in August, 1950, Joseph Fielding became acting president of the Council of the Twelve.

In 1951, as president of the Council of the Twelve, Joseph Fielding Smith, Harold Grant Heaton and their wives left on a tour of the Orient.

The *President Wilson*—their ship—stopped at Pearl Harbor, where the Japanese had attacked on December 7, 1941.

> Mute evidence of the attack still remained in the harbor as a grim reminder of the shocking event that had thrust the United States into World War II and had instantly transformed Japan into a much-maligned enemy. In the meantime, however, the shifting tides of war and peace had worked another astonishing change, converting Japan into a friendly trading partner in the burgeoning world economy. With this change had also come a relaxed Japanese attitude toward Occidental religions, with the result that the Church had begun an aggressive proselyting effort there with spectacular success.[43]

A few days out of Pearl Harbor, President Smith turned seventy-nine, with an unusual birthday celebration at sea:

> As the diners waited for their dessert that evening, an announcement came over the ship's intercom that it was the birthday of the distinguished passenger, Joseph Fielding Smith, President of the Quorum of the Twelve Apostles of the Church of Jesus Christ of Latter-day Saints. With a flourish and amid enthusiastic applause, waiters, dressed in Italian attire to carry out the Neapolitan theme of the evening, brought in a beautiful birthday cake and placed it on Elder Smith's table. Atop the cake was a single candle which Joseph ceremoniously lit and then blew out as all the diners joined in singing the traditional "Happy birthday."[44]

The *President Wilson* arrived at Tokyo on July 25. President and Sister Smith, and their party, were greeted by Hilton A. Robertson, president of the Japanese Mission, who drove them to the mission home. At a reception held later,

> a group of Japanese singers provided the entertainment. As Jessie's reputation as a singer and entertainer had preceded her, she was invited to sing. The Japanese natives were surprised and pleased that *one of her numbers was sung in their own language.*[45]

While in Japan, President Smith divided the Japanese Mission to form the Northern Far East Mission and the Southern Far East Mission. President Hilton A. Robertson assumed the presidency of the Southern Far East Mission, and his own traveling companion, Herald Grant Heaton, became the president of the Northern Far East Mission.

The apostle, the two mission presidents and two LDS officers in the military who were LDS flew to Seoul, Korea. After meeting with the Korean Saints, Elder Smith climbed to the top of a hill overlooking Seoul where he dedicated the land of Korea for the preaching of the gospel. The music for that occasion was a pleasant surprise for President Smith.

> Jessie was unable to accompany her husband there. Nevertheless, she participated in this historic event vicariously. Unknown to President Smith, the American Army Officers had brought one of her recordings with them. Attaching a speaker to a nearby pole, they played her rendition of "The Heavens Were Opened" following the dedicatory prayer.[46]

Before returning to the United States, Joseph Fielding dedicated Okinawa for the preaching of the Gospel. It was here that the last great battle of World War II was fought. He also dedicated the Philippine Islands and Guam for the preaching of the Gospel.

As President of the Quorum, Joseph Fielding—with Jessie as a traveling companion—criss-crossed the United States, traveled extensively in Europe, South and Central America and the South Seas. Repeatedly, Joseph Fielding preached and Jessie sang.

Elder Theodore Tuttle of the Seventy had traveled with Joseph Fielding when Joseph was nearly eight-five. Elder Tuttle—at half Joseph Fielding Smith's age—described President Smith as a "great traveler," who had energy to spare when other members of the party were tired."[47]

Jessie and Joseph Fielding were patrons of the arts, attending the theater (though President Smith's tastes for drama were somewhat more limited than his wife's), musicals, and concerts.

The Smiths were patrons of the Valley Music Hall and were adopted as second parents by some of the performers who appeared there. Through the Smiths they received a good introduction to the Church. When the Music Hall's production of "Sound of Music" was in the planning stage, Jessie was offered one of the lead roles, that of Mother Superior in the convent. She declined the role, feeling it would not be a very appropriate one for the wife of the president of the Council of the Twelve Apostles![48]

It became necessary, finally for the Smiths to sell their large home on Douglas Street and move into an apartment near Temple Square. The Eagle Gate Apartments were only a half block from President Smith's office and a block and a half from the Tabernacle, which Jessie visited frequently for rehearsals and performances of the Salt Lake Tabernacle Choir. [49]

The burden of responsibility for Joseph Fielding increased on October 29, 1965 when he was set apart as a third counselor to President David O. McKay. Then, for four years, he served in the First Presidency while continuing to function as the president of the Council of the Twelve, and the Church Historian.

In August, 1967 the Tabernacle Choir sang at the International Exposition in Montreal, Canada, and four months later—on December 17, the choir passed a milestone with the presentation of its 2,000th broadcast.

By this time, the performances of the choir, with the accompanying narrative and sermonettes by Elder Richard L. Evans, had become such a fixture of Sunday radio and television programming that to many these broadcasts had become their "church." The Choir's reputation and public exposure were further enhanced when, in January 1969, it was invited to perform at the inauguration of president Richard M. Nixon. Aside from his official involvement in the activities of the choir, President Smith took a personal interest because of his wife's role as one of its soloists. He never tired of hearing her sing, nor did he ever fail to laud her performances or to express pride in her talent.[50]

Besides Jessie's membership in the choir, Joseph Fielding Smith held the Tabernacle Choir in high regard. Great choral music, he believed conveys truth and is a fitting avenue for approaching God. He spoke of the place of choral music in our worship services in General Conference, October 5, 1969: [51]

> When we listen to this choir, we listen to music, *and music is truth*. Good music is gracious praise of the Lord. It is delightsome to the ear, and it is one of our most acceptable methods of worshipping.[52]

And President Smith stressed the proper attitude of those who sing.

> And those who sing in the choir and in all the choirs of the Saints should sing with understanding. They should not sing merely because it is a profession, or because they have a good voice; but they should sing also because they have the spirit of it, and enter into the spirit of prayer and praise the Lord who gave them their sweet voices. *My soul is always lifted up, and my spirit cheered and comforted, when I hear good music. I rejoice in it very much.*

Further, President Smith suggested that our voices, as well as whatever musical talent we possess, are a gift of God, and that there is an obligation with that gift to excel.

> I would like to say right here that it delights my heart to see our people everywhere improving their talents as good singers. Everywhere we go among our people we find sweet voices and talent for music. I believe that this is a manifestation to us of the purpose of the Lord in this direction toward our people, and they will excel in these things, as they should excel in every other good thing.[53]

During the last few years of his life, President David O. McKay became increasingly more frail. When he passed away on January 18, 1970, Joseph Fielding Smith—at ninety-three— became the senior apostle. Following President McKay's funeral, the Brethren met in the upper room of the temple on January 23 to reorganize the first Presidency. Joseph Fielding Smith became the tenth President of the Church—the oldest apostle of this dispensation to rise to the presidency. He was ordained "president, prophet, seer and revelator of the Church" by Harold B. Lee. He selected for his counselors Harold B. Lee and Nathan Eldon Tanner. Spencer W. Kimball became the acting president of the Twelve.

President Smith believed that sin and righteousness are separate entities, and there is plenty of space separating the two. His attitude at the pulpit conveyed an image of sternness but in reality he was warm and kind, tender-hearted and sensitive.

Following the conference session at which he was sustained as the president of the Church,

> a large crowd gathered at the General Authorities' exit of the Tabernacle. The visitors, many from out of town, were anxious to get a glimpse of President Joseph Fielding Smith or perhaps a warm handshake from the new Church president.
>
> From the crowd, wiggling between legs, came a small girl who made her way to President Smith. Soon she was in his arms for a little hug, and then back into the crowd so quickly that the Deseret News photographer was unable to get her name.
>
> The picture, unidentified, appeared in the Church News. However, her proud grandmother, Mrs. Milo Hobbs of Preston, Idaho, recognized her and promptly wrote a letter to President Smith to share the information.
>
> "I am so happy that we can identify her as our granddaughter, Venus Hobbs. She has a birthday on April 17 when she will be four years old," Grandmother Hobbs wrote.
>
> On the morning of April 17—the birthday of little Venus Hobbs, Joseph Fielding Smith and his wife called long distance "to sing 'Happy Birthday' to her."[54]

In Salt Lake City, Jessie continued to perform as a member of the Tabernacle Choir. For three hours one evening in 1970, Joseph Fielding Smith joined his wife "as an official member" of the renowned singing organization.

> When President Smith accompanied Jessie to choir practice, Richard P. Condie, conductor, said "President Smith, we consider you a member of the Choir." Condie was hardly prepared for the

President's reply. [President Smith] asked, "Then why don't you let me sing in the choir?" So Condie assigned him a seat in the choir and Joseph Fielding spent the evening singing.[55]

During his first year as President of the Church, Joseph Fielding Smith traveled to California, Idaho, Arizona, Mexico and Hawaii, expounding the principles of the Gospel and instructing the membership of the Church in their responsibilities.

As the aircraft carrying President Smith landed at the airport near Mexico City,

> thousands of men, women and children surged forward, anxious to get a glimpse of Joseph Fielding Smith. As he walked up the concourse, the huge crowd burst into song: "Te Damos, Senor, Nuestra Gracias"—"We Thank Thee, O God for a Prophet!" Tears ran down the face of many, and President Smith was deeply touched. Airport officials and other passengers watched in wonderment the elderly stranger who received such an enthusiastic greeting from so many Mexican citizens.[56]

In August, 1971, President Smith presided over the first British Area General Conference held in Manchester, England, and delivered sermons in five sessions of the conference. Before offering the keynote address of the opening sessions, his first counselor, Harold B. Lee, introduced the opening hymn, "The Morning Breaks" that was sung by the North Regional Adult Choir:

> Their singing this is very significant.... The words of this hymn were written by Parley P. Pratt, one of the original members of the Council of the Twelve in this dispensation...[T]his song written by him appeared on the front cover of the first issue of the Millennial Star, which was published in May of 1840.[57]

In his opening address to the British Saints, President Smith reflected on the early missionary activities in Great Britain, and of his own mission there many years before.

I suppose all of you know that all of the presidents of the Church except the Prophet Joseph Smith have performed missionary service in this great nation. I served as a young missionary here over seventy years ago, and many great things have transpired in the Church and in the world since that day, not the least of which is the holding of this conference here in Manchester today....

But now we are coming of age as a Church and as a people. We have attained the stature and strength that are enabling us to fulfill the commission given us by the Lord through the Prophet Joseph Smith that we should carry the glad tidings of the restoration to every nation and to all people.

And not only shall we preach the gospel in every nation before the second coming of the Son of Man, but we shall make converts and establish congregations of Saints among them.[58]

As the *first* British Area General Conference made history, so did the "Evening of Entertainment and Exhibition of Arts" that was held on Friday evening, August 27, 1971 in the Cumberland Suite at Belle Vue Gardens:

The entertainment included dancing and a grand march, with flag bearers representing each state in the British Isles and pennant bearers representing each stake and mission in the British Isles.

Following the grand march, a floor show was presented featuring the national dances and songs of Scotland, Ireland, England and Wales.

Following the floor show, there was a parade of all participants, and a grand march of the General Authorities and their wives, together with other important visitors, leading into a snowball waltz.

Refreshments were served throughout the evening.

The exhibition of arts was held in the annex to the Cumberland Suite. Exhibits were submitted by Church youth, ages 14 to 29, from all parts of the British Isles.[59]

On his ninety-fifth birthday, the Prophet was at Jessie's bedside in the hospital offering comfort. Jessie, who had given Joseph so much happiness for so many years, had become seriously ill. At sixty-nine, Jessie Evans Smith passed away quietly on August 3, 1971. Joseph Fielding Smith had now become a widower for the third time. Although he grieved deeply after Jessie's death,

> he was concerned lest his children worry unduly about him now that he was again widowed. A few days after Jessie's death a son was staying with him in his apartment. There was music playing on the radio. Joseph Fielding managed to smile and danced a little jig to the music, to show that his spirit was not vanquished. Upon his return home from a trip a few weeks later, his children had taken care to have the apartment look just like Aunt Jessie would have it for him. "See, Father, it is just the same." "No," he said, "it is not the same. Not the same. But it will have to do."[60]

Shortly after Jessie's passing, the Prophet moved in with his daughter, Amelia, and her husband, Bruce R. McConkie. On Sunday afternoon, July 2, 1972, President Smith wanted to attend fast and testimony meeting in his home ward—the Eighteenth Ward, and so Amelia took him to church at 2 o'clock in the afternoon.

> It was the weekend preceding the Fourth of July, and the chorister, announced that as a closing hymn the congregation would sing the national anthem. President Smith was one of the first to arise, and tears welled in his eyes as he joined with the others in singing "The Star Spangled Banner." He had been born in the centennial year and month of the founding of the American Republic, on July 19, 1896. And now plans were well underway for the nation's bicentennial celebration.... In 17 days he would be 96 years old.[61]

After a light supper with the McConkies, the aged Prophet relaxed in his favorite chair.

> It was the chair that Jessie had been sitting in when she died 11 months [before]. Oh, what a lonely 11 months that had been without her. How terribly he missed her. And how he missed Louie and Ethel, and his son Lewis and other loved ones who had departed this life.[62]

A little after nine, peacefully and quietly, he passed away sitting in his sweetheart's chair.

His passing was as sweet and easy, as calm and as peaceful and
as though he had fallen asleep, which he in fact had.... Truly when
the Lord took his prophet, there was no sting. President Smith did
not taste of death.[63]

Funeral Services for President Joseph Fielding Smith were
held on Thursday July 5 in the Tabernacle. Speakers included
his two counselors, Harold B. Lee and Nathan L. Tanner, and
his son-in-law, Bruce R. McConkie. The Tabernacle Choir,
directed by Richard P. Condie, sang "Does the Journey Seem
Long?,""I Know that My Redeemer Lives," and "O My
Father." Alexander Schreiner played a medley of favorite
hymns at the Tabernacle Organ, including "I Need Thee Every
Hour."

1 Joseph Fielding Smith, *Conference Report*, October 5, 1969, p. 110.
2 Leonard J. Arrington, *The Presidents of the Church* (Salt Lake City: Deseret Book Co., 1986) p. 316.
3 Ibid., p.317.
4 Ibid., p. 320.
5 Joseph Fielding Smith Jr. and John J. Stewart: *The Life of Joseph Fielding Smith* (Salt Lake City, Deseret Book Co., 1972) p. v.
6 *Conference Report*, October 5, 1969, pp. 109-110; also, Leon R. Hartshorn: *Classic Stories from the lives of the Prophets* (Salt Lake City, Deseret Book Co., 1988) p. 311.
7 Leonard J. Arrington: pp. 318-319.
8 Joseph Fielding Smith Jr. and John J. Stewart: *The Life of Joseph Fielding Smith* (Salt Lake City, Deseret Book., 1972) p. 63.
9 J. Spencer Cornwall: *A Century of Singing* (Salt Lake City: Deseret Book Co., 1958) p. 66.
10 *Conference Report*: October 2, 1964, p. 6.
11 Joseph Fielding Smith Jr. p. 67.
12 Francis Gibbons: p. 53.
13 Ibid., pp. 71-72.
14 Ibid., p. 72.
15 Joseph Fielding Smith, Jr. p. 109.
16 Francis Gibbons: p. 113.
17 Joseph Fielding Smith, Jr.: p. 149.
18 Ibid., p. 166.
19 Francis M. Gibbons: p. 144.
20 Ibid., pp. 145-146.
21 Joseph Fielding Smith, Jr.: p. 176.
22 Ibid., p. 187.
23 Op. cit. (Salt Lake City, Deseret Book., 1987) pp. 153-154.
24 Joseph Fielding Smith, Jr.: p. 201.
25 Ibid., p. 238-240.
26 Leonard J. Arrington: *The Presidents of the Church* (Salt Lake City. Deseret Book Co., 1986) p. 329-330.
27 Joseph Fielding Smith, Jr.: p. 249.
28 Francis M. Gibbons: p. 277.
29 Joseph Fielding Smith, Jr.: p. 256.
30 Ibid., p. 258.
31 Ibid., pp. 258-259.
32 Francis M. Gibbons: p. 280.
33 Joseph Fielding Smith, Jr.: p. 259.
34 Ibid., pp. 260-261.
35 Ibid., p. 261.

36 Leonard J. Arrington: p. 327.
37 J. M. Heslop and Del Van Orden, *A Prophet Among the People* (Salt Lake City, Deseret Book Co., 1971) p. 17.
38 Joseph Fielding Smith, Jr., p. 206.
39 Ibid., p. 261.
40 Ibid., pp. 283-284.
41 Francis M. Gibbons: p. 332.
42 Joseph Fielding Smith, Jr., p. 286.
43 Francis M. Gibbons: p. 392.
44 Ibid., p. 393.
45 Ibid., p. 394.
46 Ibid., p. 396.
47 *Church News*, January 14, 1961; also quoted in Gibbons, pp. 426-427.
48 Joseph Fielding Smith, Jr., p. 262.
49 Francis M. Gibbons: p. 427.
50 Ibid., pp. 451-452.
51 In his comments regarding music, particularly choral music, Joseph Fielding Smith quoted nearly verbatum the remarks of his father, Joseph F. Smith given in General Conference, October 1899.
52 *Conference Report* October 5, 1969 pp. 109-110; also, Leon R. Hartshorn: *Classic Stories from the Lives of Our Prophets* (Salt Lake City, 1988) p. 312.
53 Ibid.,.
54 Leon B. Hartshorn, p. 328; also Joseph Fielding Smith, Jr., p. 11.
55 Joseph Fielding Smith., Jr., p. 261.
56 Ibid., p. 354.
57 *British Area General Conference Report*, August 27, 1971, pp. 3-4.
58 Ibid., p. 5.
59 Ibid., p. 50.
60 Joseph Fielding Smith, Jr., p. 12.
61 Ibid., p 374.
62 Ibid., p. 375.
63 Ibid., p. 377.

Harold B. Lee

Withers '94

HAROLD B. LEE
(1899-1973)

"The most effective preaching of the gospel is when it is accompanied by beautiful, appropriate music."[1]

The presidency of Harold B. Lee was 538 days to be exact. Yet, because of his role in the development of the welfare and correlation programs of the Church, his influence church-wide in the years since his death is as great as any prophet of this dispensation.

Cliffton, Idaho was one of several small towns north of the Utah border that were settled in the 1860's by the mormon pioneers. Fifteen or so miles to the east lies the farming community of Whitney, where Ezra Taft Benson was born.

Samuel Lee was born in Nevada, but when he was very young, his mother died and he went to live with grandparents in Salt Lake City. He lived there happily until he was seventeen, when his Grandmother McMurrin passed away. After her death, Samuel moved to Clifton to live with an aunt and uncle, and there he met and married Louisa Bingham.

Harold Bingham Lee was the second of Samuel and Louisa Lee's six children. He grew up in a modest home with none of the modern conveniences—plumbing, heating, or electricity. Reflecting on his childhood, he later said, "We had everything that money could not buy."[2]

Louisa was a skilled seamstress and homemaker with an artistic sense. As such, she provided attractive clothing for her children, as well as a colorful, attractively decorated home. With a keen sensitivity towards spiritual things, Louisa acted from time to time on promptings that spared Harold danger, and sometimes even death.

The family farm was not a particularly prosperous one, and yet Samuel worked very hard to make a living for his family. Not only did he provide the physical necessities for them, he also provided "the kind of spiritual and intellectual leadership that imbued [the family] with a sense of purpose."[3] As an obsessive genealogist, he once compiled 1,500 pages of genealogical records, which he then copied, by hand, for each member of his family.

> Against this background, the home into which Harold Bingham Lee was born on March 28, 1899, was one characterized by religious conviction, intellectual interest, orderliness, and an overriding sense of urgency, which farm life induces. It was in this environment that he would begin to develop the skills, the capacities, and the qualities of character that would fit him for the prophetic office.[4]

Another writer, Leonard J. Arrington, wrote of Harold's early musical training:

> The family piano was the household gem. On that fine old instrument, sometimes with a Scottish lady by his side, Harold learned to play the lively marches he especially liked. These lessons started a diversified interest in music that he later found useful when he served as chairman on the Church Music Committee.[5]

Brother Arrington, almost poetically, describes the musical environment of the Lee home:

> New sounds were always brightening the Lee home. Sometimes it was grandma humming a hymn as she churned the butter, or mother calming a colicky baby with a soft lullaby, or Harold practicing his scales on the piano.[6]

Additional details of Harold's early musical experience are given by Francis Gibbons:

> His piano teacher (Sarah Gerard), a doughty Scottish lady...would playfully rap Harold's knuckles at the sound of a sour note. The skill he acquired at the piano and organ was one which yielded rich

rewards throughout his life, either in personal satisfaction or in the enjoyment he provided others. As a youth in Clifton, he often served as the accompanist at the Primary and Sunday School. This skill followed him into the mission field where he was frequently called on to provide the music for various gatherings.[7]

Eventually Harold extended his musical horizons beyond the piano and organ, as related by his older brother, Perry:

> Our father surprised us one day as we were convalescing from a bout with scarlet fever by bringing into our sickroom two shining instruments—a baritone horn for Harold and a cornet for me. That cured the fever in jig time, but I'm afraid the raucous sounds that came from those shining horns in the learning process gave our parents a headache.[8]

Harold eventually acquired enough skill to join the Clifton Silver Concert Band, a musical group that had been organized by a man named Cox who had moved to Clifton. The band provided music for parades and special celebrations such as the 24th of July.

One unforgettable memory for Harold was attending General Conference for the first time with his father. He was impressed to see Temple Square with his own eyes— the magnificent, granite-walled temple and the domed tabernacle, "from whose pulpit all the presidents of the Church, except Joseph Smith, had addressed the Saints."[9]

This young boy from a tiny town in Idaho sat in awe in the balcony overlooking the congregation, the General Authorities, the Tabernacle Choir, and the famous organ:

> From that vantage point, they had a close-up view of the holes in the ceiling of the building, used in the early days as apertures for ropes by which platforms were raised to the ceiling to clean or paint it. They also had a clear view of the huge organ in the west end of the building, which overshadowed the choir seats and the stand on which the General Authorities were seated. Here for the first time, Harold B. Lee saw a prophet of God in person, President Joseph F. Smith.... On the stand that day were four future presidents of the

Church, members of the twelve with whom he would later have an intimate acquaintance; Heber J. Grant, George Albert Smith, David O. McKay and Joseph Fielding Smith.[10]

After completing the first eight grades at the Clifton School at age twelve, Harold transferred to the Oneida Stake Academy at Preston. There he became acquainted with "T"—(Ezra Taft) Benson from Whitney, another nearby farmington town. Their friendship would extend, years later, as long-time associates in the Council of the Twelve Apostles.

Besides taking all of the basic courses at the Academy, Harold took special courses in "domestic science, carpentry, music, and missionary work."

> Harold gave special attention to his music during the first two years. He played both the alto and the French Horn and was a member of the academy band. Later, he took up the baritone (and the trombone)...and was good enough to be invited to join the Preston Military Band, directed by Professor Charles J. Engar. The group performed for a fee at special civic and patriotic events in communities throughout the area.[11]

After completing his studies at the Oneida Stake Academy, Harold decided to attend Albion State Normal School, near Burley, Idaho, to qualify himself to teach school. He attended summers in 1916 and 1917. He worked hard at his studies, but for recreation he played in the town band and played baseball on the school team.[12]

Harold's teaching career began at the Silver Star School, a one-room school in Weston, a neighboring town about five miles south of Clifton. He was just seventeen at the time. The next year, at eighteen, Harold became a teacher and principal at the Oxford School, another nearby town. Music remained an important part of his life, as he describes:

> A family by the name of Frew had just moved into Oxford, Idaho, and bought a large ranch. Two of the boys had played in the Lagoon Resort orchestra. One was a violinist and the other was a trap

drummer. They auditioned for others to join them, looking for a trumpet player, a piano player, and they also wanted a slide trombone player. They tried out one of the men who had a slide trombone, but he wasn't sufficiently schooled in dance time to gain acceptance, so he urged me to take his trombone and fill the position. I had been taught music in my school days at home by Mrs. Sarah Gerard, so that I played the organ and the piano with enough ability to be ward organist. Because of my ability to read both bass and treble clefs, and because I could play a wind instrument, the only other requirement I needed to play the trombone was to learn the various positions on the slide to make the various notes. This required long hours of practice day and night, mostly nights, to the distraction of my entire family, who was glad when I finally got enough ability to play with out this harrowing experience for the family.

We were the only dance orchestra from Logan, Utah on the south to Pocatello, Idaho, on the north, and it was not uncommon for us to play two and three nights a week. The roads were muddy, the nights were dark, the automobiles were poor. In the wintertime the roads were hazardous. On one occasion it was almost morning before we arrived home.

After a few hours rest I then went back to preside over the school....

For three years I played slide trombone in this five-piece orchestra which played from town to town in our valley. Known as the Frew Orchestra, it was composed of Dick Frew, violin; Chap Frew, the drums; Marion Howell, the cornet; Reese Davis, the piano; and myself on the trombone.

The Frews were always drinking when possible and indulging in conduct at a level far below what it should have been. I know that through those years, my folks, "held their breath" lest I allow this kind of association to overcome me.

For two or three years I was organist of the Clifton Ward, and in connection with this activity in music I organized and trained a group of girls into a ladies' chorus. When I left for my mission, these girls gave me a gold ring.[13]

Harold received a mission call in September, 1920 to serve in the Western States Mission, with headquarters in Denver, Colorado. His companion, Elder Willis J. Woodbury of Salt Lake City, was a cellist, "and when he discovered I could play the piano, he insisted on regular musical practices."

Tracting for the two elders was not very successful, but Harold had a plan that, he thought, would get the pair into homes to teach the gospel—his companion took his cello tracting! Once they convinced the lady of the house they weren't selling cellos, they were often invited in. If there was a piano, Elder Lee would accompany his companion. If not, he sang.

> We often carried his cello and some music with us when we went tracting, and during the day we were invited to sing and play, thereby opening the way for the preaching of the gospel. With this approach usually we succeeded in being invited into three homes a day, which was about a record for us. In every home we were complimented and invited back again. After playing and preaching, we made real friends at each visit.[14]

Elders Lee and Woodbury were frequently called upon to perform for church.

Nine months into his mission, Elder Lee was called to be the president of the Denver Conference. This meant that he was the presiding authority over all the missionaries (there were thirty-five in the Denver Conference), branch presidents, and Saints in a geographical area. A conference would be the equivalent of a district in the mission field today.

As Elder Lee traveled about the mission, besides conducting meetings, he frequently filled in conducting the music or providing accompaniment. Once when he was to accompany the mission president to Sheridan, Wyoming, President Knight had to go elsewhere and sent Elder Lee by himself to preside over the conference:

> I did the best I could—preached, played the piano, conducted the singing, and helped settle the difficulties in the branch.[15]

In another Conference, Elder Lee

> sang in a mixed Quartet, and in a male quartet, spoke in the evening, and played the accompaniments for all the musical selections.[16]

Harold had become acquainted with a lady missionary, Sister Fern L. Tanner from Salt Lake City. Though their friendship was brief, the chemistry was in place. Soon after his return to Clifton, Harold left for Salt Lake City to see her. Romance blossomed, and they were married in the Salt Lake Temple a year later.

Harold accepted a position in the Granite School District as a principal in one of the schools there. For additional income he worked at a variety of odd jobs—he pumped gas, sold groceries, and was a watchman at the local train depot. In his spare time, he attended night classes at the University of Utah. To Harold and Fern Lee, two beautiful daughters were born—Maurine and Helen, the only children that would be theirs.

Though Harold played the piano and several other instruments, he was always a little embarrassed to be called an "accomplished" musician. He had but a little specialized training by private teachers, but he worked hard to master each of these instruments simply because he enjoyed music so much. When the little family settled in a modest home on Salt Lake City's west side, music was simply part of the environment in which the children grew up. Harold enjoyed providing musical accompaniments to singing and dancing, but was insistent that the girls study music. Helen became a violinist, Maurine a pianist.

In his splendid biography of Harold B. Lee, L. Brent Goates—Helen's husband—wrote of the "fun times" at the Lee home:

> Harold frequently played the piano during fun times with the family. His girls loved him to play one of the John Philip Sousa marches, and the louder he banged it out the better they liked it. Another selection, their absolute favorite, was titled "Midnight Fire Alarm," a solo he had learned during his early years in Idaho. These were two of the few numbers he had committed to memory. Of course, he played the hymns as well.

The performances of the "Midnight Fire Alarm" have special memories for his daughters. Helen describes the scene in this manner:

> "Maurine and I would dance and prance around the room as Daddy was playing this exciting, loud music. He played with such enthusiasm that the entire house seemed to vibrate, and we loved it! Once he finished a real work-out performance with such flourish that he could see he had thoroughly delighted us, as well as some of our little friends who were with us. He felt especially pleased with his exceptional rendition when he overheard Mar's friend say, 'Gee, that was really good, wasn't it?' He was quickly deflated, however, when Mar answered honestly, "Uh, huh, and the best part about it is watching the piano shake!"
>
> Harold appreciated fine music, and for that reason he was insistent that his daughters start their musical education at ages seven and eight. He faithfully drove them back and forth from their music teacher's home some distance away, until they could drive themselves. The private music lessons continued until the girls were in college. No doubt it often strained the family's limited financial resources, but he was most willing to sacrifice for them so that they might obtain the same love for music which he possessed.[17]

As the girls became proficient, their reputation began to spread. They performed throughout the Salt Lake valley— Maurine at the piano, and Helen on the violin. Their father's role in their success, besides paying for the lessons and providing constant encouragement, was that he was always their faithful chauffeur. According to Helen:

> By the time we were married we had performed in almost every ward building then existing in the Salt Lake City area. We began responding to such requests when we were still very young and played until 1945, a period of about twelve years. I can remember my father patiently taking us everywhere we had to perform, until we could become more independent. He was a busy man, but never too busy to take us where we had to be or wait for our performance to end. It was just understood that he would take us anyplace we had to be, and he did so consistently.[18]

The Lee family lived on the west side of Salt Lake where unemployment was higher and income was lower than in other parts of the city. At twenty-eight, Harold was called to be a member of the Pioneer Stake high council, and, at thirty-one, he became the youngest stake president in the Church. During this period, a member of the Salt Lake City Commission passed away, and President Lee was asked to fill the vacancy. Reluctantly, he accepted. Later on, he was elected to the position with a rather substantial margin of votes.

In late 1929, the stock market crashed, signaling for the nation the Great Depression which would last eight years. This was not a good time to be either a stake president or a city councilman in one of the poorer sections of town. For the young Harold B. Lee, it was baptism by fire, but prophets-to-be often have their schooling in the refiner's fire.

While President Lee grappled with the problems of severe unemployment and extreme poverty in his stake, he developed programs for employing people in need, creating storehouses for goods that were grown or created in the stake, and procedures for the needy to obtain needed goods. Thus the "welfare program" in the Pioneer Stake developed—born of Harold B. Lee's creative mind, superb organization skills, and inspiration from heaven. It soon caught the attention of the First Presidency of the Church. Finally, in 1935, the First Presidency gave President Lee the assignment of introducing the welfare program church-wide. He was called into full-time service, and was given the title of Managing Director of the Church Welfare Plan.

Harold Bingham Lee, at the age of forty-two, was ordained an Apostle by Heber J. Grant on April 10, 1941. He then became the "official" organist for the Brethren in their weekly temple meetings. When Spencer W. Kimball became an Apostle two years later, he assumed that responsibility on alternate weeks with Elder Lee. Whoever was not at the organ in the Council Room of the temple directed the music. Elder Lee always kept his own personal copy of the hymnbook with him, and careful-

ly dated each hymn whenever it was sung in these holy sur-
roundings. On various pages of his hymnbook, now in possession of his daughter, Helen, appear the initials of several of the
brethren DOM (David O. McKay), MGR (Marion G. Romney),
HBB (Hugh B. Brown), SWK (Spencer W. Kimball). Apparently
the initials indicate that these were hymns of which the apostles were especially fond.[19] When Elder Lee became an apostle,
Maurine was seventeen and Helen was sixteen. They continued
to perform violin and piano duets around the valley, and, when
possible, their father still went with them. He never tired of
hearing them perform in public, or practice at home. When he
was home, which became less and less frequent, he often went
to the piano and played for his own enjoyment. In his biography
of Harold B. Lee, Francis M. Gibbons wrote:

> The family of Harold B. Lee was one characterized by love, schol-
> arship, unity, and industry, *which functioned in a gracious, well-
> ordered environment where music was frequently heard and where
> service to others and to the Church were dominant themes... It was,
> accordingly, a family that could be held up to the Church as a model
> for others to emulate.* In this fact, Elder Lee found one of the most
> potent sources of strength and justification in his apostolic ministry.[20]

As Harold B. Lee traveled around the world visiting the
stakes of Zion, it was not an uncommon occurrence at a conference to volunteer his services as an accompanist if an organist or pianist was not in place "ready to go." Sometimes, he
simply walked quietly to the piano or organ and began
playing.[21]

The four junior apostles—Spencer W. Kimball, Mark E.
Petersen, Matthew Cowley and Ezra Taft Benson—often sang
as a male quartet for socials and other programs for the general
authorities.[22] Harold B. Lee usually accompanied at the piano.

Among his various responsibilities as a general authority,
which changed from time to time, Harold B. Lee served as an
advisor to the General Music Committee in a seventeen-year

period between 1950 and 1973, sometimes sharing the responsibility with Spencer W. Kimball and Mark E. Petersen. His musical expertise probably did not qualify him for this advisory position with the Church's General Music Committee, but his life-time involvement with music and his understanding of the power of music to affect lives, most certainly did.

> With the rapid expansion of the Church around the world, the First Presidency sought to streamline the programs of the Church eliminating, where possible, duplication of effort within the various departments or programs within the Church. There was, also, concern that there be a unified voice among the auxiliaries and the publications of the Church. In 1960, the First Presidency directed the General Priesthood Committee, under the direction of Harold B. Lee of the Quorum of the Twelve, to begin "an exhaustive, prayerful study and consideration of all programs and curriculum in the light of the Church's ultimate objectives," ensuring that "the Church might reap the maximum harvest from the devotion of the faith, intelligence, skill and knowledge of our various Auxiliary Organizations and Priesthood Committees."[23]

In 1961, under the direction of Harold B. Lee, an "all-Church coordination council" was formed " to formulate policies governing the planning and operation of all Church programs." Elder Lee explained further,

> In the adoption of such a program, we may possibly and hopefully look forward to the consolidation and simplification of church curricula, church publications and buildings, church meetings, and many other aspects of the Lord's work.[24]

Anyone who has not experienced the Church "before correlation" may find it difficult to appreciate the far-reaching impact on the world-wide Church. The influence of Harold B. Lee, in this regard, is inestimable.

For some time, the already frail health of Elder Lee's beloved Fern had begun to deteriorate. Then after a brief hospitalization, Fern Tanner Lee passed away September 24, 1962. Though by this time her passing was not unexpected, it came as a shock, and the sadness and loneliness to Elder Lee was intense.

For the funeral, a double-mixed quartet comprised of members of the Tabernacle Choir, under the direction of Richard P. Condie sang two hymns that were favorites of the Lees: "O My Father" and "I Know that My Redeemer Lives." Blanche Christensen, one of Salt Lake City's finest sopranos performed "How Beautiful upon the Mountains," and Jessie Evans Smith, wife of Joseph Fielding Smith, sang a piece of which Harold and Fern were particularly fond, "The Link Divine:"[25]

> Across the moorland, bleak and bare,
> I watch the sunset sky:
> Tho' your pure soul is dwelling there,
> Sweethearts still are you and I.
> Tho' angels took you from my side
> To yonder realm divine,
> The link that bound us here below
> Still binds my heart to thine.
>
> I cannot clasp thy tender hand,
> Thy voice I cannot hear;
> Yet, in my dreams I see thy face
> Shine bright 'mid starlight clear.
> The veil may hide from me thy sphere,
> But still the link divine,
> Tho's thou art there and I am here,
> Still binds my heart to thine!
>
> But still the link divine
> Will bind my heart to thine!

Harold and Fern Lee had known Freda Joan Jensen well since before their marriage forty years before. She had been a prominent educator and supervisor of primary education in the Salt Lake Valley. As an excellent pianist, she had served on the General Music Committee and on general boards of both the Young Women's Improvement Association and the Primary. With mutual feelings of attraction, plus the conviction that Fern would approve, Harold B. Lee married Freda Joan Jensen, just eight months after Fern's death. Both Maurine and Helen were delighted to see their father married, and both approved of his selection. The tradition of a musical home continued after Joan (as she came to be known) Jensen became a member of the family.

Tragedy struck again three years later when the Lee's eldest daughter, Maurine, died suddenly from complications of her fifth pregnancy. Her husband, Ernest J. Wilkins was left to raise their four children.

When the venerable prophet, David O. McKay was finally called home to God on January 18, 1970, Joseph Fielding Smith succeeded him as the President of the Church. After thirty years as an apostle, Harold B. Lee became the President of the Quorum of the Twelve Apostles. President Smith, however, asked him to serve as his first counselor, with Nathan Eldon Tanner as second counselor. Spencer W. Kimball was then called as the Acting President of the Twelve.

Joseph Fielding Smith, at ninety-three, was the oldest apostle to assume the presidency of the Church. He died just two and a half years later on July 2, 1972.

A few weeks before President Smith's passing, Elder Lee's granddaughter, Jane, played a violin solo in her ward sacrament meeting, accompanied by a friend. The solo, "Sanctuary of the Heart," had been performed by Helen and Maurine when they were girls, and so it had been a family favorite. Elder and Sister Lee, who had wanted to hear the performance, were away at the time, but they had planned a home evening for the Goates and the Wilkins at which Jane and her friend were to perform the selection.

The day before the scheduled home evening, on Sunday, July 2, Joseph Fielding Smith passed away. Even though Elder Lee had been a counselor to President Smith, he immediately resumed his position as the senior apostle and President of the Quorum of the Twelve. Funeral arrangements were to be made under the direction of the Twelve and the senior apostle, which was Harold B. Lee, and there was a myriad of other details regarding the passing of the President of the Church that needed his attention. Moreover if tradition continued, he would become the eleventh President of the Church, the contemplation of which was as frightening to him as it was overwhelming.

Helen said to her father, "You have so many things on your mind, perhaps this is not a good time for the home evening at your home to hear Jean's violin solo." But he replied without hesitation: "By all means, come. I need all of you now more than ever!"

Ernest Wilkins brought his children from Provo (Maurine was deceased); Helen and Brent Goates brought their family:

> President Lee greeted his progeny as they arrived, but soon a rather uncomfortable pall hung over the group. All were reluctant to speak of the events that would shortly come to pass. President Lee asked Jane to play her violin. At the conclusion of the performance he expressed his pleasure and asked for a second number to be played. Jane explained that she had brought no other music with her, so she agreed to play some hymns while the rest of the family sang. Jane asked her grandfather to choose the hymns he wanted to sing. He immediately requested two, "Love at Home" and "I Need Thee Every Hour." Then President Lee said he would like to finish with "How Firm a Foundation," reciting these words from the third verse, which at that moment were particularly significant to him:
>
> > Fear not, I am with thee; oh be not dismayed.
> > For I am thy God and will still give thee aid.
> > I'll strengthen thee, help thee, and cause thee to
> >   stand,Upheld by my righteous, omnipotent
> >   hand.[26 & 27]

This humble servant—who had not aspired to the leadership of the Church, and, indeed had prayed often for President Smith's good health and long life—was now about to become the President of the Church. At this, the most difficult time in his entire life, he derived succor and strength from the melodious strains of a violin, accompanied by the piano, and some inspired lines from the songs of Zion.

On Friday morning, July 7, 1972, in the upper room of the Salt Lake Temple, Harold Bingham Lee, was ordained eleventh president of the Church by Spencer W. Kimball, President of the Quorum of the Twelve. He chose for his two counselors: Nathan Eldon Tanner and Marion G. Romney. Harold B. Lee was the youngest prophet to lead the Church in forty years.

The Sunday afternoon session of General Conference, April 8, 1973, had been a particularly spiritual occasion for the Prophet, and the music was particularly beautiful. The Tabernacle Choir had performed "Our God Is a God of Love," a musical setting by Robert Cundick to words by Delbert Stapley, and "Psalm 148" by Gustav Holst, and concluded the session with "The Link Divine" that had been sung at his first wife's funeral service, and would yet be sung at his own funeral. The congregation and choir sang the great Mormon hymn, "Come, Come, Ye Saints."

Then, in his closing remarks, President Harold B. Lee said this:

> As we come to the closing minutes of this great conference, I wish to express on behalf of all who have listened to the singing during the sessions of this General Conference our sincere appreciation and thanks to the members of the Tabernacle Choir for once again bringing to us the beautiful and inspirational music heard in this conference. And also our appreciation to the conductors and choirs and choruses who have generously rendered the beautiful, inspired music of this conference.
>
> *My experience of a lifetime, and particularly the last thirty-two years as a General Authority, convinces me that the most effective preaching of the gospel is when it is accompanied by beautiful, appropriate music.* Thank God for these wonderful musicians who give so liberally of their time.[28]

This pronouncement was given further emphasis when President Lee said elsewhere in this conference:

> *If you want to know what the Lord had for this people at the present time, I would admonish you to get and read the discourses*

*that have been delivered at this conference, for what these brethren
have spoken by the power of the Holy Ghost is the mind of the
Lord, the will of the Lord, the Voice of the Lord, and the power of
God unto Salvation*[29]

Three weeks later, on Sunday, April 29, 1973, President and
Sister Lee attended an area conference for youth and young
adults in Long Beach, California. After a stirring rendition of "I
Walked Today where Jesus Walked" by the choir, President Lee
spoke to the crowd of more than fourteen thousand young people, echoing the comment about music he had made in the
recent General Conference:

> I have a conviction that without beautiful and appropriate
> music, our sermons would not be what the Lord would want them
> to be. The beautiful singing today has been the kind of accompani-
> ment that sermons need in order to activate the spirit, as well as the
> letter of the words. This choir and your singing—all of it com-
> bined—brings profound solemnity to this great occasion that would
> probably need no embellishment of mine if the service would con-
> clude with what we have heard up to this time.[30]

A "spiritual peak" for the Prophet and his wife was reached
on a visit to Ricks College in Rexburg, Idaho, on October 6,
1973. At a devotional assembly before an audience of five
thousand, a tribute prepared by students at Ricks College was
presented to President Lee, which read in part:

> Called from the simplicity of farms and fields to stand in the
> upper rooms of the temple, where the veil is thinnest, comes such a
> man, whose life is a testimony that speaks the praises of God. This
> is a man who is more than a man, a man bearing Israel's prophetic
> inheritance, one of God's choicest sons.
> Thanks be to God that we live in a prophet's time, when his
> inspired leadership draws us close to standing in holy places where
> we prayerfully await Christ's second coming.[31]

Two members of the faculty had written a hymn in honor
of President Lee's visit to Ricks College—Donnell Hunter of

the English Department and Darwin Wolford of the Music Department—"How Glorious is the Voice We Hear." The selection was sung by the combined Ricks College Choirs:

> How glorious is the voice we hear from heaven!
> Now prophets drive the darkness from our lives.
> Hearken to their counsel; honor their priesthood;
> Receive the word our loving Father gives.
>
> Our prophet speaks to show the way to Zion,
> A refuge for the Saints whose hearts are pure.
> Follow his example, treasure his message;
> Sustain his call, and love will cast out fear.
>
> His voice now calls to every tongue and nation.
> Each ear shall hear and every eye shall see.
> Listen to the gospel; keep the commandments;
> Forsake the world. His truth will make you free.
>
> Our Father, lead and bless the living prophet.
> Protect him where he travels through this world.
> Help him while he teaches light in life's darkness,
> And guides us back to Thy eternal fold.

Noticeably moved by the performance of this piece of music, the President said:

> Oh, you young people, you who have sung so beautifully and given me that note of tribute, I wish I could think in my soul that I am worthy of all that for which you have sung. At least you have set a high water mark that I will try my best to be worthy of. If you will send that to me and let me put it high upon my memory, I will try hard to justify what you have written and what you have sung today so beautifully.[32]

Though President's Lee's address was given to a capacity congregation of more than five thousand, he spoke on a rather personal level of his own trials and struggles, the mission and destiny of our nation, and the bearing of his testimony. The Prophet concluded his remarks with these tender words and a prophet's blessing:

> There is a wonderful spirit here today. There is something
> unusual about this today. I don't know what it is. Maybe it is one of
> those occasions when we could feel and hear and see remarkable
> things happen. You have brought with you a tremendous spirit, and
> I feel it.
>
> So whatever may be here, Heavenly Father, bless this people;
> take care of them; shepherd them in the folds of this institution;
> care for its leaders, its teachers. Parents, watch these little children.
> Shepherd them from the pitfalls of evil. Father, hear our prayer, I
> humbly pray as I place this matter before you this day, in the name
> of the Lord, Jesus Christ. Amen.

Weary from his labors, exhausted from a lifetime of good
works and service to others, the Prophet was hospitalized on
the day after Christmas, 1973. A little before 9:00 in the
evening, President Lee slipped peacefully from this mortal life.

Harold B. Lee was a man of strength and gentleness. He
was a man of God, and for him the veil was very thin. He was
a visionary man, and a witness to many miracles throughout
his life. He loved good music, because it brought him nearer to
the Lord.

At his funeral service held in the historic Tabernacle
December 29, 1973, Dr. Alexander Schreiner, Tabernacle,
organist, played the great organ which Harold had seen and
heard as a boy long ago. The Tabernacle Choir sang "I Know
that My Redeemer Lives," "Lead, Kindly Light," and "How
Firm a Foundation" which had given him strength many times
in his lifetime. The choir also sang "The Link Divine" which
was sung at Fern's funeral, and which had touched him so
deeply at the April 8th General Conference of the Church.

In his tribute to the great Prophet, Spencer W. Kimball said
this:

> President Harold B. Lee was a high peak in a mighty range of
> impregnable mountains. He has become an important part of
> history.[33]

1 *Conference Report*, April 8, 1973, p. 181.
2 Leonard J. Arrington: *The Presidents of the Church* (Salt Lake City, Deseret Book Co. 1986) p. 347.
3 Francis M. Gibbons: *Harold B. Lee: Man of Vision, Prophet of God* (Salt Lake City: Deseret Book Co., 1993) p. 14.
4 Ibid., p. 18.
5 Leonard J. Arrington, p. 349.
6 Ibid., p.349.
7 Francis M. Gibbons: p. 21.
8 L. Brent Goates: *Harold B. Lee, Prophet and Seer* (Salt Lake City: Bookcraft, 1985) p. 46.
9 Francis M. Gibbons: p. 27.
10 Ibid., p. 27.
11 Ibid., p. 37.
12 Ibid., p. 37.
13 L. Brent Goates: pp. 53-55.
14 Ibid., p. 61.
15 Ibid., pp. 70-71.
16 Ibid., p. 72.
17 Ibid., p.124.
18 Ibid., p. 126.
19 Personal Conversation with Helen Lee Goates, July 18, 1994.
20 Francis M. Gibbons: p. 163.
21 Personal conversation with Helen Lee Goates.
22 Ibid., p. 225.
23 *Church History in the Fullness of Times* (Salt Lake City: The Church of Jesus Christ of Latter-day Saints, 1989) p. 562.
24 Ibid., p. 563.
25 The poem was written by Alfred H. Hyatt. The music was written by Piccolomini and arranged by John Longhurst.
26 Goates p. 456.
27 No. 85 in the current, 1985 hymnal.
28 *Conference Report*, April 8, 1973, p. 181.
29 *Ensign*, July, 1973, p.74.
30 Personal conversation with Helen Lee Goates.
31 L. Brent Goates: p. 560.
32 The text of this address was published by the Ricks College Press for campus distribution only.
33 General Conference, April 5, 1974.

SPENCER W. KIMBALL

Withers '94

SPENCER W. KIMBALL
(1895-1973)

"Instinct is like a single note of a flute, beautiful but limited, whereas the human brain contains all the notes of all the instruments in the orchestra. Man can coordinate these tones to give the world beautiful symphonies."[1]

In 1897 Andrew and Olive Kimball accepted a call to move their family of eight from Salt Lake City to the Gila Valley in Arizona where Andrew was to become the stake president. At three years of age, Spencer Wooley Kimball was the youngest of the couple's six children.

Arriving by train in Thatcher,

> a crowd of adults and children met them, intending to sing. But the wind began blowing so hard that the singing was postponed. Instead they showered the Kimball's with armfuls of roses in welcome from the 3400 scattered members of the stake.[2]

The family had little money, so the Kimball's cleared a ten-acre parcel of ground, covered mostly with mesquite, to make a home and a farm. Spencer's father began working at whatever he could do to bring in much-needed revenue. Andrew was a progressive, forward-looking church leader and father. The Kimball's, for instance, were among the first in the valley to have running water, a bathtub and a piano.

Andrew also set out to revive the Church Academy at Thatcher which had been teetering between life and death for several years. In 1914 Spencer became a graduate of the Academy.

Spencer had a near-perfect attendance record at church, *"unconsciously* absorbing the sermons," but *"consciously* absorbing the habit of being in Church."[3] He later recalled that if a testimony meeting began to lag, he "would watch for old Samuel Claridge, the short, white-haired stake patriarch, to burst spontaneously into 'Redeemer of Israel' or 'We Thank Thee, O God, for a Prophet' from the stand."[4]

> At home at special times the Kimball family knelt around the revolving piano stool to pray. Andrew put a hand on the seat. Olive covered it with hers, and so on till each hand in the family was touching. "We felt very close together on those occasions," wrote Spencer.[5]

Olive and Andrew were careful in managing the finances of home and farm. Andrew, for instance, reused old wire and staples to economize on the farm, yet he bought a piano and announced his intention for each of the children to learn to play:

> Spencer, with great enthusiasm, went to Miss Ella Heywood for his first lesson. "My fingers were short and chubby, [Spencer] remembered, "and choppy with marble playing but my father still had high hopes." Piano playing didn't look so good after a couple of weeks, however, and Spencer's career at the keyboard might had ended except for his father's persistence. He excused Spencer from hotter, "more onerous" jobs to practice music in the cool parlor. With that incentive Spencer plugged away at it. "My brothers," he admitted, "accused me of always wanting to practice when it was hottest and when there was ditch digging, plowing or weed-pulling to do. They were not far wrong." Del and Gordon teased their younger brother that his memory was perfect: every time he went through a piece he remembered the same mistakes he had made the time before. But despite his father's urging, Spencer soon stopped lessons, starting and stopping again several times in the years to follow.[6]

Though Spencer described himself "as the laziest boy that ever lived," he did his chores. He simply preferred practicing in the cool parlor to working out of doors on hot Arizona afternoons.[7]

At nine years of age, Spencer milked the cows. While practicing squirting into the mouths of the cats that regularly gathered around at milking time, he memorized the Articles of Faith and the Ten Commandments

> word perfect to the beat of milk squirts into the pail. He sang to the cows. On a one-legged stool, his head burrowed in the cow's flank, he memorized most of the songs in the hymnal from sheets of paper onto which he had copied them.[8]

Sorrow was no stranger to the Kimball family. When Spencer was eleven, his mother died from complications of her twelfth pregnancy. "The bottom dropped out of the household,"[9] leaving Andrew lost, and the children terribly lonely.

> [T]he family needed a mother. Clare, twenty-two, was gone; and Gordon, eighteen, and Del, sixteen, were fairly independent; but that left Ruth, thirteen, Spencer, eleven, Alice, nine, Helen, five and Rachel, one, still too young for Andrew to take care of alone.[10]

Andrew married Josephine Cluff soon afterward, but only after asking permission of each of the children.

In June, 1907, Andrew and Josie took the train for Salt Lake City to be sealed in the temple, leaving the children at home. Two-year-old Rachel, in the meantime, became violently ill with diphtheria. Everything the older children did to save her was futile. Upon learning of her death by telegram, Andrew and Josie hurried back to Arizona to bury little "Ray." Three other girls died in infancy.

Spencer, however, was physically very strong. He was successful at wrestling, basketball, and eventually track. He learned to type, and acted as his father's business secretary. At fourteen, he was given his first opportunity to teach a class in the ward. At fifteen, he was called to be the stake chorister.

At fourteen Spencer had only a few formal lessons behind him, but he learned to chord the music and picked up the popular songs quickly off sheet music he bought for ten cents in the drugstore. His friend Charlie McDonald played the cornet. Joe McDonald played the violin, and Leslie Clawson the bass fiddle. They formed an orchestra and asked Spencer to join them as pianist. "I did not do it well, but they kept me," he recalled. Generally they had a job every weekend. Their take was ten dollars which they split between them. Sometimes they were hired at Brier Hall in Safford, a strictly gentile dance-place, where Spencer would not have gone to dance.[11]

Modesty marked the life of Spencer W. Kimball from his boyhood in Arizona until the end of his life as a Prophet of God. Another of his fundamental character traits was his desire to be serviceable.

After the group had played "the silly games," someone would usually suggest, "Let's sing." So someone would say, "Priscilla, play the piano for us." Priscilla would answer, "Oh, I haven't my music with me." Then someone would say, "Bessie, you play." "Oh, I can't play without my music." "Well, Ella, you play." "Oh I can't play. I haven't practiced for so long." So the crowd would end up singing a cappella. Finally Spencer, out of patience, made up his mind that he "was going to be serviceable" even though the girls "could play a hundred times better than I." He began memorizing the bass chords in different keys, then practiced picking out the melody line with his right hand, until he could play tolerably well by ear. "When we'd come to the parties after I got a little bit proficient," he recalled, "they wouldn't even ask the girls anymore. They said, 'Spencer, you play.' So I'd play and they'd all sing. I sang as lustily as any of them."[12]

In 1914, after graduation from high school, Spencer received a call to serve in the Central States Mission. He remained in Salt Lake City briefly to receive his endowments at the temple and to attend General Conference. There he was ordained a seventy by his uncle, J. Golden Kimball. Spencer loved attending conference, over which another uncle, Joseph F. Smith presided. President Smith was married to his father's twin sister Alice.

Spencer was a favorite cousin to little four-year-old Thelma Wooley; he liked playing children's games with her, and would play the piano for her. By request, he played one little song again and again:

> And the little ol' Ford, it rambles right along,
> Now cut that out, you naughty tease!
> It's a left-hand turn and a right-hand squeeze.

However, once Spencer was set apart as a missionary, he refused to play it again, saying, "Oh, no. Not that song, Thelma. I have to put things like that out of my mind. I'm a missionary now."[13]

While on his mission, Spencer received word from his father that his older sister, Ruth, at age twenty-one, had passed away. It was Ruth who cared for Spencer after their mother's passing.

Spencer continued to sing and play while in the mission field. On one occasion, Spencer and five other elders

> burst out singing: "Ere you left your room this morning, did you think to pray?" aiming the words in fun at the lady missionaries. The women quipped back with "Hark, Listen to the Trumpeters." The two sides fired back and forth in a hymn duel. Later, the lady missionaries dressed in white and posed for comic photos as nurses in the act of cutting off Spencer's legs with a carpenter's saw.[14]

Spencer often used music to advantage in his missionary activities:

> While tracting in St. Louis he noticed a piano through the partly opened door, and he said to the woman, who was in the act of shutting the door in his face, "You have a nice-looking piano."
> "We just bought it," said the woman, hesitating.
> "It's a Kimball, isn't it? That's my name, too. I could play a song on it for you that you might like to hear."
> Surprised, she answered, "Surely, come in."
> Sitting on the bench, Spencer played and sang, "O My Father."
> So far as Spencer knew, she never joined the Church, but it was not because he had not tried."[15]

After completing his mission, Spencer returned to Arizona on January 1, 1917 to work and prepare for college. Camilla Eyring, whom he had met before leaving for the mission field, had accepted a position at the Gila Academy, teaching home economics. Apparently the Eyrings were as fond of Spencer as he was of their daughter. "While Spencer courted Camilla, the entire Eyring family courted him."[16] Spencer and Camilla married later that year.

> Spencer was important to the musical life of the valley. Right after his marriage he became stake Sunday School chorister. When he was made Sunday School counselor, he also led the ward choir. His journal in 1923 notes: "Drove my load of singers back up to do the rendition of the 'Holy City' oratorio at Layton. I sang a solo and assisted in three quartets and the choruses." Though a baritone, he often sang tenor, for tenors were in short supply.[17]
>
> Spencer had a beautiful voice. "It rang like a bell," said Camilla's brother Henry.
>
> Spencer performed all over the valley, solo, quartet, chorus, leading a group, accompanying someone else on the piano. He was ready at a moment's notice. In World War I, during the great flu epidemic from which Camilla suffered so heavily, Spencer sang in a quartet at many graveside funerals, held outside to prevent contamination by the dread virus. Some years later, while at a dance with Camilla, Spencer saw George Felshaw, a cowpuncher, fall dead, right in the middle of a dance. Felshaw's family asked Spencer's quartet to sing for the funeral "Get Along, Little Dogie, Get Along." When the day came and the quartet launched into their song, the whole front row of calloused, strapping, cowpunchers broke into tears, boo-hooing like babies.[18]

Like his parents, Spencer and Camilla were thrifty, but they did not hesitate to spend money on the things that were important to them.

> Spencer...worked hard to make the business succeed. He practiced thrift. He had his secretary reverse the adding machine tape and use the other side; he always saved for use as scratch paper sheets still blank on one side. Stingy, but he was selective in how he spent his money both in the business and at home. For example, early in his marriage, when he and Camilla watched every penny

and recorded every tiny purchase, *they paid $525 cash for a new piano at a time when they were paying eight dollars a month rent.*[19]

Spencer worked as a book-keeper and a bank-teller while playing piano in a dance band at night. At the same time, he spent long hours as a stake clerk, keeping records of the St. Joseph Stake. Later on, Spencer became a partner in a successful insurance agency.

After twenty-six years as stake president, Spencer's father, Andrew, passed away. In reorganizing the stake, Harry L. Payne was called as the new stake president. Spencer, twenty-nine, was then called to serve as one of his counselors.

Like his father, Spencer, too, wanted his children to learn music. And like his father, Spencer felt that he was not as successful in encouraging their musical education as he wished:

> "I believe we should do a little more for the children in their cultural development," Spencer wrote to Camilla. "If LeVan would take to a cornet or violin, or Bobbie either I believe, we should get them one and give them lessons. At least they should go on with their piano work. I believe we have been a little careless in the matter as the years are flying and they will never accomplish themselves unless done early while we can insist upon it."[20]

In 1923, as a young banker, Spencer was invited to join the newly-chartered Rotary Club in Safford.

> They needed someone who could play the piano, and Spencer could play almost anything they'd be likely to want to sing with or without music, chording his way through the song. He joined. He enjoyed the fellowship. He sang in the Club quartet, and with Camilla, attended nearly all the annual conventions within reach.[21]

> Spencer served as both the club president and district governor. On his leaving Arizona twenty years later, the Rotary newsletter would pay him tribute: "He's been so faithful and so 'on the job' all the time, we often accept him as a fixture—like the president's gavel. Ponder the past of the club for a moment. Who'll be ready to play the piano on call? Who'll put on a program on short notice?

Who'll direct community singing for our parties, and what good will
a party be without Spencer to be master of ceremonies?"[22]

In 1938, the St. Joseph Stake was divided by Elder Melvin J.
Ballard, creating the Mount Graham Stake. Spencer W. Kimball
was called to be the first Stake President of the new stake. The
area of his stake extended from Safford, Arizona, to El Paso,
Texas, and included 1,750 miles travel to each of the wards
under his jurisdiction.

On July 8, 1943, Spencer received a call from Salt Lake City.
President J. Reuben Clark called him, on behalf of the First
Presidency, to become an apostle. At first he thought of all of his
weaknesses, and all of the people in the Gila Valley whom he
might have offended throughout the years. He seriously wondered if, indeed, the Lord had authorized this important call.

For six days and nights, Spencer fasted and prayed with little sleep. He traveled to Salt Lake City, by way of Denver, to
meet with the First Presidency. Near Boulder, Colorado,
Spencer climbed a mountain to commune with the Lord and
gain a testimony of his new calling. Finally peace came to his
troubled soul, and he realized that the call, indeed, was divine.
In Salt Lake City, he met with President Heber J. Grant and his
counselors, David O. McKay and J. Reuben Clarke. Spencer
returned to Safford where he called upon every individual
whom he had ever offended, or whom he might possibly have
offended, to beg their forgiveness.

On Friday, October 1, 1943, the names of Spencer W.
Kimball and Ezra Taft Benson were presented to the Church to
fill the two vacancies in the Quorum of the Twelve. Spencer
Kimball was forty-eight years of age.

On Saturday,

Spencer and Ezra Taft Benson waited upon President Grant in
the big room next to the President's office. Elder Richard R. Lyman
prayed in behalf of the group; President David O. McKay spoke
briefly. Then Spencer Kimball knelt at the feet of the invalid

Prophet, who had been born before the Civil War and who now laid his hands on his head, joined by the other apostles, and ordained Spencer Wooley Kimball an apostle.[23]

Ezra Taft Benson's ordination as an apostle followed. Routinely, each Thursday

> the Council of the Twelve met in a room on the Temple's fourth floor. The apostles sat by seniority in twelve large oak chairs, in a crescent around an upholstered altar. Harold B. Lee played a small organ in the corner as they opened with a hymn. Then all twelve, dressed in temple clothes, formed a prayer circle around the altar. The prayer completed, they changed back to street clothes to handle the Quorum's business.[24]

Elder Kimball began playing the organ in the Quorum's weekly meetings in the temple, alternating with Harold B. Lee. After Elder Lee became the President of the Church, Spencer played the organ regularly for those meetings.

Just as he had done in Arizona, Elder Kimball often arranged musical numbers for programs among the general authorities. The programs did not always reflect the usual dignity and seriousness of the brethren:

> In 1946 Spencer was appointed chairman of a quarterly social for General Authorities and their wives. He drafted the four junior apostles—Elder Kimball, Benson, [Mark E.] Petersen, and [Matthew] Cowley—with Harold B. Lee at the piano, for a quartet. The *Deseret News* photographed them five days before the event, decorously rehearsing "Teach Me to Pray." But at the social they followed that piece with a song about a sure cure for baldness. LeGrand Richards and Milton R. Hunter, both nearly bald, were seated on stage, doused with hair tonic and their heads wrapped in towels as the quartet sang. When Bishop Richards' towel was unrolled, he sported a head of frowsy red hair. Under Elder Hunter's towel was an English barrister's wig of long solemn curls. "It created a good laugh and added a bit of merriment to the occasion."[25]

Elder Kimball's eloquent sermons covered a vast array of topics—the heritage and destiny of the Lamanites, suicide and abortion, treatment of animals, learning and the pursuit of knowledge, homosexuality, sex in marriage, effective mission-ary work, the last days, repentance and forgiveness, succession of the prophet and the twelve, maintaining tidy yards and growing good gardens. And Spencer W. Kimball spoke often about music, which he loved.

Elder Kimball spoke with ardor. His sermons were clear, direct, and beautiful. Like Isaiah, his rich vocabulary and imagery often approach poetry. On April 4, 1959, he spoke of his recent tour of South America:

> I have enjoyed greatly the touring of the missions in those coun-tries. They are like giants just yawning and stretching and ready to go to work.

On October 6, 1961 he spoke of moral transgression:

> The abyss of tragedy opens wide its mouth....
> The case of Potiphar's wife is an example of the creeping tenta-cles of sin.

Elder Kimball spoke of his beloved Lamanites on October 7, 1960:

> The gospel of Jesus Christ is neutralizing the centuries of dwin-dling unbelief.... The work is unfolding, and blinded eyes begin to see, and scattered people begin to gather.... *Truly the scales of dark-ness are falling from their eyes.*

Elder Kimball spoke of the symbolism of the seagull monu-ment on Temple Square on October 3, 1970:

> To the right of us a hundred yards is a beautiful granite monu-ment crowned with a stone globe, and on it, two bronze seagulls....
>
> *The bronze wings of the birds are spread wide, as are the great arms of the Church, to envelop all the peoples of the world; and the granite globe is prophetic of the worldwide Church.*

He spoke of the then recent death of President David O. McKay on April 6, 1970:

> It is January. *History swings on its hinges. Another page is turned and a new era comes to the front.*
> It is Sunday morning, January 18, 1970. *A great heart stops beating and an aged body relaxes and slumbers. Like an earthquake sends a tidal wave around the earth,* communications now cover the earth and millions of serious-minded people in even faraway places stop to pay saddened tribute to a mighty man of God who has passed from mortality.

The following day, April 6, 1974, President Kimball described the voices of past prophets singing beautiful melodies to us in our own time:

> As we incline our hearts to our Heavenly Father and his Son Jesus Christ, *we hear a symphony of sweet music sung by heavenly voices proclaiming the gospel of peace....*
>
> *And so with this melody of love in our hearts,* unitedly we move forward to advance the work of the Lord, knowing that it is not for a century or a millennium but forever.
>
> *Now as we listen to the sweet melody of eternity, what do we hear?* We hear the voice of God calling on our father Adam, person to person, saying:
>
> "I am God; I made the world, and men before they were in the flesh" (Moses 6:51).

Speaking about continuous revelation, he said in October, 1977:

> *The sound of the voice of the Lord is a continuous melody and a thunderous appeal.* For nearly a century and a half there has been no interruption.

In October conference of 1973, Spencer W. Kimball compared our lives to a stormy sea:

There are depths in the sea which the storms that lash the surface into fury never reach. They who reach down into the depths of life where, in the stillness, the voice of God is heard, have the stabilizing power which carries them poised and serene through the hurricane of difficulties.

Using the imagery of Spencer W. Kimball, Marylou Cunningham Leavitt created a "poetic paraphrase" of his quotation:

Oh, Father, as the steadfast undersea
Is quiet, calm and peaceful in the deep,
So I, beneath the hurricane will seek
To learn that through the tempest blessings keep.
I hear the promise of the Father's grace,
As in the depths of life, I search for Thee,
Thy word has spoken of eternal love
To guide me as I set upon life's sea.

And though I hear the fury of the story
That in its wrath doth roll the salty tide,
Beneath it there, a clear voice calls to me,
That I may cast my burdens all aside.
Oh Father, in the stillness much is heard;
Serenely poised and confident I stand.
Thy stabilizing power buoys me up
And bears me swiftly to celestial lands.

Musical setting for solo voice and piano was composed by Darwin Wolford and has been published. It has, also, been heard in a choral version.[26]

As Elder Kimball traveled throughout the Church

[h]e visited Latter-day Saints in their stakes, rode in their cars, ate their dinners, slept in their beds. On weekend assignments to stake conferences he would stay in the home of the stake president or one of his counselors. If there were a piano, he would play a song or two and sing with the children until gradually the entire family grouped around. "They'll forget my sermons," he later said, "But they'll never forget the singing."[27]

After a few years of difficulty, Elder Kimball—one of the most eloquent and poetic speakers among the general authorities—had surgery for cancer of the throat. Of his two vocal chords, only a part of one remained. For a time, it appeared his voice was gone forever. Eventually, however, after some reconstructive surgery, and with the aid of an electronic enhancement device, he was able to speak audibly, but in a faint, raspy voice. Gone was his beautiful singing voice, but not his sense of humor. He was fond of saying later on that he had gone to New York where the surgery had taken place, and "had fallen among cutthroats and thieves who had slit his throat and stolen his voice."[28]

Lamenting over his inability to sing the songs of Zion, Elder Kimball said some years later:

> I wonder if the silent [members of the congregation] can even imagine what it is like to be unable to join fellow singers in praise to their Lord in music?[29]

Through the years, Elder Kimball held a special interest in the Lamanite people and their great heritage and destiny. He loved the Indians. A niece remembered him sitting down on the dirt floor of a Navajo hogan and singing their native songs with them. On other occasions, he sang Indian songs for his grandchildren to the accompaniment of a large spoon beating on a pie pan.[30]

Though he loved the singing of natives around the world in various countries, Elder Kimball longed to see gospel themes replace superstition and war as subjects for their songs.

> Down in New Zealand, I was the recipient of many courtesies while there. They sang and danced and rolled their eyes and stuck out their tongues. And so we applaud them, you know, and think it wonderful to encourage the continuation of that culture. But as it is interpreted to me, they chant and sing battle hymns—not peace hymns. And so I said to some of the leaders: "With all your beautiful voices, your wonderful talent, why don't you develop some impres-

sive songs of the themes surrounding the coming of Christ, about
the reorganization of the gospel, about lofty ideals, the latter-day
exodus, the glories and good things which the gospel and the Church
have brought us?" In all cultures, let us perpetuate not the mating
dances, the sex stories, but the good and the beautiful and lofty as
we sing and as we dance.

We should be perpetuating Mormonism and the gospel: the true
way of life. That doesn't mean we need to bury all things of the past;
but, if there is anything associated with paganism or sectarianism or
sex, we eliminate it. As so, we are building a great culture entirely
different than out there in the sectarian world. We are building a
glorious culture of cleanliness and morality with high-minded, wonderful people. And, all the things the Church does—the singing of
the songs, the speaking in public, the organization—the everything
is devoted to this one thing: building a great spiritual culture that
the Lord wants.[31]

Developing this subject further, Elder Kimball gave a pre-
school address to the students and faculty at Brigham Young
University on September 12, 1967:

In our world, there have risen brilliant stars in drama, music,
literature, sculpture, painting, science and all the graces. For long
years I have had a vision of the BYU greatly increasing its already
strong position of excellence till the eyes of all the world will be
upon us....

With regard to masters, surely there must be many more
Wagners (Richard Wagner, 1813-1883) in the BYU, approaching him
or yet to come in the tomorrows—young people with love of art, talent supreme, and eagerness to create. I hope we at BYU may produce
men greater than this German composer, Wagner, but less eccentric,
more spiritual.

Who of us has not sat spellbound with *Aida, Il Trovaatore* or
other of the masterpieces of Verdi (1813-1900)? Can there never be
another Verdi or his superiors? Could we not find and develop a
Johann Sebastian Bach (1685-1750)—to whom music, especially organ
and choral music, owes almost as much as religion does to its
founder, say some musicians....

Would someone say that they produce singers best in Italy, in
Germany, in Poland or Sweden? Remember we draw our students
from all these places. BYU should attract many and stir their blood
with the messages of the ages. And they will sing songs of accom-

plishment, eternal marriage, exaltation, and we at BYU shall encourage and train them....

Then we remember the celebrated Jenny Lind, the Swedish singer (1820-1887), with such tone faculty, such musical memory, such supremacy, and with such unprecedented triumphs. Do you think there are no more voices like Jenny Lind's? Our day, our time, our people, our generation, our BYU should produce such as we catch the total vision of our potential and dream dreams and see visions of the future....

Our professors and instructors should be peers or superiors to those at any other school in natural ability, extended training, plus the Holy Spirit which should bring them light and truth. With hundreds of "men of God" and their associates so blessed and trained, we have the base for an increasingly efficient and worthy school.

One great artist was asked which of all his production was the greatest. His prompt answer was, "The next."

If we strive for perfection, the best and greatest, and are never satisfied with mediocrity, we can excel. In the field of both composition and performance, why cannot the students from here write a greater oratorio than Handel's *Messiah*? The best has not yet been composed nor produced. They can use the coming of Christ to the Nephites as the material for a greater masterpiece. Our...artists tomorrow may write and sing of Christ's spectacular return to the earth in power and great glory, and his establishment of the Kingdom of God on the earth in our own dispensation. No Handel (1685-1759) nor other composer of the past or present or future could ever do justice to this great event. How could one ever portray in words and music the glories of the coming of the Father and the Son and the restoration of the doctrines and the priesthood and the keys unless he were an inspired Latter-day Saint, schooled in the history and doctrines and revelations and with rich musical ability and background and training?

George Bernard Shaw, the Irish dramatist and critic (1856-1950), summed up an approach to life: "Other people," he said, "see things and say, 'WHY?' But I dream things that never were—and I say "WHY NOT?'" We need people here who can dream of things that never were, and ask "WHY NOT?"[32]

With Harold B. Lee at the head of the Church and Spencer W. Kimball serving as President of the Quorum of the Twelve,

Spencer and Camilla prayed earnestly for President Lee's welfare, not only for the usual reasons, but because the awesome

responsibility of the presidency might fall upon Spencer if the
young and more vigorous President Lee should happen to die first.[33]

But on December 26, 1973, after a brief eighteen months as President of the Church, Harold B. Lee passed away. On Sunday, December 30, Spencer Wooley Kimball, at seventy-nine, became the twelfth President of the Church. Ezra Taft Benson succeeded President Kimball as President of the Quorum.

In spite of a rather poor medical history and a continuation of medical problems—heart surgery, brain surgery, a bleeding ulcer and blindness—President Kimball was one of the most active prophets in recent history.

In his first conference address as President of the Church, on April 5, 1973, President Kimball modestly announced, *"I anticipate no major changes in the immediate future."* Yet in the course of his twelve-year presidency, the list of "changes" became most impressive. These are but a few:

1. Twenty-one new temples were dedicated in various areas of the world, including the Orient, South and central America, Europe, the South Pacific and several cities in the United States. Still other temples had been announced at the time of his passing.
2. A major thrust was given the missionary work around the globe.
3. The historic revelation was received giving the priesthood to all worthy male members, regardless of their race or color.
4. New editions of the four standard works were published, with expanded cross-referencing.
5. Two additions were made to the *Doctrine and Covenants.*
6. A new sub-title was given to the *Book of Mormon:* "Another Testament of Jesus Christ."
7. The First Quorum of the Seventy was activated.
8. Emeritus status was initiated for ailing and aged general authorities.

9. Various church meetings were consolidated into the three-hour schedule.
10. A new and revised hymnbook for the Church was published.
11. A network of 500 satellite dishes for stake centers outside of Utah was created.
12. Major changes were made in the way the church finances meetinghouse buildings and maintenance.

This modest Prophet of God became an increasing vessel receiving great inspiration from the almighty for the growth of His kingdom and the world.

Music occupied a prominent place in the life of Spencer W. Kimball, and was one of the shaping forces in his formative years. This is rather colorfully illustrated in a sermon delivered in General Priesthood Meeting, April 1, 1978.

I remember going to Sunday School, and I believe that I received a great deal of inspiration for the foundation of my life in this place. We had opening exercises in the chapel above and then went downstairs to our classwork.

I remember some of the teachers who came so devotedly and consistently to give us "the word," and they taught me many things which are so basic to my acquaintance with the Church programs and the doctrines.

My mother had a good voice and played the organ, and she and my oldest sister, Clare, sang duets. I inherited a little of the love for music from her, so I was always interested in the singing of the songs, and I generally raised my voice and sang lustily. I remember the song, "We Meet Again in Sabbath School." And we did meet again and again and again, all my life. And I remember when my mother died up in Salt Lake City when I was eleven, there had been a goal set for us to attend Sunday School every Sunday of the year. She died in October. I had never missed a Sunday School since the first of January. I had been present every week, and I had a difficult time to square myself with to miss the Sunday that her body lay in state in our home....

And then, if sometimes we had forgotten the verses, we could all join lustily in singing the chorus of the songs

Join in the jubilee; mingle in song;
Join in the joy of the Sabbath School throng.

The song "Love at Home" we sang in our home evenings, which the Kimball family always held in the early days of this century.

I remember the song "In Our Lovely Deseret," which Sister Eliza R. Snow wrote. She composed many of our songs. I can remember how lustily we sang:

Hark! Hark! Hark! 'tis children's music,
Children's voices, O, how sweet,
When in innocence and love,
Like the angels up above,
They with happy hearts and cheerful faces meet.

I am not sure how much innocence and love we had, but I remember we sang it, even straining our little voices to reach the high E which was pretty high for children's voices. I remember we sang:

That the children may live long,
And be beautiful and strong.

I wanted to live a long time and I wanted to be beautiful and strong—but I never reached it.

Tea and coffee and tobacco they despise.

And I learned to despise them. There were people in our rural community who were members of the Church who sometimes used tea and coffee and sometimes tobacco. The song goes on:

Drink no liquor, and they eat
But a very little meat

(I still don't eat very much meat.)
They are seeking to be great and good and wise.

And then we'd "Hark! Hark! Hark!" again, " When in innocence and love Like the angels up above." And then the third verse went:

They should be instructed young,
How to watch and guard the tongue,

And their tempers train, and evil passions bind;
They should always be polite,
And treat ev'rybody right
And in ev'ry place be affable and kind.

And then we'd "Hark! Hark! Hark! again.

They must not forget to pray,
Night and morning ev'ry day,
For the Lord to keep them safe from ev'ry ill,
And assist them to do right,
That with all their mind and might
They may love him and may learn to do his will.

And then we'd sing, "Hark! Hark! Hark!" again. I was never quite sure whether the angels were limited in their voice culture as we were, but we were glad to take the credit.

One of the songs that had disappeared was number 163, "Don't Kill the Little Birds," and I remember many times singing with a loud voice:

Don't kill the little birds,
That sing on bush and tree,
And thro' the summer days,
Their sweetest melody.
Don't shoot the little birds!
The earth is God's estate,
And he provideth food
For small as well as great.

I had a sling and I had a flipper. I made them myself, and they worked very well. It was my duty to walk the cows to the pasture a mile away from home. There were large cottonwood trees lining the road. I remember that it was quite a temptation to shoot the little birds "that sing on bush and tree," because I was a pretty good shot and I could hit the trunk of a tree. But I think perhaps because I sang nearly every Sunday, "Don't Kill the Little Birds," I was restrained. The second verse goes:

Don't kill the little birds,
Their plumage wings the air,
Their trill at early morn

Makes music ev'rywhere.
What tho' the cherries fall
Half eaten from the stem?
And berries disappear,
In garden, field and glen?

This made a real impression on me, so I could see no great fun in having a beautiful little bird fall at my feet.

And then there was the song that Evan Stephens wrote, "The Mormon Boy," and how proud I was when we were to sing in the congregation:

A 'Mormon' Boy, a 'Mormon' Boy,
I am a 'Mormon' Boy.
I might be envied by a king,
For I am a 'Mormon' Boy.

I liked this song; I have always gloried in those words: "I might be envied by a king, For I am a 'Mormon' Boy."

I liked the song "What Shall the Harvest Be?" because it gave us a chance to sing in parts....

"I know that God lives. I know that Jesus Christ lives," said John Taylor, my predecessor, "for I have seen him." I bear this testimony to you brethren in the name of Jesus Christ.[34]

This warm and friendly sermon was addressed to the Aaronic Priesthood of the Church—and their fathers—with a soft, but electronically amplified raspy voice. But to everyone who heard it that night, it was beautiful, because the words were spoken by a living prophet. *He testified that the songs he learned as a boy taught him important principles that shaped his life.*

President Kimball did not complain about the cancer that claimed his voice, but he lamented over the opportunity to sing the songs of Zion now gone, and he admonished the members of the church *who have voices, to sing*:

It is sad to me to see in the congregations many people standing silent when they could be "singing their hearts out." I wonder constantly if they would sing happily today if for twelve years they could only move their lips through thousands of songs and could make no sound? I wonder if the silent ones can even imagine what it is like to be unable to join fellow singers in praise to their Lord in music?[35]

He had this advice to the conductors of the congregational singing to improve their efficiency in encouraging the people to sing:

> If the conductor sings also, it will encourage the congregation and help them remember the words...In every beat of the baton should be the pleading to the Saints of God: Sing. Sing. Sing from your hearts.[36]

President Kimball adamantly believed that every ward should have a ward choir, regardless of how small the ward, or how small the choir:

> *Every congregation should have a choir. If you don't have a ward choir, you are not organized fully, any more than if you do not have a Relief Society.*
>
> There are numerous branches and small wards...where the numbers are fewer and the talent less plentiful, but there surely could be no unit without sufficient singer and reasonably competent organists and directors to carry a splendid choir even though in some cases it may have fewer numbers. I once dedicated a chapel for a ward of eighty-two persons; they had a commendable choir of thirty voices.... A general announcement asking ward members to join and support the choir will not produce the best results. Prospective choir members should be invited individually in a dignified way.[37]

Special music numbers in our sacrament meetings did not escape his attention.

> Music and instruments should induce appropriate feelings. Music sounds can be put together in such a way that they can express feelings—from the most profoundly exalted to the most abjectly vulgar. Or rather, these musical sounds induce in the listener feelings which he responds to, and the response he makes to these sounds has been called "gesture of the spirit." Thus music can act

upon our senses to produce or induce feelings of reverence, humili-
ty, fervor, assurance, or other feelings attuned to the spirit of worship. When music is performed in Church which conveys a "gesture" other than that which is associated with worship, we are dis-
turbed, upset, or shocked to the degree with the appropriate repre-
sentation of feelings of worship....

When people are invited to perform special numbers in sacred
meetings, whether ward members or others, it is important to know
in advance what numbers will be given and that they are devotional
in character and in keeping with the spirit of worship. To be avoided
are love songs, popular ballads, theatrical numbers, and songs with
words not in harmony with the doctrines of the Church.[37] Persons
invited to perform should be specifically urged to remain throughout
the service.

Musicians hold a gift in trust. The responsibility for producing,
selecting, and performing music for the Church requires discrimina-
tion, taste, knowledge, and the proper spirit; in short, it requires the
best efforts that our best musicians can give inasmuch as we are using
gifts which the Lord has given us for the purpose of building up his
kingdom and as a demonstration of the faith and love for him. We are
in a position, as musicians, to touch the souls of those who listen.[38]

The authors of, *Spencer W. Kimball*, Edward and Andrew E.
Kimball, Jr.—sons of the Prophet—conclude this splendid biography of their father with these words:

> Believing himself preserved by God for the specific purpose of
> leading the Latter-day saints, Spencer W. Kimball brought to the
> Church Presidency a combination of humility and certitude, physi-
> cal weakness and indomitable will, intelligence and spirituality. He
> responded to every call, however questioning of his own abilities,
> determined to make himself fit to serve. And as he asked others to
> lengthen their stride and quicken their step, he led the way.[39]

After a period of declining health, Spencer W. Kimball, at
ninety, passed away quietly and peacefully on November 5,
1985. On a prominent hill within the Salt Lake City cemetery
overlooking the city, this remarkable prophet of God rests
beside his beloved Camilla. The grave is marked by an upright
bluish, marble slab that stands nearly as tall as President

Kimball stood. The width is a little broader, perhaps, than his shoulders. The only printing on this beautifully simple grave-stone is near the bottom—Kimball—and below that the names of Camilla Eyring and Spencer Wooley, and the dates of their mortal lives. Set in cement on either side of the marble is a rather large chunk of petrified wood from the Arizona soil. Like this great Prophet of God, the marker is modest, beautiful and simple, strong and immovable.

1 Edward L. Kimball. *The Teachings of Spencer W. Kimball*, Salt Lake City (Bookcraft, 1982) p. 30.
2 Edward L. Kimball and Andrew E. Kimball, Jr. *Spencer W. Kimball, Twelfth President of the Church of Jesus Christ of Latter-day Saints.* Salt Lake City. (Bookcraft, 1977). P. 21.
3 Ibid., p. 32.
44. Ibid., p. 32.
5 Ibid. pp. 57-58.
6 Ibid., p. 57.
7 Ibid., p. 38.
8 Ibid., p. 39.
9 Ibid., p. 51.
10 Ibid., p. 51.
11 Ibid., p. 58.
12 Ibid., p. 61.
13 Ibid., p. 73.
14 Ibid., p. 79.
15 Ibid., pp. 79-80.
16 Ibid., p. 91.
17 Ibid., p. 112.
18 Ibid., p. 113.
19 Ibid., p. 130.
20 Ibid., p. 151.
21 Edward L. Kimball. P. 156.
22 Ibid., p. 156.
23 Ibid., p. 205.
24 Ibid., p. 207.
25 Ibid., p. 227.
26 Darwin Wolford: *Songs of Praise by American Composers* (Delaware Water Gap, PA, Harold Flammer Inc.).
27 Edward L. Kimball, p. 232.
28 Ibid., p. 311.
29 Ibid., p. 519.
30 Private conversation with Jenna Brinkerhoff Mosley.
31 *The Teachings of Spencer W. Kimball*, pp. 394.
32 Excerpts of this address are included in *The Teaching of Spencer W. Kimball*, pp. 392-394.
33 Leonard J. Arrington: *The Presidents of the Church*, (Salt Lake City: Deseret Book, 1986), pp. 407-408.
34 *Conference Report*, April 1, 1978, pp. 70-71.
35 *The Teachings of Spencer W. Kimball*, pp. 518-519.
36 Ibid., p. 519.

37 Ibid., 518-519.
38 Ibid., p. 519.
39 *Spencer W. Kimball*, p. 427.

EZRA TAFT BENSON

M Withers '94

Ezra Taft Benson
(1899-1994)

*"Rock music, with its instant physical
appeal, is an ideal door-crasher, for the
devil knows that music has the power to
ennoble or corrupt, to purify or pollute."*[1]

A farm boy from a small rural town in southern Idaho was
not a likely candidate to become the most famous farmer in
America, a prominent national, even international, political
figure, an apostle, and eventually a prophet of God. But from
his birth in Whitney, Idaho, on August 4, 1899, Ezra T. Benson,
like the Lord, "increased in wisdom and stature, and in favour
with God and man."[2] "T," as he was called, however, became a
farmer, rather than a carpenter. Along with the plowing, hoe-
ing, thinning, topping beets, milking, hay hauling, and irrigat-
ing, there was time for music, as well.

Elder Boyd K. Packer said of Ezra Taft Benson that he loved
to sing the hymns of Zion:

> He learned to sing them from his father as they milked cows.
> He learned them by watching his mother. He would spread newspa-
> pers on the floor near the coal stove, set up the ironing board and
> put the flat iron made of cast iron on the stove to heat. Then as she
> carefully ironed the white temple clothes, she would invite the spir-
> it of contentment and inspiration...by singing softly the hymns of
> the Restoration.[3]

"T" tended younger brothers and sisters every Wednesday
night as his parents, George and Sarah Benson, went to the
weekly ward choir practice. The family loved to sing—Ezra in
particular. As soon as someone else was old enough to babysit,
he joined his parents at choir practice. As Sarah sewed at the

treadle machine, she sang hymns such as "Have I Done Any Good in the World Today?" and popular tunes such as "Annie Laurie" and "In the Evening by the Moonlight." At nighttime the family gathered around the old piano for singing.[4]

On April 27, 1915, George read an announcement published in the *Deseret News* that President Joseph F. Smith and the First Presidency were initiating a program for the Church to observe one night weekly for a family to be home together for gospel study and appropriate activities. George proclaimed, "This is the word of the Lord to us!" and the program was followed religiously.

From that time forward, not a week passed without home evening. Each child had an assignment—to pray, to conduct, to give the lesson, to plan the program, to prepare refreshments. They sang songs, read from the scriptures, told pioneer stories, wrote letters to relatives and missionaries, played games, and shared talents.[4]

The Bensons of Whitney, Idaho, provided an excellent model for families throughout the Church. Ezra often recalled with fondness the closeness of the family, *"They sang together, played together, prayed together, and stayed together."*[5]

In the spring of 1912, a letter addressed to George T. Benson, Jr., arrived. The letter came from "Box B, Salt Lake City, Utah." Full of faith, George accepted a call to the Northern States Mission, leaving Sarah and the eleven children to manage the farm. At twelve, as the oldest child, Ezra took the place of his father for two years doing the work of a man.

Though the work was hard for a twelve-year old, having his father on a mission had a positive influence on Ezra. He learned how to do the work, as hard as it was. Besides, Ezra developed faith and a spirit of missionary work from his father's example. When George returned from his mission, Ezra would observe his father sitting on a one-legged milk stool, milking cows and singing at full voice "Ye Elders of Israel," "Israel, Israel, God is Calling," and "Come, All Ye Sons of God." The songs echoed through the barn and fields so often that Ezra learned every word of these and other missionary songs and could repeat them throughout his life.[6]

After graduating from elementary school in Whitney at fourteen, Ezra attended the Oneida Stake Academy at Preston. It was at the academy that Ezra met Harold B. Lee, who was a year ahead of him in school. They became good friends, and both sang in the school's first choir. Ezra also played trombone, though his major interests were agriculture and vocational training. He felt that "a man ought to be able to repair something."[7]

Ezra received a call to serve as assistant scoutmaster. But in 1918, scouting included some activities that would surprise today's scout leaders. Ezra was given the responsibility of turning twenty-four lively scouts into a boys' choir:

In those days the YMMIA[8] sponsored choruses for the teenage boys, and the Scoutmaster was expected to get them to practice. The choirs sang not only for pleasure and entertainment but also in competitions. After weeks of practice and pushing and prodding on Ezra's part, his choir won first place in the Franklin Stake competition against six other winning groups.[9]

On the night of the competition each choir drew lots for placement. The Whitney chorus drew 6th place which prolonged their anxiety. When they were finally announced, twenty-four boys marched up the aisle and on stage while the pianist played "Stars and Stripes Forever." Ezra crouched between two benches to direct their performance. "They sang as I'd never heard them sing, and of course I'd not tell the story had we not won first place in Logan," he said.[10]

Ezra's experience as assistant scoutmaster in the Whitney Ward began a lifetime of involvement in scouting. He later became the scoutmaster, and many years later, served as a member of the National Executive Board of the Boy Scouts of America. Believing that "It's better to build boys than mend men," Ezra received some of scouting's highest awards—the Silver Beaver, the Silver Antelope, the Silver Buffalo and the world scouting's highest honor, the Bronze Wolf.[11]

Ezra met his future wife, Flora Amussen, while attending Utah State Agricultural College (later named Utah State University) in Logan, Utah. But marriage had to wait, however, as he accepted a call to serve a mission to the British Isles.

Because there was considerable anti-Mormon sentiment in England, Ezra's mission was difficult, and the successes were meager. He did consider his experience a great blessing in his life, serving under two great mission presidents—both apostles—Orson F. Whitney, after whom his home town was named, and David O. McKay, who later became the President of the Church.

Completing his mission, Ezra looked forward to renewing his friendship with Flora Amussen. Much to his disappointment, however, Flora was about to leave on a mission to the Hawaiian Islands. Marriage had to wait.

Meanwhile, Ezra transferred to Brigham Young University where he completed a dual major: animal husbandry and marketing. And in his spare time, he served as president of the Agricultural Club and president of the Men's Glee Club.

Ezra and Flora were finally married in the Salt Lake Temple on September 8, 1926. They packed up *all* of their belongings in a Model T Ford pickup and headed for Ames, Iowa, where he attended Iowa State College as a scholarship student in agricultural economics. He received a master's degree from Iowa State College in the spring of 1927.

The young couple returned to the farm in Whitney where they hoped to spend "the rest of our lives." His success on the farm, however, earned him the job as county agricultural agent. He took one year's leave of absence from that position to work on a doctorate at the University of California at Berkeley. He returned to Idaho, where the excellence of his work as the Franklin Agricultural Agent, as well as his graduate training, earned for him the position of Agricultural Economist and Extension Agent in Boise.

The weight of responsibility working for the State of Idaho in this position during the years of the Great Depression was enormous. But in addition to this, Ezra later served as the Boise Stake President. No doubt, these challenges were preparation for things yet to come.

Sarah, Ezra's mother, became ill during the years he and Flora were in Boise. Her health worsened, and on June 1, 1933, she passed away, leaving behind a grieving husband and ten children who were still at home. Many marveled at Ezra's strength, when on the following Sunday, he sang "O Mother of Mine" in Church. Just fourteen months later, in August, the family lost their father.

While in Boise, four children were born to Ezra and Flora. As the family grew, music became an integral part of their growing up. "Over the years various children took piano, voice, organ, art, dance, ice skating, swimming and sculpture lessons."[12] They loved playing games, reading poetry, and having frequent gospel discussions. But especially did the Benson family enjoy singing together around the piano at home.

Ezra's reputation in agriculture spread from Boise to Washington, and in January, 1939, he was offered a position as executive secretary to the National Council of Farmer's Cooperatives. He accepted, but first he had to be released from the stake presidency. Six weeks after Ezra left for Washington, his family joined him in the nation's capitol.

With each new career move, the demands on Ezra's time increased. Even though he was away frequently, family home evenings were held often.

> A typical evening went something like this: a song by the family, minutes read from the previous meeting, a story read by Flora entitled "How I Became a Mormon," a scripture reading by Mark, a song by the girls, a clarinet solo by Reed, closing thoughts by Ezra on "The Meaning of Family Loyalty," and a discussion of family problems."[13]

Less than one year after the Benson's move to Washington, a district conference was held. The Washington Stake was organized from the Capitol District of the Eastern States Mission, and Ezra was called to be the first stake president. In his new calling, Ezra placed a great emphasis on missionary work, and music assumed a place of great importance in the missionary effort.

Cleone Skousen was stake mission president. Ezra assigned Sterling Wheelwright to give organ recitals and conduct tours through the building, interspersing the music with the gospel message. Ezra invited associates to visit church meetings.[14]

While Ezra was serving as the President of the Washington Stake, the Second World War intensified. On the dreadful morning of December 7, 1941, when the Japanese bombed Pearl Harbor, America was immediately drawn into the war. Suddenly Washington was in turmoil. There was added weight upon the shoulders of Ezra as the stake president in the nation's capitol with the nation at war. Moreover, his work responsibilities increased greatly.

Ezra had spent some time in Utah in the summer of 1943. When he was about to catch a return train to Washington, he was summoned to the home of President Heber J. Grant. And there he was issued the greatest calling of his life to date:

> "Brother Benson, with all of my heart I congratulate you and pray God's blessing to attend you. You have been chosen as the youngest member of the Council of the Twelve apostles."[15]

President Grant invited Ezra to attend conference in October when he would be sustained by the members of the Church. The announcement of his divine call was announced in the *Deseret News* on July 27, noting that he was a descendent of Ezra T. Benson, an earlier apostle who served as a counselor to President Brigham Young. President Grant advised him to begin using his entire name *Ezra Taft Benson*, to avoid any confusion with the earlier apostle.

On October 6, 1943, Spencer W. Kimball and Ezra Taft Benson were presented to the 114th semi-annual conference of the Church for their sustaining vote as the newest members of the Quorum of the Twelve. On the morning of October 7, Heber J. Grant ordained Spencer W. Kimball an apostle, and following him, President Grant ordained Ezra Taft Benson.

War raged on in Europe and in the Pacific for another two years. Finally, on May 8, 1945, Germany surrendered. One week later Heber J. Grant passed away and George Albert Smith became the next president of the Church. Three months later, on August 6, 1945, a United States Army plane dropped the first atomic bomb on the Japanese city of Hiroshima; three days later, another bomb was dropped on the city of Nagasaki. August 14, Japan accepted the unconditional terms of surrender. The war was over!

President Smith called a special meeting of the First Presidency and the Twelve on Saturday morning, December 22nd. Elder Benson related details of that important meeting:

> After the prayer President Smith referred to the fact that announcement had been made that Brothers [John A.] Widstoe and [David O.] McKay would go to Europe, but he said that on further investigation they found conditions so bad in Europe that it would not be wise to send these two brethren but to select a younger man....
>
> After outlining the magnitude of the job, President Smith announced that I had been chosen to go and preside over the European Mission and take charge also of the distribution of relief help for our people in those war-torn countries."[16]

With Europe just emerging from a World War that devastated much of the continent, the President of the European Mission would have overwhelming challenges. The youngest apostle with the largest family, Elder Benson had only five weeks to prepare for a mission of indeterminate length. Frederick Babbel was selected as his private secretary, and the two of them departed from Salt Lake City on January 30th. In a general conference held after his return, Elder Benson summarized what his four-point charge had been:

> First, to attend to the spiritual affairs of the Church in Europe;
> second, to work to make available food, clothing, and bedding to our
> suffering Saints in all parts of Europe; third, to direct the reorganization of the various missions of Europe; and, fourth, to prepare for the
> return of missionaries to those countries.[17]

Arriving in Europe, the brethren decided to locate their headquarters in London. The account of what turned out to be a ten-and-a-half month odyssey is published in the book, *On Wings of Faith* by Elder Benson's companion, Frederick Babbel. He wrote of "being directed" in finding a place:

> Our search finally took us to one of London's most fashionable
> sections—the area of Bond and Brook Streets. We walked into an
> old dismal-looking courtyard through a narrow alley. From the
> exterior, the place we examined looked very plain and uninteresting, but the interior of the apartment exceeded our fondest expectations. Both of us felt that it was the Lord's answer to our fervent
> prayers. The following morning we moved into our new headquarters.
>   It turned out that we had rented a section of the home of the
> noted musician, George Frederick Handel where he had composed
> his great masterpiece, the *Messiah*.... Here we set up our home and
> our office. With a typewriter, plus discarded dictaphone equipment I
> had salvaged from the damp attic of the British Mission office and
> then laboriously rejuvenated, we were ready to go.[18]

Within these walls in 1741, George Frederick Handel composed *Messiah*, one of the world's greatest religious masterworks. After completing it in the seemingly impossible period of twenty-five days, he remarked, "I think God has visited me."[19] Is it a mere coincidence that two hundred years later a future prophet of the Lord should occupy these quarters?

As the brethren approached their assignment, they saw massive destruction in every direction. Beautiful, historic buildings were no longer recognizable. Whole cities were reduced to rubble. Many church members were among the casualties. Survivors were without food, clothing or shelter. And there were still other conditions that had to be met. Elder Benson wrote surveying the problems of reconstruction:

> The worst...is not the physical combat but that which follows— the abandonment of moral and religious restraints; the increase of sin, disease, the increase in infant mortality; and all the suffering which accompanies famine, disease, and immorality. We saw these things on every side. We saw nations prostrate, flat on their back economically. We found it difficult even to get a phone call through from London to many of our missions on the continent. We could not even make a telephone call to Holland, let alone countries like Poland, Czechoslovakia, and other nations. Almost the only type of transportation available was that under the control of the military.[20]

Yet, Elder Benson met every challenge fearlessly and with total faith in the Lord—miracles unfolded daily before their eyes.

An LDS chaplain, Howard C. Badger, of the U. S. Army, received authorization to accompany the brethren on the first leg of their mission. Elder Babbel writes of their travels together:

> As we traveled toward Switzerland, we spent many pleasant hours in conversation and in singing together. Brother Badger sang bass, President Benson sang the melody, I provided suitable harmony. President Benson did most of the driving.[21]

Elder Babbel describes one incident that took place in Karlsühe, Germany, in which he and Elder Benson had a difficult time locating a conference they planned to attend:

> Upon arriving at Karlsühe, we made inquiries to learn where our saints might be meeting in district conference. Finally, there was pointed out to us a sizeable area of almost completely demolished buildings and we were told that they were probably meeting somewhere in that section.
> Parking the car near massive heaps of twisted steel and concrete, we climbed over several large piles of rubble and threaded our way between the naked blasted walls in the general direction which

had been pointed out to us. As we viewed the desolation on all sides of us, our task seemed hopeless. Then we heard the distant strains of "Come, Come, Ye Saints" being sung in German. We were overjoyed. No strains of music were ever more welcome!

We hurried in the direction of the sound of the singing and arrived at a badly scarred building which still had several useable rooms. In one of the rooms we found 260 joyous saints still in conference, although it was already long past their dismissal time. (They had already been in session over three hours that afternoon, but had been hoping and praying that we might arrive in time to meet them.)

As we entered the room, the closing strains of this beloved Mormon hymn swelled to a crescendo of joyousness that overwhelmed us.[22]

While traveling to Berlin, Elder Benson and his two travel companions decided to remain in Hannover overnight:

Arrangements were hurriedly made to hold an evening meeting with the saints in a room of a bombed-out schoolhouse. There was no electricity. When we arrived at dusk, we found the room overflowing with assembled saints. All the window panes had been shattered by repeated bombings and had been replaced with sections of cardboard opened wide to admit the fading daylight. We had barely begun our meeting when a violent rain and windstorm broke out. This necessitated quickly closing all of the windows and continuing our services in almost total darkness. In spite of this condition, the hastily formed choir, which [Elder Babbel] had been invited to join, sang fervently, even though we could barely see our director.

The meeting opened with the singing of "We Thank Thee, O God, for a Prophet." And how they sang that song! After President Benson's stirring remarks...the choir appropriately sang "Come, O Thou King of Kings." I believe the very heavens were moved by the spirited singing.[23]

"Come, O Thou King of Kings" reflects the pain and suffering of the Saints of an earlier time, writes Alexander Schreiner:

Brother Pratt's inventive mind was frequently triggered by the many trials he was forced to undergo. The hymn, "Come, O Thou

King of Kings," is a plea to the Father of all mankind to come quickly to set his people free from the suffering which seemed a part of their daily existence—a plea for him to gather them within the shelter of his arm. It is a prayer that wickedness might not prevail on earth.[24]

> Come, O thou King of Kings! We've waited long for
> thee,
> With healing in thy wings To set thy people free.
> Come, thou desire of nations, come; Let Israel now
> be gathered home.
>
> Come, make an end to sin, And cleanse the earth
> by fire,
> And righteousness bring in, That Saints may tune
> the lyre
> With songs of joy, a happier strain, To welcome in
> thy peaceful reign.

In traveling through East Germany to Berlin, President Benson, Elder Babbel and the Chaplain were joined by Max Zimmer, president of the Swiss Mission.

> For the first time the four of us traveling together formed a male quartet. We sang all the songs we knew to make the time pass more quickly and pleasantly. President Benson sang melody, President Zimmer the high tenor, Chaplain the bass, and I filled in with the tenor or baritone parts as needed. We nicknamed ourselves the "K-Ration Quartet," since we were subsisting largely on K-Rations during our entire trip.[25]

The K-Ration Quartet, with President Benson singing lead, performed for a variety of occasions in a number of countries, much to the delight of those in attendance. President Benson customarily preached a sermon on the program where the quartet sang. Apparently, the audiences were moved by the sermons and the singing.

Although Elder Benson and his traveling companions had gone to the distressed Saints to encourage them and bring comfort, frequently, however, choral singing, rehearsed in less-than-ideal conditions, brought strength and joy to the visiting

Elders. In Norway, they were thrilled by a chorus of eighty singers, accompanied by a string orchestra.

> Our evening meeting with saints and friends was a spiritual feast. Beautiful music was furnished by a chorus of eight voices accompanied by a well-balanced string orchestra. We learned that this Oslo choir is famous throughout Scandinavia, and even President Benson volunteered that it was the best choir he had ever heard except for the Salt Lake Tabernacle Choir![26]

Elder Benson commented further about the two musical organizations in his journal,

> September 7, 1946:
>
> The choir, in addition to rendering musical numbers for every Sunday evening service, holds two concerts yearly. These concerts have become traditional, and the attendance fills the chapel to overflowing. The choir has also made a practice of visiting various hospitals from time to time to sing for the patients.
>
> The Oslo Branch orchestra was organized on November 20, 1944.... The orchestra's aim was not only to assist in accompanying the choir but also to stimulate musical interests among the Saints. It now consists of seventeen active members. One of their former members, Brother Eris Drunn, was a leader of the Norwegian underground during the war. Upon being discovered, he was shot to death, his body thrown in the ocean and never recovered.
>
> These two outstanding musical organizations, products of a mission branch, should be a challenge to the entire Church membership and an inspiration as well. What they have done and are continuing to do might well be duplicated in other missions, wards, and stakes throughout the Church.[27]

Elder Babbel wrote of their visit to Amsterdam:

> I was greatly impressed by the enthusiastic singing of the Dutch. I do not believe there was a person in the audience in any one of our meetings who was not singing with all his heart. For this occasion there was a special "Singing Mothers" chorus. And—wonder of wonders!—the singers were all dressed in the traditional black skirts and white blouses, so characteristic of this singing group

throughout the world. Nearly all of these skirts and blouses had been received from America in Welfare packages. Some were rather ill-fitting—some skirts were wrapped around the wearer for about a time and a half for example—but the sisters looked lovely to me and sang with as much power and harmony as I have ever heard a group of women sing. It was inspirational.[28]

A most interesting experience took place in Herne, Germany:

> In the Sunday morning session of our conference...the finest spirit we had ever enjoyed was richly manifest. While a children's chorus was singing, President Benson looked at them several times with a most intense expression on his face.
>
> No sooner had the children finished their singing than we heard the Salt Lake Tabernacle Choir and organ burst forth in all their glory. Without our knowledge, some of the brethren had concealed radio speakers in the chandeliers. They had tuned in the weekly rebroadcast of this program over Radio Stuttgart, where Captain Fred G. Tailor, one of our fine servicemen, was in charge. Since he was a former missionary in Germany and had an excellent command of the language, he relayed Elder Richard L. Evans' sermonette to us in German.
>
> Many were weeping for joy as the music and singing proceeded. This signified Zion and all that it meant to Latter-day Saints. The spirit on this occasion was tender and sweet, yet overpowering in its impact.
>
> When the music ended, President Benson took me by the arm and led me to the pulpit so that I might serve as his translator. He said, in effect: "I hope you were listening carefully as the children were singing. Let me assure you that they were not singing alone. *The angels were singing with them. And if the Lord would touch your spiritual eyes and understanding, you would see that many of our loved ones, whom you have lost during the war, are assembled with us today."*[29]

With all of the stirring, spiritual experiences involving music, some were less serious. For instance:

> While we were dining at the officers' mess in Frankfurt, a spirited string ensemble was playing sweet music. The leader of the group approached our table and asked if we had any special request.

President Benson said he would like to hear them play "When It's Springtime in the Rockies." The leader being unfamiliar with this song, President Benson hummed the tune to their leader, whereupon he returned to his gifted companions, humming the tune to them, then led them in playing the song beautifully and with scarcely a mistake. This performance pleased our group very much.[30]

Did President Benson have a sense of humor? Brother Babbel relates another incident that proves he did. Before returning to the United States, President Benson invited Elder and Mrs. Alma Sonne and Elder and Mrs. Selvoy J. Boyer to join Elder Babbel as his guests at Royal Albert Hall to hear a performance of the London International Orchestra:

As the orchestra was playing Rossini's *William Tell Overture*, I noticed that President Benson's eyes were sparkling as he recognized the theme song for "The Lone Ranger." What happened next was entirely unexpected. As the conductor brought down his baton to conclude this stirring number, and during the brief pause before the thunderous applause which followed, President Benson leaned over to his guests and said in a voice which could be heard for quite a distance, "Hi, Ho, Silver away!"[31]

With his remarkable post-war experiences behind him, Ezra Taft Benson returned hating war and oppression. Even more, he despised governments, or government actions, that would rob individuals of their basic human rights. He returned a staunch champion of the Constitution of our land, and a passionate defender of freedom. So impassioned were his sermons and writings regarding these matters, some believed he had crossed the line into politics. But to Ezra Taft Benson, America had a divine mission in human history—past and present—and freedom, he felt, rests at the very heart of the Gospel plan.

In the fall of 1953, President-elect Dwight D. Eisenhower asked Ezra to serve in his cabinet as Secretary of Agriculture. This meant taking a leave of absence from his ecclesiastical duties, which Ezra did not want to do. With encouragement from David O. McKay, however, he accepted President

Eisenhower's invitation to serve in the United States government.

Moving from the administration of recovery efforts after the war to cabinet position with government was like moving from the frying pan into the fire. A "conservative's conservative," as Elder Benson described himself, he opposed big government, government controls and subsidies. "The Federal Government has no funds which it does not, in some manner, take from the people. And a dollar cannot make the round trip from Oklahoma, Iowa, California, or even Maryland, to Washington and back, without shrinking in the process."[32]

While not compromising his church standards in any way, nor soft-pedaling his conservative views on government, Ezra was the object of intense praise and criticism. Repeatedly he appeared on the cover of national magazines and on network television. His religious views, as well as his position on government matters were well-known.

> President Eisenhower, at Secretary Benson's suggestion, saw that each Friday morning cabinet meeting was opened with silent or verbal prayer. Secretary Benson insisted that his own Department of Agriculture staff meetings on Thursday be opened with a verbal prayer.[33]

Ezra's family followed him to Washington six months after he assumed his cabinet responsibilities, moving into a modest home about fifteen minutes from the White House. "Prominently featured in the living room were an old spinet piano and a leather-bound volume of the *Book of Mormon*. The children soon became involved in musical activities and study. Beverly continued her vocal training in New York City and made her formal singing debut at a private concert for dignitaries and congressmen."[34] Frequently, to relieve pressure for her father, she would give "her father a private organ recital at the Washington Ward chapel. The music seemed to soothe his nerves."[35]

The Bensons became well-known as a close-knit family that held high standards of conduct. Music seemed always to be an important part of their family life. Edward R. Murrow, host of a popular Friday-night television program, "Person to Person," approached Secretary Benson about featuring his family at home on one of his programs. At first Ezra was reluctant to have national television invading the privacy of his home and family. When he realized this to be an opportunity to show the nation what an LDS home and family are like, he accepted.

> The show was televised on September 24, 1954, with only an informal run-through—no rehearsal. Three television cameras were set up in the Benson's living room and library. The garage was filled with electronic equipment, and a production crew of ten was on hand. On the show, Flora introduced the family. The girls sang "Sittin' on Top of the World," Barbara sang "Italian Street Song," Beth tap-danced and sang, Reed and Mark explained the church's missionary program, and the family sang "Love at Home."
>
> With time winding down on the program, and realizing this as her last opportunity to cover a few salient points, Flora responded to Murrow's question, "So do you have any domestic help?" with a spirited reply: "No, we do not have a maid. We feel that we learn by doing. We prepare all of our own meals, and plan them...*We play together, sing together*. We're a very religious family. We have prayer—individual and together—because we feel that a family that prays together stays together. I feel that's true of a nation."[36]

Murrow was happy to report back to Secretary Benson that the program was a great success, having generated more fan mail than any other program he had done.

From time to time, the wives of cabinet members met for luncheons that were generally catered and usually rather formal. When it was Flora's turn to host the women, she invited them, as well as Mamie Eisenhower, to her home. With help from her daughters, Flora prepared everything herself. She explained to her guests that there were no cocktails, playing cards, smoking, or tea and coffee. But "we'll try to make it up to you in our way, and we hope you enjoy our home."

The girls helped serve the meal, and all of the children performed. BYU's Madrigal Singers were in Washington on tour, and they also sang (with Barbara as soloist). Mamie Eisenhower was so taken with the BYU group that she promptly invited them to the White House that afternoon, accompanying them on the tour of the mansion.[37]

On at least one occasion, the Bensons invited President and Mrs. Eisenhower to attend a Mormon home evening at the Virginia ranch of J. Willard Marriott and his wife, active LDS people and close friends of the Bensons.

> So, by a roaring fireplace on a cold winter night the Benson family performed, with musical numbers by the four Benson daughters, comic skits, readings, and group singing that included the Eisenhowers.[38]

During the eight years the Bensons were in Washington, Ezra and Flora mingled frequently with world leaders, including Nikita Khrushchev, prime minister of the Soviet Union. He proclaimed to Ezra, "Your grandchildren will live under communism." "On the contrary," Ezra responded, "my grandchildren will live in freedom as I hope that all people will."[39]

A week after Krushchev's visit to this country, Secretary Benson, accompanied by his wife, Beverly and Bonnie and four members of his staff, left for a trip to seven European countries, including the Soviet Union. In Moscow, the Secretary was shown "the best" of Soviet farms and equipment, which were poor by our standards. Several times, he asked to see one of the Protestant churches in Moscow, but his requests were conveniently ignored. While the party was en route to the airport, Ezra once again asked to visit a church. Reluctantly, the driver took them to the Central Baptist Church. The experience which followed was one of the most deeply moving spiritual experiences of Ezra's life:

> It was raining, but the chill left as the Secretary's party entered the church which was filled to overflowing with mostly middle-age and elderly people. Ezra understood that Soviet citizens

attended these services at some risk; anyone who looked to a career of any kind avoided the slightest suspicion of belief in Christianity.

The American group caused an immediate stir in the old church. A newsman present described the scene:

"Every face in the old sanctuary gaped incredulously as our obviously American group was led down the aisle. They grabbed for our hands as we proceeded to our pews which were gladly vacated.... Their wrinkled old faces looked at us pleasingly. They reached out to touch us almost as one would reach out for the last final caress of one's most-beloved just before the casket is lowered. They were in misery and yet a light shown through the misery. They gripped our hands like frightened children."

Surprisingly, the minister invited Secretary Benson to speak.

Never had he stood before an audience like this. As he scanned the crowd of anxious faces, it took some moments for him to control his emotions. These were good people, he felt immediately, subjected to a society that deprived them of unrestricted worship. The emotional impact was almost more than he could bear. Then he began to speak about hope and truth and love. As he talked about the Savior and the hope of life after death, tears flowed freely throughout the church.

"Our Heavenly Father is not far away," the secretary promised. "He is our Father. Jesus Christ, the Redeemer of the world, watches over this earth.... Be unafraid, Keep His commandments, love one another, pray for peace, and all will be well."

By this time tears were streaming down Ezra's face. When his entourage finally filed down the aisle, men and women waved handkerchiefs and grasped the visitors' hands in an action that spoke more than words. Spontaneously they began to sing *God Be With You Till We Meet Again*. The language was foreign, but the tune and meaning were unmistakable. The Americans entered their cars with not a dry eye among them. Finally a newsman broke the silence, commenting, "I believe they were the only really happy people we saw in Russia."[40]

Ezra Taft Benson completed eight years in Washington as a member of the president's cabinet—two full terms, which may be some kind of record in Washington.

After Dwight D. Eisenhower's second term as President, Ezra Taft Benson returned to his full responsibilities as a member of the Quorum of the Twelve. More than ever, he preached that the Constitution of the United States is a divinely inspired document. He denounced totalitarianism in any form, and he spoke repeatedly of the adversary and his successes in the world. He continually warned the Saints of Satan's efforts to destroy God's children.

Elder Benson recognized the evil influence of Satan in much of the entertainment of the day: movies, magazines, books, and even music. In the Philippine Islands Area Conference, August 12, 1975, he said:

> Now, what of the entertainment that is available to our young people today? Are you being undermined right in your homes through your television, radio, slick magazines, and rock music records? Much of the rock music is purposely designed to push immorality, narcotics, revolution, atheism, and nihilism through language that often carries a double meaning and with which parents are not familiar.[41]

His message in the Scandinavia and Finland Area Conference, August 16-18, 1974, was the same:

> The devil-inspired destructive forces are present in our literature, in our art, in the movies, on the radio, in our dress, in our dances, on the television screen, and even in our modern so-called popular music. Satan uses many tools to weaken and destroy the home and the family, and especially our young people. Today, as never before, the devil's thrust is directed at you, our precious youth.[42]

In General Conference, April 1969, he attacked rock music once again:

> Have you been listening to the music that many young folks are hearing today? Some of it is nerve-jamming in nature and much of it has been deliberately designed to promote revolution, dope, immorality, and a gap between parent and child. And some of this music has invaded our Church cultural halls.[43]

Again, he spoke of the devil's influence in popular music at a BYU Ten-Stake Fireside held May 7, 1972:

> Rock music, with its instant physical appeal, is an ideal door-crasher, for the devil knows that music has the power to ennoble or corrupt, to purify or pollute. He will not forget to use its subtle power against you. His sounds come from the dark world of drugs, immorality, obscenity, and anarchy. His sounds are flooding the earth. It is his day—a day that is to become as the days of Noah before the Second Coming, for the prophets have so predicted. The signs are clear. The signs are here in this blessed land. You cannot escape this mass media environment which is controlled by finan-cial censorship. Records, radio, television, movies, magazines—are monopolized by the money managers who are guided by one ethic, the words are *wealth* and *power*.[44]

His strongest denunciation of rock music, however, was given in General Conference on October 1, 1971:

> A letter from a concerned father about the evil effects of some popular music is one of many. I quote from this well-informed teacher of youth:
>
> "Music creates atmosphere Atmosphere creates environment. Environment influences behavior. What are the mechanics of this process?
>
> "*Rhythm* is the most physical element in music. It is the only element in music that can exist in bodily movement without the benefit of sound. A mind dulled by drugs or alcohol can still respond to the beat.
>
> "*Loudness* adds to muddling the mind. Sound magnified to the threshold of pain is of such physical violence as to block the higher processes of thought and reason.
>
> "*Repetition* to the extreme is another primitive rock device....
>
> "*Gyrations*, a twin to rock rhythm, are such that even clean hands and a pure heart cannot misinterpret their insinuations....
>
> "*Darkness* is another facet of the rock scene. It is a black mass that deadens the conscience in a mask of anonymity....
>
> "*Strobe lights* split the darkness in blinding shafts that reduce resistance like the lights of an interrogator's third degree or the swinging pendulum of the hypnotist who would control your behavior....

"The whole psychedelic design (this father continues) is a swinging door to drugs, sex, rebellion, and Godlessness. Combined with the screaming obscenities of the lyrics, this mesmerizing music has borne the fruit of filth. Leaders of the rock society readily proclaim their degeneracy....

The Spirit of the Lord blesses that which edifies and leads men to Christ. Would his Spirit bless with its presence these festering festivals of human degradation cured in LSD, marijuana, and Speed? Would He be pleased by the vulgar display of unashamed nudity and immorality? The speech of the rock festival is often obscene. Its music, crushing the sensibilities in a din of primitive idolatry, is in glorification of the physical to the debasement of the spirit. In the long panorama of man's history, these youthful rock music festivals are among Satan's greatest success. The legendary orgies of Greece and Rome cannot compare to the monumental obscenities found in these cesspools of drugs, immorality, rebellion, and pornophonic sound. The famed Woodstock festival was a gigantic manifestation of a sick nation. Yet the lurid movie and rock recordings of its unprecedented filth were big business in our own mountain home.

And now a music scholar points to "a new direction in the rock-drug culture (which is) hailed by many ministers and the music industry as a silver lining in the Top Ten charts. The growing resistance to the rock-drug scene is being diverted by this wholesome-appearing retreat from the new morality. But a review of religious rock materials unmasks an insidiously disguised anti-Christ. By reducing revealed religion to mythology, rock assumes the mantle of righteousness while rejecting the reality of sin. Without sin the new morality can continue in its Godless revel behind the pretense of religious robes. By reversing the roles of Jesus and Judas, one fast-selling album fits perfectly the warning of Isaiah (5:20): "Woe unto them that call evil good, and good evil; that put darkness for light, and light for darkness."

Little wonder that the leadership of the Church felt impelled to speak out against this sacrilegious, apostate deception by calling this wickedness to the attention of the members of the Church in a special item in the Church *Priesthood Bulletin* of August 1971.

Yes, we live in the best of times when the restored gospel of Jesus Christ brings hope to all the world. And the worst of times, for

Satan is raging. With relentless vigor he plunges in the harvest.

How can we thwart his designs? The MIA scriptural recitation for last year gives us a pattern to follow. The Thirteenth Article of Faith of the Church contains an important key: "If there is anything virtuous, lovely, or of good report or praiseworthy, we seek after these things."

But will we really seek? To seek requires effort.

The record bins that beckon our young people with their colorful and often off-color jackets bury many masterworks that are virtuous or lovely under a vast bulk of crass commercialism.

The magnetism of TV and radio is in the accessibility of their mediocrity. Lovely is not an adjective to describe most of their products. The inventors of these wonders were inspired by the Lord. But once their good works were introduced to the world, the powers of darkness began to employ them for our destruction. In each medium—the phonograph, motion pictures, radio, and television—the evolution of decline from the inventor's intentions can be easily traced.

Ezra Taft Benson also talked about music as a means of overcoming despair in General Conference of October 5, 1974. He said:

To help us from being overcome by the devil's designs of despair, discouragement, depression, and despondency, the Lord has provided at least a dozen ways which, if followed, will lift our spirits and send us on our way rejoicing.[45]

Among these ways of overcoming despair and depression, Elder Benson discussed repentance, prayer, work, maintaining good physical health, reading, priesthood blessings, fasting, friends, music, endurance, and setting goals. Under the subject of music, he said this:

Inspiring music may fill the soul with heavenly thoughts, move one to righteous action, or speak peace to the soul. When Saul was troubled with an evil spirit, David played for him with his harp and Saul was refreshed and the evil spirit departed (I Samuel 16:23). Elder Boyd K. Packer has wisely suggested memorizing some of the inspiring songs of Zion and then, when the mind is afflicted with temptations, to sing aloud, to keep before your mind the inspiring words and thus crowd out the evil thoughts. This could also be done to crowd out debilitating depressive thoughts.[46]

After a long, productive and brilliant career, both in and out of the Church, Ezra Taft Benson became President of the Council of the Twelve on December 30, 1973, when Spencer W. Kimball became the twelfth president of the Church. Apostle Benson was seventy-four.

Upon the death of President Spencer W. Kimball, Ezra Taft Benson became the thirteenth president of the Church. He was ordained by his brethren on November 10, 1985.

After becoming president of the Church, Ezra Taft Benson met with Ronald Reagan in the Oval office, in January 1986, to report on a $10 million contribution the Church was making to aid world hunger. At this meeting, President Benson presented to President Reagan a copy of the 1985 hymnbook from a limited edition, with a handsome leather binding, in royal blue with silver organ pipes on the cover.

Before his health began to fail, President Benson gave conference addresses, especially to the elderly of the Church, including those who are alone, the children of the Church, drawing from *I Am a Child of God, Teach Me to Walk in the Light, Let the Little Children Come,* and *Dare to do Right!,* to the mothers and fathers of the Church, the young men and the young women, and to the single adult sisters and single adult brethren.

During his nine years as the prophet, the Church saw unprecedented growth around the world. There was an increase in missionary work abroad and spirituality among the members, due, no doubt, to the increase in our *Book of Mormon* study. There was also increase in temple work.

Soon after becoming the President of the Church, the new Prophet said,

My heart has been filled with an overwhelming love and compassion for all members of the Church and our Heavenly Father's

children everywhere. I love all our Heavenly Father's children of
every color, creed, and political persuasion.[47]

He also loved the United States of America, the Book of
Mormon, and he loved good music.

President Benson appeared in public for the last time in
August, 1992, at the funeral of his companion of sixty-six
years. As members of his family learned that the end was near,
they visited him "singing hymns and favorite songs to him."[48]
On Memorial Day, May 30, 1994, the Prophet passed away at
his home in Salt Lake City. His mortal body was taken to a little cemetery in Whitney, Idaho, to rest along side of his
beloved Flora.

1.Ezra Taft Benson: *The Teaching of Ezra Taft Benson* (Salt Lake City: Bookcraft, 1988) p. 326.

2 Luke 2:52.

3 Spoken at the funeral services for President Benson, June 1, 1994.

4 Ibid. p. 25.

5 Leonard J. Arrington: *The President of the Church* (Salt Lake City: Deseret Book Co. 1986) p. 423.

6 Sheri L. Dew, p. 37.

7 Ibid., p. 38.

8 Young Mens Mutual Improvement Association.

9 Ibid., p. 43.

10 Ibid., p. 43.

11 Elaine Cannon: *Boy of the Land, Man of the Lord* (Salt Lake City Bookcraft, 1989) p. 69.

12 Sheri Dew: pp. 136-137.

13 Ibid., p. 150.

14 Ibid., p. 158.

15 Ibid., p. 174.

16 Ezra Taft Benson: *A Labor of Love, the 1946 European Mission of Ezra Taft Benson* (Salt Lake City: Deseret Book Co., 1989) pp. 6-7.

17 Ibid., p. 248.

18 Frederick W. Babbel: *On Wings of Faith* (Salt Lake City, Bookcraft, 1972) p. 24.

19 David Ewen: *The Complete Book of Classical Music* (Englewood Cliffs, N. J.: Prentice-Hall, Inc. 1965) p. 142.

20 Ezra Taft Benson: *A Labor of Love*, p. 249.

21 Babel: p. 34.

22 Ibid., p. 36.

23 Ibid., p. 54.

24 Darwin Wolford, ed., "Selections from the Writing of Alexander Schreiner" in *Music and the Gospel*, Springville, Utah, 1991, pp. 110-111.

25 Babel, p. 55.

26 Ibid., p. 20.

27 Ezra Taft Benson: *A Labor of Love*, p. 184.

28 Babbel: pp. 75-76.

29 Ibid., p. 116.

30 Ibid.

31 Ibid., p. 167.

32 Leonard J. Arrington: *The Presidents of the Church*, p. 434.

33 Ibid., pp. 436-437.

34 Sheri Dew: p. 283.

35 Ibid., p. 295.
36 Ibid., p. 297-298.
37 Ibid..
38 Ibid., pp. 301-302.
39 Arrington: *The Presidents of the Church*, p. 438.
40 Sheri L. Dew: p. 339.
41 Ibid., pp. 342-344.
42 *The Teachings of Ezra Taft Benson*, p. 322; *Conference Report*, October 1982.
43 Ibid., p. 325.
44 Ibid., p. 326.
45 *General Conference Report*, April 5, 1986, p. 91.
46 Ibid., p. 93.
47 *Conference Report*, April 1, 1989, pp. 10-105.
48 *Ensign*, January 1986, back cover.

HOWARD W. HUNTER

M. Withers '94

HOWARD W. HUNTER
(1907-1995)

*"Pablo Casals, the great cellist, spent the
morning on the day he died—at the age of
ninety-five—practicing scales on his cello.
Giving consistent effort in the little things
in day-to-day life leads to true greatness."*[1]

Howard W. Hunter, President of the Quorum of the
Twelve, stood at the pulpit to address a nineteen-stake fireside
at Brigham Young University. As he was about to begin, an
angry voice screamed, "Stop right there!" Carrying what he
claimed to be a bomb, the assailant rushed to the stage and
shoved a written statement at President Hunter, and demanded
that he read it aloud. Maintaining his composure, Elder Hunter
stood firmly at the podium and ignored the demand of the man
who wildly flaunted what he claimed to be a gun in one hand
and a bomb in the other.

Spontaneously, the audience of nearly twenty thousand
began singing "We Thank Thee, O God for a Prophet," and
then "I Am a Child of God." The singing startled the would-
be-attacker, permitting the security guards to subdue him and
remove him from the auditorium.

Then, as if nothing had happened, President Howard W.
Hunter began his prepared address: "Life has a fair number of
challenges in it." Pausing slightly, he looked up at the vast congregation and added, "As demonstrated."

The oldest of two children, Howard William Hunter was
born in Boise, Idaho. His mother, Nellie Rasmussen, a faithful
Latter-day Saint, nevertheless had married John William
Hunter—a good man who was not a member of the Church.

Refusing to allow Howard and his younger sister, Dorothy, to be baptized at eight, Will Hunter wanted his children to be old enough to make that decision on their own. At twelve, Howard still was not a baptized member, even though he attended regularly and participated in all of the activities for the youth. Envious of his friends who now were passing the sacrament, Howard continued to beg for his father's permission. Howard and his younger sister, Dorothy, finally received permission to be baptized—Howard had turned twelve and Dorothy was ten.

Howard was soon ordained a deacon and given the Aaronic Priesthood.

As a deacon, he could perform other services in the small ward besides pull the curtain for Sunday School. "Occasionally I had the assignment to pump the bellows for the organist by putting my weight to the pump handle at the end of the organ," [Howard] remembers.

"The job I didn't like was to cut kindling on cold mornings and light the fire in the stove in the room behind the choir loft."[2]

Scouting in America had been in existence about ten years when Howard became a deacon and entered the scouting program. There were no Eagle Scouts in Idaho when Howard and his friend, Edwin Phipps, began earning the required merit badges. Edwin became the first scout in Idaho to receive the Eagle Award. Howard completed the requirements two months later, and became Idaho's second Eagle Scout.

The Boise First Ward was divided to make two wards when Howard was fifteen and a newly ordained Teacher. The Boise Second Ward, of which the Hunters were members, began meeting in the Jewish Synagogue.

Soon after this, the Saints in Boise met to discuss a proposal to build a tabernacle, which would serve as a center for both the stake and the new ward. When an appeal for pledges was made, Howard raised his hand and made the *first one*—twenty-five dollars, a substantial sum for that time, especially for a teenager. "I worked and saved until I was able to pay my commitment in full," he remembers.[3]

During high school, Howard developed a strong, active interest in music. "When name bands came to Boise, Dorothy's friends wished Howard would take them to the dances, but more often than not he would go alone to listen to the music."[4]

During his second year in high school, Howard, entered a sales contest sponsored by Sampson Music Company.

> Purchasers of merchandise in the store received one point for every dollar spent and could designate which contest entrant would receive the points. Howard encouraged all of his friends and acquaintances to shop at Sampson's, and the points credited to him gave him the second-place prize, a marimba. He soon taught himself to play it well enough to perform at school, church, and other programs, and then as part of a dance orchestra.
>
> "Most orchestras were not large enough to have a marimba player unless he doubled on other instruments," Howard explained, "so I commenced to play drums as well. As I played more and more on a professional basis, I started to play saxophone and clarinet and later added the trumpet." He also played the piano and the violin, which he had studied for about a year each while in elementary school.[5]

After school and on Saturdays, Howard worked at a variety of jobs. He particularly enjoyed working in an art store, making picture frames, cutting mats and glass. But Howard discovered he was color blind. Not being able to distinguish between shade of certain colors, he had to select mat and frame colors strictly mechanically. The owners of the store were both professional artists and taught Howard his framing techniques as well as an appreciation of fine art that he would enjoy the rest of his life.

Howard's musical talents—and especially his versatility on a number of instruments—came to be recognized in Boise and in the surrounding communities. Several orchestras asked him to join them, playing one instrument or another. Finally, in 1924—*at seventeen*—Howard organized his own dance orchestra, which he named Howard's Croonaders. They began playing rather late in the year. As their reputation spread, so did the frequency of their engagements.

That November and December the group played for six dances, and the next year they had fifty-three dance engagements at public halls and restaurants, private parties and wedding receptions, schools and churches, civic clubs and fraternities.⁶

Traveling with the group of musicians—especially late at night was not without its dangers. Returning from an engagement in Idaho City, a former mining town in the mountains about forty miles north of Boise, near disaster took place.

> The open touring car in which Howard was a passenger was going up a steep hill on a narrow, winding road when the driver suddenly had to swerve to avoid colliding with an approaching car. The driver managed to jump out, but Howard was thrown out on the last roll-over. The car crashed down on him and he was crushed into the sand, but because one corner of the vehicle rested on a large rock, he had no broken bones.
>
> The other musicians, following in another car, raced down the hill and managed to raise the roadster so that Howard could crawl out. Dazed, he got to his feet, staggered about fifty feet into the bushes, and fell, unconscious, to the ground. The group carried him up the hill to the road and were relieved when he regained consciousness and was able to stand up. The only thing broken was his bass drum, which had been tied to the running board of the roadster; it was, he said, "smashed beyond recognition."⁷

One week after the accident, Howard was back on his feet and the orchestra played another dance.

After graduating from Boise High in June, 1926, he worked as assistant to the soda-fountain manager at a drug store, still performing with the Croonaders evenings and weekends. Their reputation earned them a contract for a two-month cruise on the S. S. President Jackson.

> The Group was hired to play classical music at dinner, background music for movies shown on board the ship, and music for dinner and ballroom dancing....
>
> Howard selected four musicians to go with him: a piano player, a tenor saxophone and clarinet player, a trumpet player and a violin and banjo player, each of whom could also play most of the other

instruments. Howard played alto and soprano saxophone, clarinet, trumpet, and drums. He also pulled together a library of music, and they began rehearsing.[8]

The *President Jackson* set sail from Seattle on January 5th.

> It was mid-winter on the north Pacific, and that night a major storm struck. By morning the ship was tossing wildly amid high waves. "Nearly every person on board is seasick," Howard reported. "It was said that the captain is seasick for the first time in twenty-five years."[9]

The harsh weather continued until the ship had crossed the International Dateline. On January 13th, the ship had entered the eastern hemisphere, and that evening

> Hunter's Croonaders played their first gala party, the Meridian Costume Ball and dinner, with passengers dressed in costumes representing mythical and real sea creatures. From then on, there was a full schedule of programs, parties, movies, and other activities.[10]

The ship docked at Tokyo, Yokohama and Kobe in Japan, Shanghai in China, Hong Kong, and Manila in the Philippines, allowing the passengers to visit these famous cities and savor their exotic beauty. Between ports, there was a full schedule of playing.

Howard and his fellow musicians took every opportunity to enjoy the sights, sample the food, and mingle with the people. Howard made friends easily. In Manila, he visited a music store, where he and his companion

> met a man from Boise, who took them to lunch and sight-seeing. Howard began to see how small the world really is when he learned that their new friend was the man who had delivered the player piano on Dorothy's eighth birthday.[11]

Before leaving Manila, Howard

> ran into two friends from Boise who were stationed at the U. S. airbase...They also visited the radio station known as the Voice of

> Manila, on the roof of the Manila Hotel, where they played a few numbers and sent messages home by radio.[12]

After visiting the Philippines, the *President Jackson* headed back, visiting once again the port cities they had visited earlier. But not all of the performances of Hunter's Croonaders were aboard ship.

> At Kobe, the Croonaders played an engagement in the dining room of the Oriental Hotel, and at Yokohama they played for a dinner dance at the Tent Hotel.[13]

The political situation in China was ominous, with signs that a civil war was about to break out. Many American residents there were leaving as the opportunity presented itself. The ship

> had taken on scores of new passengers in the Orient, mostly American missionaries from various Christian churches who were being evacuated from China because of the war. "Not many of them participate in the dancing and in the activities," Howard wrote, "so there is a more subdued crowd on this return trip. The missionaries comprised nearly 70 percent of the passenger list. While they didn't participate in many social activities, they did guarantee a large attendance at the religious services. And when the orchestra played classical music at dinner, they stayed late and listened and "were generous with their applause."[14]

Returning home, Howard learned that during his absence his father had been baptized. On the first Sunday at home, Howard and his father attended priesthood meeting together for the first time.

> Within a few days, the Croonaders played for a radio broadcast, a popular restaurant in downtown Boise, and for dances as far away as Ontario, Oregon. Before long, Howard got a job at Falk's Department Store, "selling shoes all day, [while] playing dinner music five evenings a week," leaving him little free time. Commenting on the old expression, "All work and no play makes Jack a dull boy," Howard wrote in his journal, "*I am not dull, because I do both.*"[15]

But to reduce stress in his life,

> Howard transferred to Falk's music department where he super-
> vised outside sales. His responsibilities included demonstrating and
> repairing radios, which were quickly becoming a favorite source of
> family entertainment, and selling other instruments.[16]

Bill Salisbury—who had played piano with the Croonaders
when they traveled to the Orient—moved to Southern
California. Writing to Howard, he invited him to come for a
visit. Accepting the offer, Howard hitch hiked all the way to
Upland—near Los Angeles—where Bill lived. Howard enjoyed
the excitement of the great California metropolis, and since he
had no particular obligations in Idaho, he decided to stay.
Before long, he was working at a variety of odd jobs, including
that of selling shoes and sorting lemons for the Sunkist pack-
ing plant. Due to his color blindness, the *only* job in which
Howard was not successful was sorting lemons, which
required the ability to distinguish shades of yellow and green
to determine their ripeness.

Perhaps as a compensation for his color-blindness,
Howard was born with *perfect pitch*[17]—the special gift to
"hear" exact pitches found on a page of printed music, and
the ability to sing accurately any pitch on demand.

Howard applied for a job at the Bank of Italy—later becoming part of Bank of America—and was hired on the spot. He
began taking banking classes at night to improve his opportunities for advancement. Once he had settled into a routine, he
wrote to his parents and asked them to ship his musical instruments to California.

> After weighing several offers, he signed on as a drummer for a
> dance band that also had a contract to perform on radio.
> Occasionally he played with other groups as well.[18]

Howard made friends with a returned missionary, Ned
Redding, who was also enrolled in the same banking class

Howard was taking. Howard discovered that he and Ned shared a love for the Gospel as well as a love for music. The two of them joined a popular Church-sponsored choral group—the Los Angeles Thrift Chorus.

> Singers came from wards and stakes all over Los Angeles to rehearse on Thursday evening at the Adams Ward. For many it was both a social and a musical experience. The year before Howard moved to California, the chorus had sung at the Arizona Temple dedication in Mesa. He and Ned joined the group after their banking class ended in June and were preparing for the chorus's summer appearance at the Hollywood Bowl.[19]

In the fall of 1928, Howard's parents sold their home in Boise—and with Howard's sister, Dorothy—moved to Los Angeles. Howard moved into the same apartment, and all four members of the Hunter family became members of the Adams Ward.

Because Howard had worked days, taken night classes and played for dances on his free nights and on weekends, he had not held a church position. Though he had a testimony of the Gospel, it was in Sunday School class taught by Brother Peter A. Clayton that his first real awakening to the beauties of the Gospel principles began to unfold. A lesson on patriarchal blessings kindled a desire in him to have such a blessing. In the blessing given to him soon afterward, the kindly patriarch stated:

> Howard was one "whom the Lord foreknew," and that he had shown "strong leadership among the hosts of heaven" and had been ordained "to perform an important work in mortality in bringing to pass [the Lord's] purposes with relation to His chosen people...." He was promised that if he remained faithful, he would be "a master of worldly skill and a teacher of worldly wisdom as well as a priest of the most high God," and he would use his talents in serving the Church, and would *sit in its councils*.[20]

Howard had noticed Claire Jeffs at the Thrift Chorus rehearsals. Then he became better acquainted with her when she attended a dance sponsored by the Wilshire Ward as Ned Redding's date. For a while they were together as part of larger groups, then later on, she accompanied Howard on some of his dance jobs. Gradually their relationship became more serious, and their conversations turned to the subject of marriage.

After a three-year courtship, Howard and Claire Jeffs were married in the Salt Lake Temple. Prior to their wedding, however, Howard made another major decision. For several years he had played with orchestras at dances and parties in public ballrooms, and on radio and the stage. "It was glamorous in some respects," he reflected, "and I made good money, but the association with many of the musicians was not enjoyable because of their drinking and moral standards." Such associations were not compatible with the lifestyle he envisioned with a wife and family, so he decided to give up professional music.

> On June 6, 1931, four days before their wedding, Howard played his last engagement at the Virginia Ballroom In Huntington Park. After he got home that night, he packed up his saxophones and clarinets, and his music and put them away. He had already sold his drums and marimba and packed up his trumpet and violin.
>
> "Since that night," he said, "I have never touched my musical instruments except on a few occasions, when the children were home, [and] we sang Christmas carols and I accompanied on the clarinet. Although this left a void of something I had enjoyed, the decision had never been regretted."[21]

With the coming of the depression, Howard's bank was closed. Out of a work, he was back to "odd jobs," this time selling soap and painting highway bridges. Later on, he accepted a position with the title department of the Los Angeles County Flood Control District. Soon thereafter, he began attending night classes that would lead toward a law degree. Though he worked full-time and attended law school at night, while fulfilling a variety of church assignments, Howard graduated in 1939 from Southwestern University, the third in his class.

During his law school years, Howard and Claire became the parents of three sons—William Howard, Jr., John and Richard. Then tragedy struck: Billy, the first child, suffered from an intestinal disorder, which—at seven months—claimed his life.

Howard passed the state bar examination, and established a successful law practice, earning the respect of the legal community of southern California.Within a year of completing law school and passing the state bar, Howard W. Hunter—at thirty-two—became the first bishop of the newly-created El Sereno Ward. Bishop Hunter was young, vigorous and *creative* in the way he fulfilled his stewardship. The new ward met in a rented building next door to a drug store with a soda fountain. The Aaronic Priesthood were accustomed to leaving sacrament meeting for a malted milk after discharging their duties at the sacrament table.

Seeing the quiet exodus of the boys from the chapel, and learning the reason for their leaving, Bishop Hunter

> fumed for a few moments, then left the stand and marched out the door and over to the drugstore. "Brethren," he announced, "when you have finished your malts, we will continue the meeting."
>
> Those boys who had already been served hurriedly gulped down their malts, while the others, still waiting to be served, plunked down their money and followed their bishop back next door. Without saying a word about the incident, he proceeded to announce the rest of the sacrament meeting.[22]

Thus ended the problem.

One of priests in his ward had difficulty getting out of bed Sunday mornings to attend priesthood meeting. After trying other approaches one Sunday,

> [Bishop Hunter] took the entire priests quorum to the home...The young man was still in bed, and so they held priesthood meeting in his bedroom.[23]

Reportedly, the young man did not sleep in on Sunday mornings after that.

Four-year-old Richard enjoyed visiting his grandparents, Will and Nellie Hunter, who managed some apartments. Richard became friends with a little girl—just a few months older than he—who, with her mother, lived in one of the apartments. His friend, Margaret O'Brien, was a famous child actress.

> At the time the Metro-Goldwyn-Mayer studio was casting parts for a movie starring Margaret O'Brien. The director had tested several boys for a role as one of her playmates but had not yet found one who suited him. One day when the children were playing together, Margaret's mother taught Richard some lines from the script and had him act out the part.
>
> She liked what she saw and called the director, who agreed to test him.
>
> Nellie took Richard to the studio, where he worked for two days with the cast and crew. When MGM agents told Nellie they wanted to talk with Richard's parents about a possible movie contract, she contacted Howard and Claire. After discussing the matter at length, they decided they did not want their son to be in the movies.
>
> "Margaret's mother was upset and my mother thought we were not very appreciative after all the work and effort," Howard remembered, adding, "I had been around enough people of the motion picture industry to cause me to dislike the environment, so Richard's movie life was short lived."[24-25]

Though the Hunters went to their Grandmother Jeffs for Thanksgiving,

> On Christmas Eve they stayed home and sang carols, with Howard accompanying them on the piano or his clarinet. Then he would open the Bible and read the second chapter of Luke. Christmas Day they went to Grandmother and Grandfather Hunter's home for turkey dinner and to exchange gifts with Dorothy's family."[26]

In 1950 there were ten stakes in Metropolitan Los Angeles. The Pasadena Stake, with over nine thousand members, was divided. Howard W. Hunter at forty-three was called to be the

President of the Pasadena Stake. The years he served as stake president were a period of great growth for the Church, with attendant building projects and fund raising. The weight of his responsibilities increased in 1952 when he was called to serve as chairman of the regional council of stake presidents.

On November 14, 1952—Howard's forty-sixth birthday—Howard and Claire were in Mesa, Arizona, with other members of the Pasadena Stake participating in a temple excursion. In a meeting prior to the session, Howard spoke to the members of his stake assembled in the chapel. He described what happened during his address:

> While I was speaking to the congregation, my father and mother came into the chapel dressed in white. I had no idea my father was prepared for his temple blessings, although Mother had been anxious about it for some time. I was so overcome with emotion that I was unable to continue to speak...This birthday I have never forgotten because on that day they were endowed and I had the privilege of witnessing their sealing, following which I was sealed to them.[27]

As chairman of the regional council of the stake presidents, Howard was the chairman of the first MIA conference held outside of Salt Lake City. Leaders and youth from sixteen stakes participated in the event that was patterned after the annual all-Church June conferences.

> Many general board members came to Los Angeles to conduct departmental sessions for the leader, and thousands of young people performed in cultural events. These included a music festival at the Hollywood Bowl featuring a 1452-voice choir and a 75-piece symphony orchestra, with over 17,000 persons in the audience; a dance festival in the stadium of the East Los Angeles Junior College; and a closing session that filled the Hollywood Bowl for an address by President David O. McKay.[28]

One of the great milestones in the history of the Church in southern California was the dedication of the Los Angeles Temple. At the dedicatory sessions held each day between

Sunday, March 11, through Wednesday, March 14, 1965, music was provided by the Mormon Choir of Southern California. As regional chairman, Howard W. Hunter was supervisor for the music for the services. Claire, who had attended the Mesa Temple dedication in 1927 as a member of the Los Angeles Thrift Chorus, now "had the privilege of singing at a temple dedication in...[her] own area."[29]

Claire went to Utah one week before general conference in October to assist with their first grandchild. Howard flew into Salt Lake City Friday morning, October 9, arriving at the Tabernacle when the first session was half over. After the session he was told that President McKay wanted to see him in his office as soon as possible.

Arriving at the office of the President of the Church, Howard was greeted by President McKay who said to him:

> "Sit down, President Hunter, I want to talk to you. The Lord has spoken. You are called to be one of His special witnesses, and tomorrow you will be sustained as a member of the Council of the Twelve."
>
> Tears came to my eyes and I could not speak. I have never felt so completely humbled as when I sat in the presence of this great, sweet, kindly man—the Prophet of the Lord.[30]

At the Saturday morning session, the name of Howard W. Hunter was presented for the sustaining vote of the Church to become the newest apostle. On Thursday morning, October 15, President McKay gave Howard the traditional apostolic charge then ordained him an apostle and set him apart as a member of the Council of the Twelve Apostles. He was the seventy-fourth man to be ordained to this high calling in this dispensation.

Reflecting his love for the hymns of Zion and the important gospel messages taught in them, Elder Hunter often turned to the hymnbook for inspiration of his addresses. At the opening session of general conference, September 30, 1978, Howard W.

Hunter spoke on the meaning of "true religion," and drew inspiration from the hymn "A Poor Wayfaring Man of Grief":

> It was during the last two hours of [Joseph Smith's] life, confined behind bars in Carthage, that his close friend, President John Taylor, sang a song to cheer him on that melancholy occasion. The song had a number of verses commencing with helping the unfortunate and sharing a crust with one perishing for want of bread. These are some of the words:

> > A poor wayfaring man of grief
> > Had often crossed me on my way,
> > Who sued so humbly for relief
> > That I could never answer, Nay.

> > I had not power to ask his name;
> > Whither he went or whence he came;
> > Yet there was something in his eye
> > That won my love, I knew not why.

> > Once, when my scanty meal was spread,
> > He entered—not a word he spake.
> > Just perishing for want of bread;
> > I gave him all; he blessed it, brake.

> > And ate, but gave me part again;
> > Mine was an angel's portion then,
> > For while I fed with eager haste,
> > The crust was manna to my taste.

> The verses continue to tell of a drink given to quench the thirst of a sufferer, clothing and rest for the naked and weary, caring for the injured and wounded, sharing the condemnation of a prisoner. Then the last verses recognize the appearance of the Master:

> > Then in a moment to my view,
> > The stranger started from disguise:
> > The tokens in his hands I knew,
> > The Savior stood before mine eyes.

> > He spake—and my poor name he named—
> > "Of me thou hast not been asham'd;

These deeds shall thy memorial be;
Fear not thou didst them unto me."

Poor, indeed, and destitute is the man who disclaims being religious because he does not have sufficient love for his fellowmen to be concerned and have compassion. The Lord will say: "Inasmuch as ye did it not unto one of the least of these, ye did it not to me.

"And these shall go away into everlasting punishment: but the righteous into life eternal" (Matt. 25: 45-46).[31]

Howard W. Hunter spoke of faith, and of the troubled waters in our lives, in the morning session of General Conference, October 6, 1984:

Let me recall for you the story of Mary Ann Baker. Her beloved and only brother suffered from the same respiratory disease that had taken their parents' lives, and he left their home in Chicago to find a warmer climate in the southern part of the United States.

For a time he seemed to be improving, but then a sudden turn in his health came and he died almost immediately. Mary Ann and her sister were heartbroken. It only added to their deep grief that neither their own health nor their personal finances allowed them to claim their brother's body or to finance its return to Chicago for burial.

The Baker family had been raised as faithful Christians, but Mary's trust in a loving God broke under the strain of her brother's death and her own diminished circumstances. "God does not care for me or mine," said Mary Ann. "This particular manifestation of what they call 'divine providence' is unworthy of a God of love." Does that sound at all familiar?

"I have always tried to believe in Christ and give the Master a consecrated life," she said, "but this is more than I can bear. What have I done to deserve this? What have I left undone that God should wreak His vengeance upon me in this way?" (Ernest K. Emurian, Living Stories of Famous Hymns [Boston: W. A. Widdle Co., 1955] pp. 83-85)

I suppose we have all had occasion, individually or collectively, to cry out on some stormy sea, "Master, carest thou not that we perish?" And so cried Mary Ann Baker.

But as the days and the weeks went by, the God of life and love began to calm the winds and the waves of what this sweet young woman called her unsanctified heart." Her faith not only returned but it flourished, and like Job of old, she learned new things, things "too wonderful to have known before her despair. On the Sea of Galilee, the stirring of the disciples' faith was ultimately more important than the stilling of the sea, and so it was with her.

Later, as something of a personal testimonial and caring very much for the faith of others who would be tried by personal despair, she wrote the words of the hymn we have all sung, "Master, the Tempest Is Raging." May I share it with you?

> Master, the tempest is raging!
> The billows are tossing high!
> The sky is o'ershadowed with blackness.
> No shelter or help is nigh.
>
> Carest thou not that we perish?
> How canst thou lie asleep
> When each moment so madly is threatening
> A grave in the angry deep?
>
> Master, with anguish of spirit
> I bow in my grief today.
> The depths of my sad heart are troubled.
> Oh, waken and save, I pray!
>
> Torrents of sin and of anguish
> Sweep o'er my sinking soul,
> And I perish! I perish! dear Master.
> Oh, waked and save, I pray!

Then this beautiful, moving refrain:

> The winds and the waves shall obey my will;
> Peace, be still! Peace be still!
> Whether the wrath of the storm-tossed sea
> Or demons or men or whatever it be,
> No waters can swallow the ship where lies
> The Master of ocean and earth and skies.
>
> They all shall sweetly obey my will:
> Peace, be still! Peace, be still!
> They all shall sweetly obey my will:
> Peace, peace, be still!

Too often, I fear, both in the living of life and in singing of this hymn, we fail to emphasize the sweet peace of this concluding verse:

> *Master, the terror is over.*
> *The elements sweetly rest.*
> *Earth's sun in the calm lake is mirrored,*
> *And heaven's within my breast.*
>
> *Linger, Oh blessed Redeemer!*
> *Leave me alone no more,*
> *And with joy I shall make the blest harbor*
> *And rest on the blissful shore.*

Whether the wrath of the storm-tossed sea or demons or men or whatever it be, no waters can swallow the ship where lies the Master of ocean and earth and skies. They all shall sweetly obey his will. Peace, be still![32]

In a priesthood leadership meeting held April 4, 1986 in connection with general conference, Howard W. Hunter spoke eloquently to the topic "Make Us Thy True Undershepherds." In part, he said:

What should we do to help those who have lost their way in the wilderness?

Because of what the Master said about leaving the ninety-nine and going into the wilderness to seek the one that is lost, and because of the invitation of the First Presidency to those who have ceased activity or have been critical to "come back," we invite you to become involved in saving souls. Reach out to the less active and realize the joy that will come to you and those you help if you and they will take part in extending invitations to come back and feast at the table of the Lord.

The Lord, our Good Shepherd, expects us to be his Undershepherds and recover those who are struggling or are lost. We can't tell you how to do it, but as you become involved and seek inspiration success will result from efforts in your areas, regions, stakes, and wards. Some stakes have responded to previous pleadings and have had remarkable success.

To conclude his deep, heart-felt petition to the brethren President Hunter turns to the hymn, "Dear to the Heart of the Shepherd."

> The words of a familiar hymn contain the Savior's appeal to us:
>
> > *Hark! he is earnestly calling,*
> > *Tenderly pleading today:*
> > *"Will you not seek for my lost ones,*
> > *Off from my shelter astray?*
>
> And the hymn, sung often, indicates what our response should be:
>
> > *Make us thy true undershepherds:*
> > *Give us a love that is deep.*
> > *Send us out into the Deseret,*
> > *Seeking thy wandering sheep.*
>
> If we do this, eternal blessings will come to us.[33]

Unable to stand at the pulpit, President Howard W. Hunter spoke in the Sunday session of conference, April, 1987, about adversity.

> Forgive me if I remain seated while I present these few remarks. It is not by choice that I speak from a wheelchair. I notice that the rest of you seem to enjoy conference sitting down, so I will follow your example.
>
> With reference to both standing and sitting, I have observed that life—every life—has a full share of ups and down. Indeed, we see many joys and sorrows in the world, many changed plans and new directions, many blessings that do not always look or feel like blessings, and much that humbles and improves our patience and our faith. We have all had those experiences form time to time, and I suppose we always will.

And to conclude his remarks, President Hunter turned to the seventh verse of "How Firm a Foundation."

> If you have troubles at home with children who stray, if you suffer financial reverses and emotional strain that threaten your homes

and your happiness, if you must face the loss of life or health, may peace be unto your souls. We will not be tempted beyond our ability to withstand. Our detours and disappointments are the straight and narrow path to Him, as we sing in one of our favorite hymns:

> *When through fiery trials thy pathway shall lie,*
> *My grace, all sufficient, shall be they supply.*
> *The flame shall not hurt thee; I only design*
> *Thy dross to consume and thy gold to refine.*[34]

President Hunter turned to the popular hymn, "Lord, I would Follow Thee," for the text of his conference address, April 5, 1992.

In an important message to the Latter-day Saints in Nauvoo just one year before his tragic and untimely martyrdom, the Prophet Joseph Smith said:

"If we would secure and cultivate the love of others, we must love others, even our enemies as well as friends...Christians should cease wrangling and contending with each other, and cultivate the principles of union and friendship in their midst" (History of the Church, 5: 498-99.)

That is magnificent counsel today, even as it was 150 years ago. The world in which we live, whether close to home or far away, needs the gospel of Jesus Christ. It provides the only way the world will ever know peace. We need to be kinder with one another, more gentle and forgiving. We need to be slower to anger and more prompt to help. We need to extend the hand of friendship and resist the hand of retribution. In short, we need to love one another with the pure love of Christ, and genuine charity and compassion and, if necessary, share suffering, for that is the way God loves us.

In our worship services, we often sing a lovely hymn with text written by Susan Evans McCloud. May I recall a few lines of that hymn for you?

> *Savior, may I learn to love thee,*
> *Walk the path that thou hast shown,*
> *Pause to help and lift another,*
> *Finding strength beyond my own...*

Who am I to judge another
When I walk imperfectly?
In the quiet heart is hidden
Sorrow that the eye can't see...

I would be my brother's keeper;
I would learn the healer's art.
To the wounded and the weary
I would show a gentle heart.
I would be my brother's keeper—
Lord, I would follow thee.

We need to walk more resolutely and more charitably the path that Jesus has shown. We need to pause to help and lift another," and surely we will find "strength beyond [our] own." If we would do more to learn "the healer's art," there would be untold chances to use it, to touch the "wounded and the weary" and show to all "a gentle[r] heart." Yes, Lord, we should follow thee.[35]

If there is one underlying theme to the sermons and writings of Howard W. Hunter, it is to center our lives around the Lord Jesus Christ. His sermon given on the Sunday morning session of General Conference, April 4, 1993, is an elaboration of one of his favorite hymns, "Jesus, the Very Thought of Thee":

Jesus, the very thought of thee
With sweetness fills my breast;
But sweeter far thy face to see
And in thy presence rest.

Nor voice can sing, nor heart can frame,
Nor can the mem'ry find
A sweeter sound than thy blest name,
O Savior of mankind!

O hope of ev'ry contrite heart,
O joy of all the meek,
To those who fall, how kind thou art!
How good to those who seek!

> Jesus, our only joy be thou,
> As thou our prize wilt be;
> Jesus, be thou our glory now,
> And thru eternity.

The First Presidency Preface to the Church's most recent hymnbook, published in 1985, states:

> *We hope leaders, teachers, and members who are called upon to speak will turn often to the hymnbook to find sermons presented powerfully and beautifully in verse.*

President Howard W. Hunter did this repeatedly in his addresses to the members of the Church. This powerful address given April 4, 1993—Palm Sunday—is the perfect example. Those who teach classes or speak in sacrament meeting could follow President Hunter's example.

The First Presidency, later in their preface to the hymnbook, indicates their desire to see the hymnbook *"take a prominent place among the scriptures and other religious books in our homes."* Howard W. Hunter drew inspiration from the hymnbook as well as the scriptures, and provides an example for all of the members of the Church.

Howard W. Hunter did not talk about himself, nor did he draw from personal experience in his writings on sermons. But occasionally his sermons revealed his appreciation for music and his understanding of the dedication of an accomplished musician. Speaking to the student body at Brigham Young University, February 10, 1987, he drew an important lesson from the life of the celebrated Pablo Cabals, one of the greatest musicians of the twentieth century:

> Pablo Casals, the great cellist, spent the morning of the day he died—at the age of ninety-five—practicing scales on his cello. Giving consistent effort in the little things in day-to-day life leads to true greatness. Specifically, it is the thousands of little deeds and acts of service and sacrifice that constitute the giving, or losing, of one's life for others and for the Lord[36]

Similarly Howard W. Hunter taught that to seek and find God, one must pay some price paid by an accomplished musician, or a scholar or scientist who succeeds.

> It is the general rule that we do not get things of value unless we are willing to pay a price. The scholar does not become learned unless he puts forth the work and effort to succeed. If he is not willing to do so, can he say there is no such thing as scholarship? Musicians, mathematicians, scientists, athletes, and skilled people in many fields spend years in study, practice, and hard work to acquire their ability. Can others who are not willing to make the effort say there are no such things as music, mathematics, science, or athletics? It is just as foolish for man to say there is no God simply because he has not had to inclination to seek him.[37]

From the remarkable life of Howard W. Hunter we see a vivid lesson in commitment, when—at fifteen—he pledged twenty-five dollars to the ward building fund. Repeatedly, we see exemplified creativity and ingenuity, such as when he set out to "win" a marimba, or sold soap door-to-door during the depression. Or, when as a bishop he "reformed" or reactivated members of Aaronic Priesthood under his stewardship. We see energy and ambition in learning ten musical instruments, or working days as a banker, while attending law school at night and playing for dances on the weekend.

In Howard W. Hunter we saw the rare combination of meekness and strength, as well as total dedication to the Lord Jesus Christ and the principles of His Gospel.

From June 5, 1994, when he was ordained and set apart as the fourteenth president of the Church, Howard W. Hunter served as the Lord's spokesman on earth for a mere eight months and twenty four days, the shortest tenure of any prophet of this dispensation. President Hunter, however, traveled widely throughout the world conducting the business of the Church and bearing witness of the Savior.

Three weeks after his ordination to the holy calling of prophet, he accompanied Gordon B. Hinckley and M. Russell

Ballard to Carthage, Illinois to commemorate the sesquicenten-
nial of the assassination of Joseph and Hyrum Smith. In
August,President Hunter attended meetings in Lausanne and
Geneva, Switzerland, as well the temple at Bern. In September,
he attended a regional conference in Tuscon, Arizona. Beween
October 9th and 11th, he dedicated the Orlando, Florida Temple
in twelve sessions. Later, in October, he returned to the
Pasadena California Stake, over which he once presided. In
November, President Hunter traveled to Hawaii to officially
install a new president of the Brigham Young University-Hawaii
campus. In December, he spoke at the First Presidency's annual
Christmas Fireside heard throughout the world via sattelite.
Then after the first of the new year, beginning January 8th, he
presided over six dedicatory sessions of the Bountiful Temple.

After the dedication of the Bountiful Temple, the Prophet
checked into the hospital for "exhaustion." On January 18,
1995 the Church issued a statement that quoted President
Hunter's attending physician, Dr. William F. Reilly: "President
Hunter's condition is a serious one. He has cancer of the
prostate gland, metastic [spread] to the bone, for which he is
currently being treated." The cancer, first diagnosed in 1980,
had now returned.

Unable to take adequate medication for pain because of
another condition, the ailing prophet endured the intense pain
quietly. On Friday morning, March 3—ever gracious—
President Hunter said to those attending to him, "Thank you."
And he was gone.

President Hunter's ministry—like that of the Savior—was
brief, but it was long enough to articulate the Savior's message
to His people:

> We are at a time in the history of the world and the growth of
> the Church when we must think more of holy things and act more
> like the Savior would expect his disciples to act. We should at every
> opportunity ask ourselves, "What would Jesus do?" and then act
> more courageously upon the answer.[38]

Funeral services for Howard William Hunter were held March 8, 1995 in the tabernacle on Temple Square. All of the details—including the music, the talks, and the prayers—had been carefully planned by the Prophet in the weeks before his death. Since Temple Square organist Bonnie Goodliffe had been the organist for the Solemn Assembly at which Howard W. Hunter first presided as the fourteenth president of the Church, the Prophet planned to have the other Temple Square organist, Linda Margetts, play the prelude and postlude at his funeral. President Hunter prepared a list of favorite hymns for Sister Margetts to play.

These hymns, which Sister Margetts played artistically and sensitively, painted a musical portrait of the late prophet. "The Spirit of God Like a Fire is Burning" reflected his abiding love for the temple and the work that is done therein. Other hymns expressed his deep affection for the Lord: "I Believe in Christ," "Come Unto Jesus," "Come Follow Me," and "Savior, Redeemer of my Soul." One was reminded of his strong commitment to keep the Lord's commands with "Lord, I Would Follow Thee," and serving "even the least of these, my brethren" with "A Poor Wayfaring Man of Grief."

President Hunter's gentleness and kindness toward others were reflected in "Nay, Speak No Ill" and "Let Us Oft Speak Kind Words." "O My Father," "Sweet Hour of Prayer" and "Secret Prayer" were a reminder of President Hunter's relationship with Deity.

The Tabernacle Choir, which Howard W. Hunter dearly loved, sang three hymns in simple, but moving renditions from the hymnbook—"I Need Thee Every Hour," "Nearer My God to Thee," and "How Great Thou Art." The funeral concluded with a simple, but sublime setting of "Abide with Me, Tis Eventide," composed by tabernacle organist, John Longhurst. Its tender, transparent beauty beckoned the listeners, for a few brief moments, into paradise, where our beloved prophet had gone.

Thomas Monson, Second Counselor in the First Presidency, referred to the heavenly music, as well as the sounds of mourning heard at the services, with these eloquent words:

> The heavenly music of this angelic choir, accompanied by the almost silent sobbings of little children and the rustling of a thousand handkerchiefs pressed to weeping eyes, bespeak our love for our prophet dear, President Howard W. Hunter (Ensign, April 1995, p. 31).

The membership of the Church grieved because they had lost a close friend, but drew solace from having lived during the short time that Howard W. Hunter was President of the Church.

1 Howard W. Hunter: *That We Might Have Joy* (Salt Lake City, Deseret Book Co. 1994) p. 105.
2 Eleanor Knowles: *Howard W. Hunter* (Salt Lake City, Deseret Book Co., 1994) pp. 38-39.
3 Ibid., p. 41.
4 Ibid., p. 43.
5 Ibid., p. 45-46.
6 Ibid., p. 46.
7 Ibid., p. 46-47.
8 Ibid., p. 48.
9 Ibid., p. 49.
10 Ibid., p. 49.
11 Ibid., p. 53.
12 Ibid., p. 53.
13 Ibid., p. 54.
14 Ibid., pp. 55-56.
15 Ibid., p. 58.
16 Ibid., p. 60.
17 *Ensign*, August, 1994, p. 6.
18 Knowles, p. 66.
19 Ibid., p. 67.
20 Ibid., p. 71.
21 Ibid., p. 81.
22 Ibid., p. 99.
23 Ibid., p. 100.
24 Ibid., p. 106.
25 Richard eventually grew up to marry Nan Greene, who is the author of "Father, This Hour Has Been One of Joy." No. 154 of the 1985 hymnal.
26 Ibid., p. 108.
27 Ibid., p. 153.
28 Ibid., p. 133.
29 Ibid., p. 134.
30 Ibid., p. 144.
31 *Conference Report*, September 30, 1978, pp. 15-16.
32 *Conference Report*, October 6, 1984, pp. 41-43.
33 Howard W. Hunter: *That We Might Have Joy* (Salt Lake City, Deseret Book. Co, 1994) pp. 85-86.
34 *Conference Report*, April , 1987, p.
35 *Conference Report*, April 5, 1992, pp. 84-85.
36 *Howard W. Hunter*: p. 105.
37 *Conference Report*, April , 1970, p.
38 *Ensign*, April 1995, back cover.

GORDON B. HINCKLEY

MARIE
WITHERS '95

GORDON B. HINCKLEY
(1910-   )

*"Can anyone doubt that good music is
godly or that there can be something of
the essence of heaven in great art?"*[1]

On the morning of March 13, 1995, in the foyer of the
Joseph Smith Memorial Building, Gordon Bitner Hinckley
was introduced to the public and press as the fifteenth
President of the Church. He had been ordained to that high
calling the day before—Sunday March 12th—in the Salt Lake
Temple. A press conference then followed—the first such
occasion since Spencer W. Kimball became the President of
the Church. With his typical "warm, often witty, always winning exchange" with reporters, he answered questions on a
variety of topics.

"What will be your focus? What will be the theme of your
administration?" asked one reporter. The President responded,
"Carry on. Yes. Our theme will be to carry on the great work
which has been furthered by our predecessors."

Elder Jeffrey R. Holland, of the Quorum of the Twelve,
reflected on his answer:

That simple answer—crisp, clear, unpremeditated, inspiring—
says much about our new prophet, seer and revelator. "Carry on" is
a familiar phrase taken from the text of a hymn written by Ruth
May Fox some sixty-five years ago, a musical rallying cry filled with
joy and determination. Its opening line and sometimes title "Firm as
the mountains around us!" Its bold declaration? "Stalwart and brave
we stand!" Where? "On the rock our fathers planted For us in this
goodly land—The rock of honor and virtue, Of faith in the living
God...Carry on, carry on, carry on!" (*Hymns*, 1985, no. 255)

Then Elder Holland added these two interesting sentences:

So many hymns, like so many scriptures and sermons, could be cited to underscore the qualities and cast light upon the strengths of the prophets of God. But perhaps no hymn does better at catching something of the essence of Gordon B. Hinckley than does this forthright and optimistic call to "carry on."

Gordon B. Hinckley's father, Bryant S. Hinckley, was the the principal of what is now known as LDS Business College. He had lost his wife and was struggling to care for his small family. Ada Bitner returned from Chicago where she had learned the Gregg system of shorthand. She joined the faculty at the business college—where Bryant was principal—to become the first person in Utah to teach Gregg shorthand. Bryant and Ada fell in love and were married in 1909. One year later, on June 23, 1910, a son was born to the couple—Gordon Bitner Hinckley.

With both parents professional teachers, Gordon grew up in an environment of learning, and of good books. In their home was a library of well over 1,000 volumes—books of history and great literature, and books on a variety of technical subjects. From an early age Gordon had a thirst for knowledge and he read widely from these and other books, including books dealing with church history, and, of course, the scriptures.

Soon after he became a deacon, Gordon accompanied his father—a member of the stake presidency—to a stake priesthood meeting:

My father went to the stand and I sat on the back row. The meeting was called to order, and the opening song was "Praise to the Man Who Communed with Jehovah." All of the men stood to sing. The hall was filled. Many had come as converts from Europe. They lifted their voices in unison in that great hymn:

Praise to the man who communed with Jehovah!
Jesus anointed that Prophet and Seer.
Blessed to open the last dispensation,
Kings shall extol him, and nations revere.

It touched my heart. It gave me a feeling that was difficult to describe. I'd never had it previously in terms of any church experience. There came into my heart a conviction that the man of whom they sang was really a prophet of God. And I'm grateful to say that the conviction—that I believe came by the power of the Holy Ghost—has never left me."[2]

Like so many others, Gordon B. Hinckley's first spiritual experience was also a musical experience!

"Even today," wrote then-Elder Boyd K. Packer in a 1986 Ensign article about President Hinckley, "more than six decades later, he cannot tell of that experience without slipping a finger under his glasses to prevent a tear from rolling down his cheek."[2]

The Hinckley's lived in the same ward as the elderly George Careless, a former director of the Tabernacle Choir. Brother Careless was a well-known composer of many of our most beloved hymns, including "The Morning Breaks," "Though Deepening Trials," "Prayer Is the Soul's Sincere Desire," "Behold the Great Redeemer Die," and several others. As a holder of the Aaronic Priesthood, Gordon had the frequent assignment of going to the Careless home on Sunday mornings to administer the sacrament to Brother Careless when he was no longer able to come to church. His Sunday morning assignment at the home of this distinguished Church musician made a lasting impression on Gordon:

[Brother Careless] was a shriveled up man, as I remember him to whom we took the sacrament on Sunday.... I can still see his hand looking like the claws of a bird, if you'll pardon the expression, reaching for the sacrament as we handed it to him. He had been the chorister in our ward. Mark Petersen [who later became an apostle] succeeded him as the chorister. Mark loved such songs as "In our Lovely Deseret" and George Careless loved such songs as "The Morning Breaks." He was a product of the choral schools of England, a tremendous musician. I can still see him leading the ward choir.

And I can still see Mark Petersen leading us in singing "In Our Lovely Deseret." I'm glad they've included it [in the new hymnbook].

Reflecting the candor for which he is so well-known (as well as the observation that "In Our Lovely Deseret" does not measure up to those hymns by Alexander Schreiner, or Frank Asper), President Hinckley continued:

> I guess it wasn't included for the music, but I'm glad it's here. I can still sing those words as a little tow-headed kid sitting on the hard benches—and they were miserably hard—of the First Ward where we were so restless:
>
>> That the children may live long And be beautiful
>>   and strong,
>> Tea and coffee and tobacco they despise,
>> Drink no liquor, and they eat But a very little
>>   meat;
>> They are seeking to be great and good and wise.
>>
>> They should be instructed young How to watch
>>   and guard the tongue,
>> And their tempers train and evil passions bind;
>> They should always be polite and treat everybody
>>   right,
>> And in every place be affable and kind.

Elder Hinckley recalled, "Well, that's just a delightful memory for me and a bit of a bore for you, I suppose." He seemed pleased to point out the composer of "The Light Divine" was written by his junior high music teacher:

> [It]...was written by Mathilda Watts Cahoon. She was my music teacher in junior high school. The only claim I have to musical fame is that I was a part of the boys chorus in junior high which won two district championships of the Salt Lake and Granite school districts. Since then I've forgotten how to read music...but I do hold up my hand to Mathilda Watts Cahoon who somehow coaxed a tune out of me as a part of the boys chorus of that junior high school. She was a great and delightful and lovely teacher.[4]

After graduating from high school, Gordon enrolled at the University of Utah. Majoring in English, he took every writing course that was offered, and enjoyed a wide exposure to the works by the world's great authors:

> I read Carlyle and Emerson, Milton and Longfellow, Shakespeare and all the others. And from there I went on to study Latin and Greek. I couldn't do it now, but once I could have read you the *Iliad* and the *Odyssey* in the original Greek. I finished up my work at the university with a minor in ancient languages.[5]

Gordon worked nights at the Deseret Gym in the key room. And in the summers he performed various kinds of maintenance work, including plumbing and electrical work. "I learned to use tools," he said, "and I have loved them ever since."[6]

Writer for the *Church News*, John L. Hart, described Gordon B. Hinckley this way:

> If it was work, young Gordon did it. He wasn't afraid of grease or slivers. He made stalled cars run, did household repairs, carpentry, plumbing.[7]

As a youth, Gordon Hinckley developed a reputation as a hard-working, dependable and focused young man. He also became known as a remarkable public speaker. Reed Smoot—an Apostle as well a U. S. Senator from Utah—was to be the featured speaker in the First Ward one Sunday evening. At the last minute, however, an emergency prevented him from filling that assignment. With little time to make other plans for the meeting, Bishop John Duncan called two young men in the ward to "fill in" for the distinguished Apostle and Senator: Robert Sonntag and Gordon Hinckley. Before Church, Gordon had to complete a watering assignment on the family farm. Then, with little time to prepare for his speaking assignment, he hurried home, changed, and was off to the First Ward to speak. The large crowd of people who came to hear the famous Reed Smoot was no doubt disappointed to hear, instead, two young men of the ward. Robert

Sonntag reported, however: "When Gordon had finished speaking, the people had forgotten all about Senator Smoot's absence."[8]

In 1930, after a six-month illness, Gordon's mother died of cancer. Elder Hinckley later recalled:

> I remember the grey November day of her funeral. We put on a front of bravery, and fought back the tears. But inside the wounds were deep and painful.[9]

In the depths of the depression, Gordon graduated in English from the University of Utah in 1932. Half of the nation's banks had failed, including *his* bank. *Gone was his missionary savings account!* Once again, however, he began to work and save towards a mission. In 1933, Gordon accepted a call to serve a mission in the British Isles. Taking all of his savings, he still did not have enough. Reluctantly, he took the contents of a large bottle of change that his mother had saved for many years. He considered her savings "sacred," and would not have used it for any other purpose.

Elder Hinckley's first assignment took him to Preston at Lancashire, where the early apostles inaugurated the Church's missionary work in Europe. After a few months, however, he was transferred to the mission home in London to work as an assistant to Joseph F. Merrill of the Council of the Twelve and president of the European Mission. One day, reviews of an anti-Mormon book appeared in the London papers. Though the book was alleged to be a history of the Church, it was not. It was pure fiction. President Merrill was very upset by what he read. But *obviously* impressed by Elder Hinckley's superb skills in dealing with people, he asked Gordon to go to the publisher to protest the publication of this potentially damaging book.

Naturally, this difficult assignment frightened Gordon, and he was puzzled why President Merrill—an apostle—did not personally handle the problem.

My inclination was to say, "Why me? Why don't you go. You are an older man, and I'm just a boy. I didn't say it. I said, "Yes sir. I got on my knees and asked for the blessings of the Lord. [Then] I arrived at the office of the publisher and handed my card to the receptionist and told her that I would like to see the president of the company. "Mr. Skeffington is very busy," [she answered.] And I said, "Well I've come about 5,000 miles. I think I'll wait for him. Well I sat there and she went in and out of his office several times. Finally she concluded that I would wait there. [She] went in again, and she came out and said, "He'll see you."

Well, I'll never forget the picture. He was seated behind a big desk, had a cigar out of the corner of his mouth. He seemed to be saying, "What do you want, kid?" I don't know what I said to him after that. At first he was defensive and belligerent. Then he began to soften.... And he said finally, "I'll recall all those books and slip in a page on which we will say this book is fiction, [and] it is not in any sense history." He did that. It was a tremendous thing.

Not only did Elder Hinckley handle a difficult problem with the publisher, he made a friend for life.

[Mr. Skeffington]...sent me a Christmas card after that as long as he lived. It was a tremendous lesson to me: *I came to know that if we would put our faith in the Lord, and go forward in trust that he would open the way.*[10]

Even then, *as a green missionary*, Gordon B. Hinckley exemplified a remarkable gift of leadership and diplomacy.

One of Gordon's childhood friends from the ward, G. Homer Durham was called to the same mission at the same time as Gordon; and for a time, the two served together as companions. Then, completing their missions at the same time, they returned to New York together in June, 1935, and to Detroit by train. By previous arrangement, they picked up a new 1935 Plymouth which had been purchased by Gordon's father, and made the sixteen hundred mile journey to Salt Lake City in the new automobile.

A member of one of the Church's best-known musical families, G. Homer Durham was an able pianist. He nevertheless chose a different career, going into political science and history. Years later he would become the vice president of one university and president of another. He would later become the director of the Historical department of the Church, and one of the presidents of the First Quorum of the Seventy.

President Merrill had arranged for Gordon to meet with the First Presidency to report on conditions in the European Mission. The meeting with President Heber J. Grant and his two counselors, J. Reuben Clark and David O. McKay, was to have lasted fifteen minutes. "They began to ask questions and I was there for over an hour," Gordon later recalled.

Obviously impressed with the returned missionary, President McKay called a few days later to offer Gordon a position as secretary and producer with the Church's newly organized Radio, Publicity and Mission Literature Committee. That auspicious committee, of which he was now a part, consisted of six members of the Quorum of the Twelve!

Though his title was impressive, his circumstances were not.

> He was given an empty office, bare of furniture. Undaunted, he found a cast-off table from a furniture store. One leg was short, but he elevated that corner with a block of wood. He brought his typewriter from home and talked a frugal supply clerk out of an entire ream of typing paper.

The supply clerk was not impressed with Gordon and wondered if he could ever use that much paper.

"Do you know how much paper is in a ream? But to the clerk's surprise who dispensed the paper, and perhaps others too,

> with his first touch of the typewriter keyboard was launched a prolific writing endeavor that would fill many volumes, and which has advanced the kingdom in many ways.[11]

The young Gordon Hinckley wrote *and produced* thirty nine half-hour radio dramatizations of the history of the

Church. Produced in Hollywood, *The Fullness of Times*—as the series was entitled—employed both music and dialogue, and was heard over hundreds of radio stations throughout the nation. With these dramatizations, Brother Hinckley became a pioneer in the use of the media in the Church. And in addition to *The Fullness of Times*, he also wrote and produced another series of radio programs based on the Book of Mormon—*New Witness for Christ.*

Church News writer, John L. Hart, said of Gordon B. Hinckley:

> [He]...became a sort of one-man Church Office Building staff as he wrote and produced *The Fullness of Times*, and *New Witness for Christ* series of recordings. Some of these aired on some 400 radio stations nation-wide, forerunners of today's media efforts.[12]

Arch L. Madsen, long-time KSL radio executive and President Emeritus of Bonneville International, spoke of Gordon B. Hinckley's enormous contribution in the use of the media to preach the gospel:

> He organized the first use of the media by the Church years ago, [and] he has retained that interest. It is amazing...his quick insight and panoramic view of any media situation. The Church broadcasting today has been greatly influenced by this great man.[13]

The San Francisco World's Fair was held in 1939 on Treasure Island. Brother Hinckley was directed to create the Church's exhibit for the fair. He decided to build a small-scale model of the Salt Lake Tabernacle. Fair goers, tired from walking, could come in and sit down, listen to a short organ recital—as if they were on Temple Square—and receive a brief introduction to the Church. A "small, but fine organ" was purchased for the "Little Tabernacle"—an Everett Orgathon, with two keyboards and full pedal board. One of the missionaries, G. William Richards—an accomplished organist—was invited to present recitals each day. "Much good came from our efforts at the World's Fair," said Elder Hinckley modestly. Gordon B. Hinckley understood then—as he does still—the power of music to attract people and prepare them for the spoken word.

When Gordon returned from his mission, he rediscovered Marjorie Pay, the girl who lived across the street. He had known her since she was a little girl in Primary. Marjorie had, in the meantime, blossomed into a beautiful young woman, and, as President Hinckley later recalled, "I had the good sense to marry her!"[14] The couple was married in the Salt Lake Temple on April 29, 1937.

Later that year, he was appointed to the Deseret Sunday School Board, on which he served for nine years. Another member of that committee was one of the most prominent musicians of the Church, Tracy Y. Cannon. One of Brigham Young's grandsons, Tracy Y. Cannon had served as a tabernacle organist for twenty years, and—for twenty-five years—he had been the Director of the McCune School of Music and Art. Brother Cannon was a kind and wise man with flowing white hair that made him look like Moses or Elijah. While he was a member of the Sunday School Board, he served, also as the chairman of the General Music Committee of the Church. Brother Hinckley worked closely with this great musician, but in later years he and Tracy Cannon would enjoy even a closer relationship.

Later on, Brother Cannon hired a new secretary for the General Music Committee: Carol Hinckley, daughter of Gordon's father and his first wife.

After Brother Cannon became a widower for the second time, his interest in his secretary began to deepen. Then in 1944, they were married in the Salt Lake Temple. Gradually, Carol H. Cannon's responsibilities with the General Music Committee increased. Eventually she was named Executive Secretary to the Church's General Music Committee of the Church.

During the "Cannon years" of the General Music Committee, a massive music training program in the Church was developed. William Foxley, Darwin Wolford and several others, travelled throughout the western states teaching courses in the basics of conducting and organ playing in the stakes of the Church. Music instructions for organists and choristers in the Church were taught from Lovell, Wyoming to Los Angeles; from Durango, Colorado, to Salmon, Idaho; from Logan, Salt Lake City and Provo to Tuscon, Arizona. As Tracy Y. Cannon grew older and more frail, the work of organizing and administrating that work fell to his wife, Carol. Through the years, she and Gordon enjoyed a close, personal relationship. He was well aware of his sister's work in administering the training courses for musicians in the Church, and he understood the importance of it.

Brother Hinckley was called to serve as a counselor in the East Millcreek Stake presidency in 1946. Five years later— while serving still in the stake presidency—he was appointed Executive Secretary of the General Missionary Committee. Within the year of that appointment, uniform missionary lessons for use around the world were established. With the reorganization of the East Millcreek Stake in 1956, he was called to be the new stake president. Having demonstrated exceptional leadership skills through the years in various callings, he was called as an Assistant to the Council of the Twelve on April 6, 1958. Three years later, on October 5, 1961, President David O. McKay called Gordon B. Hinckley to be an apostle.

As a member of the Quorum of the Twelve, Elder Hinckley eventually became one of the most widely traveled General authorities, visiting *many times* Asia, the Pacific Islands, Europe and the Americas. As he traveled throughout the world, instructing and blessing the Saints, bringing strength and comfort, he always seemed to derive strength from the members of the Church, and inspiration from their music.

In the summer of 1981, President Spencer W. Kimball called Elder Hinckley to become a third counselor in the First Presidency, joining N. Eldon Tanner and Marion G. Romney. Though the First Presidency was already complete, Elder Jeffrey R. Holland wrote,

> in a moment of clear revelatory inspiration and good health, President Kimball asked Elder Hinckley to join the First Presidency.[15]

Elder Hinckley commented on his becoming a third counselor to the presidency:

> When I accepted President Kimball's call to join them, I did not know exactly how I would function or fit in, and perhaps they did not at the time. But the circumstances called for additional help, and I was more than willing to give it. I did not know whether it would be for a few days or a few months.[16]

President Kimball, as well as presidents Tanner and Romney, "were in varying degrees of declining health," wrote Elder Holland.[17] N. Eldon Tanner died in November 1982 at the age of 84. As the health of the Prophet, as well as President Romney began to fail, President Hinckley began to assume more of the burden of the work of the First Presidency.

For many years, the musicians in the Church looked forward to the publication of a new hymnbook. Though it had served the Church well since 1948, as time went on its deficiencies became more and more obvious. In September, 1983, the First Presidency issued the long-awaited authorization to revise the hymnbook. They were anxious to have the work done "quietly and quickly." With an eye to the needs of the world Church, the Brethren wanted the new book "as simple as possible." More doctrinal coverage in the topics of the hymns was needed. It was determined that the nine members of the General Music Committee would serve as the Executive Hymnbook Committee. Michael F. Moody, chairman of the

General Music Committee would be the over-all chairman. Elder Hugh Pinnock, advisor to the General Music Committee, became the advisor to the entire work of publishing a new hymnbook for the Church.

From the beginning, President Hinckley took a particular interest in the hymnbook. In the early stages of the committee's work, a dinner was held for committee members and spouses at the home of one of the members, Vanja Watkins. Since the Watkins were neighbors to the Hinckleys, President and Sister Hinckley were extended an invitation to attend. This gathering provided an excellent opportunity to introduce the Hinckleys to some of the proposed new additions to the hymnbook. As the new "discoveries" were sung, the Hinckleys listened intently and responded positively. The committee decided to end with "Hark, All Ye Nations!" Since this hymn was borrowed from the German Saints, everyone *assumed* President Hinckley would not know it. Cautious about how he would respond to the vigorous tempo and rhythm, the committee decided to sing it in a more restrained style. He listened quietly to the entire hymn and then exclaimed: "Wonderful hymn!" Then, without hesitation, he added to everyone's surprise, "But the Germans sing it with much more gusto!"[18]

One challenge that faced the committee was to determine which hymns from the old book should be deleted. Infrequency of use became the main reason for deletion. The committee was anxious to learn which hymns from the old hymnbook were sung often by the Brethren in their weekly temple meetings, or not at all. One of the musicians asked President Hinckley if the Brethren in the temple ever sing "Ye Chosen Twelve," number 211 in the 1948 hymnbook, which addresses the Quorum of the Twelve and reminds them of their duties to teach the Gospel to all of the nations of the earth. His answer was short: "Never!" Then as he thought about the hymn further, he said: "You know, the Twelve know their calling, but they do not know how to sing about it."

Another time, the committee had been involved in a day-long work session in the Church Office Building, and in the evening, the spouses joined the committee for a fine meal in the Lion House. On that occasion, Elder Pinnock spoke to those gathered there about the importance of the work in which they were engaged. In his remarks, he said:

> I got a phone call last night after ten o'clock from President Hinckley. He had xerox copies of the revisions and new hymns that had been finalized so far sitting on his piano. He had gone through them all very carefully. He was most enthusiastic, but, at the same time he has some very specific concerns.[19]

The committee was pleased with President Hinckley's enthusiasm for their progress. The "specific concerns," however, indicated that his examination of the manuscripts was anything but superficial. Nothing had escaped his attention!

Hymn No. 135 in the new 1985 Hymnbook bears the title, "My Redeemer Lives," with words written by President Gordon B. Hinckley. Herbert Klopfer explains the genesis of this hymn:

> An original poem "My Redeemer Lives" by President Gordon B. Hinckley of the First Presidency was printed in the April 1983 issue of the *New Era*. In the ensuing months, several musical settings of this poem were received at Church headquarters. At one point, President Hinckley was asked for his opinion regarding the various tunes submitted to [his poem]. Members of the General Music Committee felt strongly that one version of this beautiful text and tune ought to be included in the new hymnbook, but also desired some input of personal feelings from the author of the text.

Two different settings of President Hinckley's poem had been culled from the others by the committee and had been sent to him to see how well he liked either of them. In a phone call to a committee member, which he initiated, President Hinkley said that he was not totally satisfied with either of them. He agreed with President Benson, who always liked a hymn he could sing while milking the cows. Both of these settings "lacked the common touch."

This may not please the "purists" among the musicians of the Church, but the scope of usage of the hymns of Zion goes well beyond our church meetings. When the hymnbook was ready for publication, the "First Presidency Preface" included these lines:

> Teach your children to love the hymns. Sing them on the Sabbath, in home evening, during scripture study, at prayer time. *Sing as you work, as you play, and as you travel together.* Sing hymns as lullabies to build faith and testimony in your young ones.[20]

"Can they be easily sung to the cows?" became a consideration for selecting new additions for the hymnbook.

Brother Klopfer wrote further about "My Redeemer Lives":

> I received fourteen musical settings to President Hinckley's poem in November, 1983, [including] one by general authority, G. Homer Durham. The tune ultimately selected was the one by his fellow general authority G. Homer Durham.
>
> [When] President Hinckley heard this hymn sung for this first time, he had not known which tune was ultimately chosen and who the composer of the tune was. After having heard the new hymn, he leaned back in his easy chair and thought for a moment. His response was warm, gracious, and gratifying. He shared his feelings about this new hymn and his pleasure of being named together with his lifelong friend, G. Homer Durham, on the same page of the new hymnbook. None of us knew of this close friendship until this moment. "Homer and I grew up together. We are the same age. We went to the same grade school and Roosevelt Junior High School. We were the shortest boys in the school with the same shoe size. Whenever my shoes were missing, I knew who had stolen them. We went to college together and graduated in the same class. We went to the same mission in England together, and we labored together in London. We taught seminary together for one year after our missions."[21]

Sadly, G. Homer Durham passed away January 10, 1985. seven months before the hymnbook was published.

Copies of the hymnbook, in English, rolled from the presses in early August, 1985—150 years since the publication of Emma Smith's original hymnbook, *to the very month*. Typesetting of each hymn—*both words and music*—was accomplished by computer, allowing each of the foreign language editions to come from the established format. The continuation of the hymnbook—which has been described as a "fifth standard work"—into all other languages where the Church is established could then be done accurately and *efficiently*. The preparation of this volume seemed to inspire unanimous interest among the Brethren. Its completion was second only to the publication of the scriptures—that had been cross referenced and indexed—in its significance to the Church. Finally, the Church has a hymnbook that is now cross referenced and indexed with the four standard works, as if it were an extension of the scriptures.

A near capacity crowd filled the Assembly Hall on Temple Square to attend the Hymnbook Celebration on September 3, 1985. Presided over by President Gordon B. Hinckley, scores of individuals who were involved in the revision, editing, research, computer type-setting, printing and binding, as well as poets and composers represented in the book, gathered for the celebration. Between talks given by Gordon B. Hinckley of the First Presidency, Neal A. Maxwell and Thomas S. Monson of the Council of the Twelve, Elder Hugh Pinnock—advisor to the entire project, Michael Moody and Karen Lynn Davidson who represented the hymnbook committee, a sampling of hymns from various sections of the hymnbook were introduced to and sung by the enthusiastic audience. With Bonnie Goodliffe at the organ and Vanja Watkins directing—both were members of the hymnbook committee—a sampling of new hymns was introduced and sung by the congregation.

Karen Lynn Davidson, a member of the committee,[22] spoke of the work from the standpoint of the people who had con-

tributed so generously. She recalled a statement made by Elder
Dean L. Larsen at one of the meetings of the committee:
*"When the singing in the congregation has slipped, it often
means that other spiritual matters have slipped as well."*
Elder Neal A. Maxwell described a meeting of Latter-day
Saint soldiers at a battle scene on the island of Okinawa:

> [A] battered group of infantrymen assembled on a little hill on
> Okinawa, our division having been relieved for an LDS service, the
> first we'd had since the fighting had begun. We were anxious to be
> there to see who had survived and who would not show. As we
> began that meeting singing "Come, Come, Ye Saints," we watched
> carefully to see who might yet show up a bit tardy. And we knew
> when they didn't come it meant they'd been killed or had been
> wounded. *I don't remember a thing that was said at that meeting,
> but I remember what we sang.* And so often in life this is true of
> us."[23]

Elder Thomas S. Monson, who had been involved in the
printing industry before becoming a general authority, over-
saw with great interest the publication of the hymnbook from
a printer's point of view.

> "My heart goes out tonight to some with whom I've served for a
> long period on this particular project. For some reason...I've become
> involved in some of the more difficult things like a Bible reprinting,
> a hymnbook reprinting, the two most difficult that I know anything
> about.

Elder Monson related an incident that took place on a cold
morning in Leipzig. Inside, he was interviewing brethren for
leadership for a stake that was about to be created. Outside,

> 30 of the brethren were singing in beautiful four-part harmony
> from the hymnbook. I said to Brother Ringger, my associate, "Do
> these brethren represent a priesthood choir for the meeting this
> evening?" Brother Ringger said, "Oh, no, they're just the brethren
> that we're going to interview this afternoon. They would prefer
> singing to chatting." And they sang for four hours! As we would
> interview some of the tenor section, the tenors became a little weak

and then they would return and the bass would come in for the interviews. But all in all, *we learned a lesson that if you love the Lord, if you love his doctrine, you'll love the hymns. And when you love them, then you sing them.* And this is the spirit that I hope we could inculcate in the heart of every person.[24]

Elder Hugh Pinnock, who successfully guided this mammoth project from the start, conducted the meeting. In his brief remarks, he pointed out that Elder Mark E. Petersen of the Quorum of the Twelve, had looked forward *for years*—like a child in March or April anticipates Christmas—to the publication of a new hymnbook. Elder Petersen was a trained musician, but professionally he was a newspaper publisher. At the time he was called to be a general authority, he was the general manager of Deseret News. This gave him a double reason for wanting a new hymnbook for the Church. Many times, *unsuccessfully*, he tried to initiate the work on a revision among the Brethren. Elder Petersen suffered for a lengthy period of time with cancer. He passed away, finally, on January 11, 1984—after the work on his "pet project" was irreversibly going forward. Perhaps the Lord had extended his life, at least, to see this work in progress!

President Gordon B. Hinckley offered closing remarks on this most auspicious occasion. With his candid humor and friendly demeanor, he began:

Vanja Watkins [who introduced and directed each of the fourteen hymns] is the music director in our ward, and it's like going to Sunday School to be here. This is what she does in our ward.

People in the Church like new things: They like new cars. They like new boats. They like new debt. They like new meeting houses. Some of them would even like some new scripture! They like new hymnbooks, and this is the fulfillment of a dream of many people over a long period of time.

The first hymn we sang, "The Morning Breaks, the Shadows Flee," sets forth those marvelous words of Parley P. Pratt. None like them, really, concerning the opening of this, the dispensation of the fullness of times, written by a man who was a convert to the

Church as a result of reading the Book of Mormon, and who spent his life preaching the gospel.

A few years back I was in Fort Smith, Arkansas, to organize a new stake there. The mission president said, "Would you like to see where Parley P. Pratt is buried? And I said, "Yes." We arose at 5:00 Sunday morning, and drove out into the country to a little dusty town, Alma, Arkansas. Beyond that a little ways, out into the really rural area where the roosters were crowing, we came to a beautiful, little fenced-in plot where stood a great shaft of granite, in which were incised the words:

PARLEY PARKER PRATT:

The morning breaks, the shadows flee,
Lo' Zion's standard is unfurled.
The dawning of a brighter day
Majestic rises on the world.

It was riding out of that little town on horseback that he was shot in the back by an angry man who hated the Church and Parley Pratt as a missionary. The music to that hymn was written by George Careless, who I think contributed very generously to this hymnbook.

President Hinckley related how, as a boy he used to take the sacrament to George Careless at his home when he was no longer able to come to Church. He reminisced about singing in the junior high chorus directed by Mathilda Watts Cahoon who wrote "The Light Divine."

President Hinckley then referred to the closing hymn, "The Spirit of God."

The hymn which we will sing to close this meeting—the words were written by W. W. Phelps. What a great and marvelous statement that is, sung for the first time, I suppose, at least that's the record of our history, at the dedication of the Kirtland Temple in 1836, "The Spirit of God Like a Fire is Burning."

It's been my opportunity in the last twenty eight months to participate in the dedication of 17 new temples. And in every one of those dedicatory services, incidentally, we have sung, "The Morning Breaks, the Shadows Flee," that is, the choirs have sung. And the great concluding number is the "Hosanna Anthem" sung by the choir in the dedicatory service, which was written by Evan Stephens, the shepherd from the Welsh hills who joined the Church and came to Zion and composed much of our greatest music—distinctive, beautiful Latter-day Saint music.

We sing the "Hosannah Anthem" and the congregations in each of these dedicatory services has then joined in singing, "The Spirit of God Like a Fire Is Burning." In each of these situations I have sat with the choir immediately behind me, and the choir has always had difficulty singing because of the tears that choke their voices as they try to express themselves in a newly dedicated House of God

In those dedicatory services we have joined through the music three great events in the history of the Church: the dedication of the first temple in 1836, the dedication of the Salt Lake Temple in 1893; and the dedication a week ago, or whatever it was, of the Johannesburg South Africa Temple, far away in that troubled, but beautiful land, and felt of the marvelous spirit of the Saints who live there, and whose lives will be blessed by reason of that House of the Lord.

President Hinckley concluded by saying:

"The song of the righteous is a prayer unto me and it will be answered with a blessing upon their heads." *May this new hymnbook motivate our people to sing the songs of Zion, that they may be worthy of the blessing of the Lord promised through revelation, as I express in behalf of the entire Church our appreciation to the very many who have worked so hard to bring to pass this great accomplishment.*

President Gordon B. Hinckley also presided at the General Women's meeting held in the Tabernacle Saturday evening, September 28, 1985.

President Kimball is not with us. I wish he were. What a wonderful man he is. What a wonderful life he has lived. Now he is elderly, trapped by the infirmities of age.... We bring you his love, his blessing.

President Romney celebrated his eighty-eighth birthday only a week ago. He, too, has been touched and bent by the storms of life. He also sends his love to each of you.

President Hinckley concluded by reminding the women of the Church of ten great blessings and opportunities that are theirs:

> I conclude with the tenth great privilege and opportunity you have. This is the opportunity and the encouragement to educate your minds and hands, to refine your talents, and to so qualify yourself to work in the society in which you live.
>
> I am grateful that women today are afforded the same opportunity to study for science, for the professions, and for every other facet of human knowledge. You are as entitled as are men to the Spirit of Christ, which enlightens every man and woman who comes into the world (See D&C 84:46.). Set your priorities in terms of marriage and family, but also pursue the educational programs which will lead to satisfying work and productive employment in case you do not marry, or to a sense of security and fulfillment in the event you do marry.
>
> *It is also important to enhance one's appreciations of the arts and culture which are of the very substance of our civilization. Can anyone doubt that good music is godly or that there can be something of the essence of heaven in great art! Education will increase your appreciation and refine your talent.*[25]

In General Conference, April 3, 1988, Gordon B. Hinckley spoke these original words as part of his address:

> What is this thing that men call death,
> This quiet passing in the night?
> 'Tis not the end, but genesis
> Of better worlds and greater light.
>
> O God, touch Thou my aching heart,
> And calm my troubled, haunting fears.
> Let hope and faith, transcendent, pure,
> Give strength and peace beyond my tears.
>
> There is no death, but only change
> With recompense for vict'ry won;
> The gift of Him who loved all men,
> The Son of God, the Holy One.[26]

This poem was given a beautiful musical setting by Herbert Klopfer. Then on the Tabernacle Choir's CBS broadcast Sunday morning, April 5, 1992—immediately before the opening of General Conference—this hymn became the inspiration for the "Spoken Word" given by Lloyd Newell. In it, he spoke of despair and hope, and reminded the radio listeners, *"failure is an event; it is never a person."* Then he concluded with these lines:

> It takes great courage to be imperfect and yet hopeful. It takes real faith to live with hope amid despair. But, when we have faith in the Lord, we have power in the present and hope in the future. And that hope will help give us "peace in this life, and eternal life in the world to come" (Doctrine and Covenants 59: 23.) Let us sing, with hope, the words of the song [by Gordon B. Hinckley]:
>
> > O God, touch Thou my aching heart,
> > And calm my troubled, haunting fears.
> > Let hope and faith, transcendent, pure,
> > Give strength and peace beyond my tears.

As Ezra Taft Benson's health began to fail, the weight on the shoulders of Gordon B. Hinckley increased. Ezra Taft Benson passed away on Memorial day—May 30, 1994. During the short administration of Howard W. Hunter, Gordon B. Hinckley served as first counselor, with Thomas S. Monson as the second counselor.

Upon the death of President Hunter on March 3, 1995, Gordon Bitner Hinckley became the fifteenth President of the Church, the holy calling to which he had been fore-ordained millennia, no doubt, before he was born into mortality, and to which he had been preparing all of his life. Gordon B. Hinckley was ordained and set apart as the fifteenth President of the Church in the Salt Lake Temple, March 12, 1995 by the next senior apostle, Elder Thomas S. Monson, who then became his first counselor. Elder James E. Faust joined the First Presidency as the Second Counselor. With Elder Monson, *officially* the president of the Quorum of the Twelve, now serving as First Counselor, Elder Boyd K. Packer became the *acting* President of the Quorum of the Twelve.

Elder Jeffrey R. Holland wrote of Gordon B. Hinckley's preparation to become the President of the Church:

> Perhaps no man has ever come to the Presidency of the Church who has been so well prepared for the responsibility. Through sixty years of Church administration he has known personally, been taught by, and in one capacity or other served with every President of the Church from Heber J. Grant to Howard W. Hunter. As one of his associates says, "no man in the history of the Church has traveled so far to so many places in the world with such a single purpose in mind—to preach the gospel, to bless and lift up the Saints, and to foster the redemption of the dead."[27]

Speaking of his administrative experience, Elder Boyd K. Packer wrote of Gordon B. Hinckley in 1986, when he became the first counselor to President Ezra Taft Benson:

> At one time or another he has been chairman or acting chairman of important committees of General Authorities. These include the General Priesthood Committee, the Missionary Committee, the Temple Committee, Church Correlation Committee, Personnel Committee, Budget and Appropriations Committee, the Board of Education and Board of Trustees of Bright Young University (and the executive committees of both), Publications and Communications Committee, Special Affairs Committee, and the Information and Communications Systems Committee.[28]

Following the formal announcement of the reorganization of the First Presidency on March 13, 1995, in the Joseph Smith Memorial Building, prepared statements were given by the new president and his two counselors.

President Hinckley—self-assured, but dependent on the Lord for whom he would now be His voice to the Church and the world, began:

> One cannot come to this sacred office without almost overwhelming feelings of inadequacy. Strengthened resolution to go forward comes from the knowledge that this is the work of God, that he is watching over it, that he will direct us in our efforts if we will be true and faithful, and that our accountability is to him.

With that assurance we reach out to our own people and to those of goodwill throughout the world, in that spirit of love and brotherhood which comes from the Lord Jesus Christ.

As the Church moves forward on its divinely appointed mission, I do not anticipate any dramatic change in course. Procedures and programs may be altered from time to time, but the doctrine is constant. *We are dedicated, as have been those before us, to teaching the gospel of peace, to the promotion of civility and mutual respect among people everywhere, to bearing witness to the living reality of the Lord Jesus Christ, and to the practice of his teachings in our daily lives.*[29]

With the warmth and humor that has characterized Gordon B. Hinckley through the many years of public service, the new prophet answered questions about the Church's direction in the world, women who have to work outside the home, the educational needs of our younger members, temples and family values. Asked about his health, he replied that in his eighty-five years, he had only spent two nights in a hospital...and one of them was with a sick grandchild. "But," he clarified, "that doesn't mean I can run the hundred-yard dash!"

Near the end of the news conference, a reporter asked what the Church would do to foster the arts. What would the Church do

> to have a great Mormon writer, a great Mormon singer? Are we going to have a great Renoir? What will the LDS Church do to promote artists within the LDS Church?

Perhaps a little surprised at that question, President Hinckley answered, "I don't know...and you can quote me on that!" He then continued:

> Of course we'll give encouragement, as we traditionally have done. This Church has always encouraged the arts—the finer things of life. In its early days, young aspiring artists were sent from this community to France to learn the finest techniques[30] of painting. We've cultivated music. The Tabernacle Choir has become a great, world famed organization, and this is the home of that choir. We

have encouraged the arts of all kinds, and will continue to do so. We've fostered them. We have given of our means to encourage them. *We want to cultivate the finer elements in our society.*[31]

As an apostle, he became the advisor to the Tabernacle Choir in the late 1970s. Because of his intense interest in the choir, he has retained that responsibility after becoming a counselor in the First Presidency, *and* does so today as the President of the Church! "President Gordon B. Hinckley has referred to the Tabernacle as 'the crown jewel of the Church,'" said Jerold Ottley, director of the choir. "He points to the specific mission of the choir in the outreach of the Church, both as an *ambassador* and as a *missionary.*"[32]

President Hinckley accompanied the Tabernacle Choir to Japan in 1979. He went with the choir to Toronto, Canada first in 1984, and then again in 1992. On that latter concert tour, the choir sang at Richmond, Virginia, Kirtland, Ohio, Cleveland, Springfield, Illinois, and at the RLDS Auditorium in Independence, Missouri.

As the fifteenth president of the Church, Gordon Bitner Hinckley presided over the 165th annual General Conference, held April 1 and 2, 1995 in the Tabernacle. The traditional Solemn Assembly—at which the new prophet is sustained by the membership of the Church—took place during the Saturday morning session.

One week later, the Tabernacle Choir performed at the opening of the Tuacahn Art Complex near St. George, Utah. With President and Sister Hinckley attending, the Choir presented an outdoor concert Saturday evening, April 8, in the amphitheater that is part of the art complex. The Choir presented their regular Sunday morning broadcast, April 9, "beneath the shadow of the everlasting [red sandstone] hills" of Tuacahn. Because it was windy and very cold, blankets had been passed out to the audience before the broadcast to help them stay a little warmer. At the conclusion of the broadcast,

President Hinckley, spoke to the vast audience—huddled in their blankets. True to form, the Prophet looked upon the crowd and said, "You look like *one giant unmade bed!*" Then he observed, "How appropriate for the Tabernacle Choir to come here to present *their music and the frozen word!*"[33]

Once, at the home of Jack and Vanja Watkins, neighbors of the Hinckleys, President Hinckley enjoyed listening to an autoharp that Sister Watkins had there. Declining an invitation to strum the instrument himself, he seemed content to appreciate and encourage the efforts of the performer. Such a small incident as this seemed to show how focused he is on the things he does best as he serves the Lord in the Church, at the same time encouraging others to do what they do best.[34]

Virginia H. Pearce, daughter of the prophet—almost apologetically—said:

> We are not a particularly musical family. My father doesn't perform musically, *but he does understand the power of music to change lives!*[35]

Perhaps as the leader of the Lord's Church on earth, it is only necessary to understand the power of music to affect the soul, and to know that music is an important part of the religious experience.

One of the greatest operas ever written is *Die Meistersinger von Nürnberg* (The Mastersingers from Nuremberg) by Richard Wagner. The setting is sixteenth-century Germany—the time of the guilds. To be successful, the suitor of the beautiful Eva Pogner must become a master singer in the musician's guild by composing a perfect song and singing it flawlessly. Bechmesser wants Eva and the glory of becoming a master singer, but he resorts to underhanded means to accomplish this. Walther aspires to excellence in his art and labors arduously to accomplish it. With the help of Hans Sachs, a poet-cobbler and Walther's mentor, Walther composes the winning song and sings it beautifully. Hans, who wanted no glory for himself, found his greatest joy in coaching and encouraging Walther. Walther and Eva were married.

There are Walthers today who aspire for perfection in their art, who toil constantly to achieve it. There are, perhaps, those musicians who want the glory, but who are not disciplined enough to work for excellence. Then, there are those like Hans Sachs—however few there may be—whose personal happiness comes from the successes of the true artist, who inspire and promote excellence in the music of others. Such a man is Gordon B. Hinckley.

1 General Women's Meeting, September 28, 1985, *Conference Report*, October 1985, p. 116.
2 From the video: *Gordon B. Hinckley: A Man of Integrity, Fifteenth President of the Church*.
3 *Church News*, March 18, 1995, p. 4.
4 Transcript of Hymnbook Celebration, held in the Assembly Hall on September 3, 1985, after the publication of our latest hymnbook.
5 *Ensign*, June, 1995, p. 7.
6 Video: *Gordon B. Hinckley*.
7 *Church News*, March 18, 1995, p. 4.
8 Video: *Gordon B. Hinckley*.
9 Video: *Gordon B. Hinckley*.
10 Video: *Gordon B. Hinckley*.
11 John L. Hart,"Roots are Embedded in Responsibility", *Church News*, March 18, 1995, p. 4.
12 Ibid.
13 Video: *Gordon B. Hinckley*.
14 *Ensign*, June, 1995, p.11.
15 *Ensign*, June 1995, p. 12.
16 Ibid.
17 Ibid p. 12.
18 According to Herbert Klopfer, a member of the hymnbook committee and counselor in the Ensign Stake Presidency related this incident: "In September 1985, the Ensign Stake Choir sang this hymn beautifully and with *enthusiasm* at our stake conference. President Ezra Taft Benson, sitting two chairs to my right, had a broad smile on his face and said somewhat loudly to me: 'This is a good German song.' As soon as the choir had finished, he jumped to his feet (he had already spoken earlier), stepped to the pulpit and declared: 'This is a most beautiful hymn. You ought to hear the German-speaking saints sing this hymn! They'll bring the roof down!' And he sat back down." (From a conversation with Herbert Klopfer.)
19 From the author's personal journal.
20 *Hymns of the Church of Jesus-Christ of Latter-Day Saints*, 1985, First Presidency Preface, p. x.
21 From the journal of Herbert Klopfer that was shared with the author.
22 She is the author of *Our Latter-day Hymns* that was written after the hymnbook was published.
23 From a Transcript of the Hymnbook Celebration.
24 Transcript of the Hymnbook Celebration.
25 *Conference Report*, April, 1985, p. 116.
26 *Conference Report*, April, 1988, p. 76.

27 *Ensign*, June, 1995, p. 13.

28 "President Gordon B. Hinckley—First Counselor", *Ensign*, February, 1986, p. 9.

29 *Ensign*, April 1995, p. 5.

30 In the early 1920s, the Church made it possible for the young Alexander Schreiner to spend two years in Paris to study with some of the finest organists in the world, including Charles M. Widor and Louis Vierne.

31 Transcribed from a video recording of the broadcast.

32 From a personal conversation with Jerold Ottley, May 23, 1995.

33 From a telephone conversation with Jerold Ottley.

34 From a personal telephone conversation with Vanja Watkins, May 27, 1995.

35 From a telephone conversation on May 23, 1995.

Appendix I

AS GOD IS MAN MAY BECOME

About ten years before Lorenzo Snow passed away, he composed a hymn text in which he described man's journey to godhood—as man is, God once was; as God is, man may become—for which he is so famous. This inspired poem may be sung to the tune of "The Morning Breaks" by George Careless.

MAN'S DESTINY

Has thou not been unwisely bold,
Man's destiny to thus unfold?
To raise, promote such high desire,
To raise, promote such high desire,
Such vast ambition thus inspire?

Still 'tis no phantom that we trace
Man's ultimatum in life's race;
This royal path has long been trod
This royal path has long been trod
By righteous men, each now a God:

As Abra'm, Isaac, Jacob, too,
First babes, then men—to Gods they grew.
As Man now is, our God once was;
As now God is, so man may be,—
Which doth unfold man's destiny.

The boy, like to his father grown,
Has but attained unto his own;
To grow to sire from state of son,
To grow to sire from state of son,
Is not 'gainst Nature's course to run.

As son of God, like God to be,
Would not be robbing Deity;
And he who has this hope within,
And he who has this hope within
Will purify himself from sin.

(*The Improvement Era*, June 1919, pp. 660-61)

Appendix II

THE PARABLE OF THE TALENTS

The special talents with which we have been blessed—our intelligence, physical abilities, time and money, and the many opportunities given to us—have come from the Lord. They have been entrusted to us to be used, not for safekeeping or to be hidden away. They were given to us according to our ability to use—not for our own gain, but for the Lord's purposes here upon earth. We are like tenant farmers, who, given the use of the land, make their own selection as to the crop they will raise, and they work according to their own skill and desire to work. Some have the ability to sow, cultivate, and raise a bounteous crop, but others are less successful. There are some persons who will work hard and produce, while others, lacking initiative and desire, will fail. The day comes, however, when an accounting must be made.

So it was in the parable [of the talents]. "After a long time the Lord of those servants cometh, and reckoneth with them" (Matthew 25:19.) The five-talent servant was the first to speak. "Lord, thou deliveredst unto me five talents: behold, I have gained besides them five talents more. His lord said unto him, Well done, thou good and faithful servant: thou hast been faithful over a few things, I will make thee ruler over many things: enter thou into the joy of thy Lord" (Matthew 25: 20-21). One can feel the delight of that servant in those words; he wanted to please his master. The master expressed appreciation by telling him that because of his faithfulness he would be given the opportunity for greater things and, the invitation, "enter thou into the joy of thy Lord." To *enter into* means to share. He was invited to share the joy of his master. The master invited him to partake of the feast in celebration of his homecoming, and perhaps he was more of a friend than a servant.

The two-talent servant was next. He had been entrusted with fewer talents, but he had doubled those given to him. He too seemed pleased to be able to hand over the gain which he had made. The master made the same reply to him as to the five-talent servant. Herein lies an interesting principle. The Lord had given to the first, five, and to the second, two, "to each man according to his several ability." But now the difference between the two amounts, as far as ability is concerned, seems to have disappeared. The master praised and rewarded the second servant in exactly the same way as he did the first. Even though he had been entrusted with less, he had been faithful to that trust.

Now we come to the one-talent servant. We are saddened and disappointed in this part of the drama because first there was an excuse, then a display of the fear that caused him to hide the talent. He had been afraid to assume the responsibility. His attitude was one of resentment and faultfinding, saying he found the master to be a hard man, even harvesting where he had not sown. There are many in the world like this servant, idle and unwilling to work for the master—interested only in themselves. There are those who become so involved in the things of the world and their own selfish interests that they will not make the attempt or put forth the effort to magnify one little talent entrusted to them by the Lord.

To the one-talent servant, "His lord answered and said unto him, Thou wicked and slothful servant....Take therefore the talent from him, and give it unto him which hath ten talents...And cast ye the unprofitable servant into outer darkness: there shall be weeping and gnashing of teeth" (Matthew 25:26,28, 30). At first glance this would appear to be a hard judgment, nevertheless we would expect a man to use his talent. If not, it should be given to one who has proven himself willing and anxious to work for his master.

Near the conclusion of the parable, the Lord stated what has become known as the law of increase in these words: "For unto every one that hath shall be given, and he shall have abundance: but from him that hath not shall be taken away even that which he hath" (Matthew 25:29). Does the law of increase seem to be harsh? In effect, it is that the rich will become richer and the poor will become poorer. In the parable, more was given to both the five-talent servant and the two-talent servant, but to the one-talent servant, the one who had been given less, it was taken away.

Those who use their talents find they will grow. One who exercises his strength finds it will increase. If we sow a seed, it will grow; if we fail to plant, it will be lost. One who posesses some insight and is attentive to his teacher will gain more knowledge and insight and will have growth in mind and spiritual understanding. Understanding increases as it is used. As we learn, we acquire greater capacity to learn. As we use our opportunities for knowledge, more opportunities come to us. *How sad it is when the opposite course is followed, and the talent and capacity is wasted and not used. "From him that hath not shall be taken away even that which he hath."*

Talents are not given to us to be put on display or to be hidden away, but to be used. The Master expects us to make use of them. He expects us to venture forth and increase what we have been given according to our capacities and abilities. *As servants of the Lord, we should use every opportunity to employ our talents in his service. To fail to do so means to lose them.* If we do not increase, we decrease. Our quest is to seek out the talents the Lord has given us and to develop and multiply them, whether they be five, two, or one. We need not attempt to imitate the talents given to other persons.

—Howard W. Hunter British Area General
Conference held in Manchester, England
August 29, 1971

Appendix III

STATEMENTS ABOUT MUSIC BY APOSTLES

Music is part of the language of the Gods. It has been given to man so he can sing praises to the Lord. It is a means of expressing, with poetic words and in melodious tunes, the deep feelings of rejoicing and thanksgiving found in the hearts of those who havae testimonies of music is both in the voice and in the heart. *Every true saint finds his feart full of songs of praise to his Maker. Those whose voices can sing forth the praises found in their hearts are twice blest.* "Be filled with the Spirit," Paul counseled, "Speaking to yourselves in psalms and hymns, and spiritual songs, singing and making melody in your heart to the Lord" (Ephesians 5: 18-19). Also: "Let the word of Christ dwell in you richly in all wisdom; teaching and admonishing one another in psalms and hymns and spiritual songs, singing with grace in your hearts to the Lord" (Colossians 3:16).

Unfortunately not all music is good and edifying. Lucifer uses much that goes by the name of music to lead people to that which does not edify and is not of God. Just as language can be used to bless or curse, so music is a means of singing praises to the Lord or of planting evil thoughts and desires in the minds of men. Of that music which meets the divine standard and has the Lord's approval, he says: "My Soul delighteth in the song of the heart; yea, the song of the righteous is a prayer unto me, and it shall be answered with a blessing upon their heads." (D&C 25:12)

—Bruce R. McConkie, *The Promised Messiah*
(Deseret Book, 1978) pp. 553-554

[We must] learn once again in The Church of Jesus Christ of Latter-day Saints to really sing...If you love the Lord, if you love His doctrine, you'll love the hymns; and when you love them, then you sing them.

> —Thomas S. Monson, Hymnbook Celebration,
> The Assembly Hall, September 3, 1985

Singing our beautiful, worshipful hymns is food for our souls. We become of one heart and one mind when we sing praises to the Lord. Among other influences, worshipping in song has the effect of spiritually unifying the participants in an attitude of reverence.

> —James E. Faust, *Ensign*, May, 1992, p. 8

The Spirit does not ratify speech nor confirm music which lacks spiritual substance.

> —Boyd K. Packer, *Ensign*, November 1991, p. 21

We are able to feel and learn very quickly through music, through art, through poetry some spiritual things that we would other-wise learn very slowly."

> —Boyd K. Packer, Brigham Young University,
> February 1, 1976

There come to one's soul heavenly thoughts as he joins in heavenly expressions coupled with heavenly melody.

> —David B. Haight, *Ensign*, May 1993, p. 12

When we rejoice in beautiful scenery, great art, and great music, it is but the flexing of instincts acquired in another place and another time."

—Neal A. Maxwell, *Ensign*, May, 1984, p. 21

[L]ife is largely what we choose to make of it and of our inborn talents. The same musical scale was available to Beethoven for composing his Fifth Symphony as to the composer of "Chopsticks." These compositions even share several opening notes of melody. But what an enormous difference in substance and effect.

—Neal A. Maxwell, *A Wonderful Flood of Light*
(Bookcraft, 1990), p. 47

The soul is like a violin string: it makes music only when it is stretched. (Eric Hoffer)

—Eric Hoffer as quoted by Neal A. Maxwell, *All
These Things Shall Give Thee Experience*
(Deseret Book. Co., 1980) p. 28

The spirit of the listener [is] moved most by melodies soft and simple, sung with sweet sincerity.

—Russell M. Nelson, *Ensign*, November, 1995, p. 32

Select music that will strengthen your spirit.

—Russell M. Nelson, Ensign, November, 1985, p. 32

The singing of hymns is one of the best ways to learn the

doctrines of the restored gospel.

Our hymns contain matchless doctrinal sermons, surpassed only by the scriptures in their truth and poetic impact.

—Dallin H. Oaks, General Conference, October 1, 1994

When I hear these choirs, I am impressed that there is more volume of sound than there are numbers [of singers].... I believe that there is help from angelic choirs from the other side of the veil....

[In the hymn "Sweet Is the Work"], the phrase ["When in the realms of joy I see] thy face in full felicity" is a beautiful expression of what this is all about."

—Jeffrey R. Holland, from remarks spoken at the Bountiful Temple dedication, January 12, 1995, 8:00 a.m. session

INDEX